FROM CONCEPT
TO MARKET

Gary S. Lynn

WILEY

John Wiley & Sons

New York • Chichester • Brisbane • Toronto • Singapore

This publication is designed to provide accurate and
authoritative information in regard to the subject
matter covered. It is sold with the understanding that
the publisher is not engaged in rendering legal, accounting,
or other professional service. If legal advice or other
expert assistance is required, the services of a competent
professional person should be sought. *From a Declaration
of Principles jointly adopted by a Committee of the
American Bar Association and a Committee of Publishers.*

Library of Congress Cataloging in Publication Data:

Lynn, Gary S.
    From concept to market.

    Bibliography: p.
    Includes index.
    1. New products. 2. Innovation. 3. Invention. 4. Product Management. I. Title.
HF5415.153.L96 1988   658.5′038   88-27851
ISBN 0-471-50126-3 (cloth)
ISBN 0-471-50125-5 (paperback)

Printed in the United States of America

10 9 8 7 6 5 4 3 2

To individuals with an idea and
the belief, courage, and commitment
to see their vision become a reality.

Success is not measured by what you have
attained, but rather by how far you have come.

Confucius

Foreword

The dream of America is the dream of opportunity: Opportunity to try, opportunity to innovate, opportunity to succeed or fail.

When enthusiastic, innovative entrepreneurs have failed, the cause most frequently may be traced to inadequate financing, or imprudent or inexperienced management.

Out of these dilemmas, *From Concept to Market* was born. In simple, but in complete and logical sequence, Gary Lynn guides the inexperienced entrepreneur through and around the myriad of inevitable obstacles and decisions. Here in concise but interesting dialogue, questions, methods and answers are probed. *From Concept to Market* draws on Mr. Lynn's own real life experiences in bringing new products into the marketplace. This book will save would-be entrepreneurs from hours and days of grief and costly mistakes.

As a business primer or as a checklist for the veteran, *From Concept to Market* is a welcome and valuable addition to any library. It will help Americans rediscover the adventures and challenges of entrepreneurship.

PHILIP KOTLER

S.C. Johnson and Son Distinguished Professor of International Marketing at the J. L. Kellogg Graduate School of Management, Northwestern University.

Preface

This book will show you step-by-step how to take a concept, such as a new product idea, and bring it to market. *From Concept to Market* is a practical handbook to guide you through the entire new product innovation process. After reading this book, you will know how to: document, evaluate, test, perform a patent search, complete a market research, locate a potential licensee, write a business plan, and raise money. In short, you will learn how to make money from your new product idea.

The goal of this book is not to provide legal counsel. Although every effort has been made to accurately state the law, be aware that laws differ from state to state and court to court. In addition, practices change with new court decisions. You are strongly urged to consult a patent attorney on matters concerning intellectual property and a general corporate attorney on matters dealing with business issues, such as hiring a distributor or entering into any contractual agreement.

This book was written as an easy-to-follow story to facilitate the understanding of a myriad of complex and confusing principles.

It is my hope that you were able to glean one concept from this book that made it worth both your time and money. If you have any thoughts, suggestions, or experiences that you would like to share, I'd be delighted to hear from you. Address all correspondence to GSL and Associates, Technology Commercialization Center, Northwestern University, 906 University Place, Evanston, Illinois 60201.

GARY S. LYNN

February, 1989

Acknowledgments

I'd like to thank Philip Kotler, of the J. L. Kellogg Graduate School of Management at Northwestern University, my first mentor.

The talented staff at John Wiley and Sons deserves praise, Michael Hamilton, Senior Editor, in particular, for cutting through the red tape and approving this book in 3½ weeks. I would also like to thank Nancy Land for her fine editorial work and David Ainscough for his creative graphic design.

I would also like to thank the following people who read this book while it was in manuscript form and offered their ideas and suggestions: Marty Bernard, Jack Bishop, Bruce Buteyn, Carol Butterfield, Ted DeBoer, Dave Dullum, John Farady, Stephen Gnass, Fred Grissom, George Gruenwald, Dipak Jain, William Konold, Calvin MacCracken, Stuart Meyer, Benjamin Mosier, Don Moyer, Kevin O'Grady, Mitchell Olan, Carol Pladsen, Anne Rabin, Martin Rachmeler, Judith Ratner, Gary Ropski, Dudley Rosborough, Euegene Step, Alan Tratner, Karl Vesper, and Terry White.

In addition to my mother, I am indebted to these people who helped me both personally and professionally: Brenda Band, Robert Bies, C. Anne Brooks, Richard Chandler, Douglas Conroy, Louis Dehmlow, Alan Garfin, Walter Herbold, James Hill, Ralph Jindrich, Glen Johnson, Stuart Kaye, Robert Kincaid, Douglas Lamont, Esther Maloblocki, Luis Maldonado, Jay McGuerty, David Mosier, Mitchell Olan, Mike "Whacker" Step, Lester Teichner, and Miles Townsend.

A special thanks to Ruth (Fong-Hsi) Chiang for her tireless effort in typing this book and for offering insightful suggestions, even though English is her second language.

My overriding thanks is to my father, Norman; it was through his love, support, and enough red ink in his pen that turned my manuscript into this book.

Contents

Contents

Introduction

A paper clip: So simple, so versatile, so useful! Amazing! What a great idea! Why didn't you think of it? Why didn't I?

Frankly, I don't know who thought of that idea first; but chances are more than one person did. Sometimes the only difference between action and inaction is merely knowing what to do, and how.

Someone did more than think about the paper clip. Someone was able to convert a concept into a reality—a real benefit. That somebody could have been you!

Have you ever thought of a new product but didn't know what to do with the idea? You are in good company.

Often the only difference between having an idea and doing something with it is knowing *what* to do and *how* to do it. To address these questions, *From Concept to Market* was written. In language easy to understand and with steps that are clearly defined, you will learn how to develop and market your new product. This book is for you—the innovator.

Throughout the book, important forms are shown often with filled out examples for you to follow. The story used to illustrate the steps to follow is a success story in every sense. This is not always the case. I have worked with many concepts, some made it to the market, some did not. From experience, I have drawn on the ideas, the procedures, and the techniques that are most likely to achieve success. These attributes are woven into the fabric of the success story you will follow.

I have chosen to illustrate positively, but have not lost sight, nor should you, of the possibility of failure. If, however, you believe in your concept and are willing to work through all the steps illustrated, your chances for success will be greatly improved.

1

The Search

There was once a bright young man who we'll call Jim who had a brilliant idea for a new product. He was convinced his idea was marketable and had vast potential. All of his friends thought it was a fantastic idea also. Interestingly enough, creating the design for a new product did not vex Jim as much as other questions that popped immediately into his mind:

▶ What is the market potential for my idea?

▶ Has someone already thought of it and patented it before?

▶ Is my idea unique? Is it patentable?

▶ What is involved in getting a patent and how much will it cost?

▶ How can I find a company who would make and sell my product and pay me a royalty?

▶ How can I raise money if I would like to start my own company and manufacture and sell my product myself?

Finding questions to ask was easy; finding answers was difficult. And Jim set out to find the answers.

He went to libraries and scoured everything written on new product marketing and licensing. He was discouraged because the materials he found were much too general and of little help. Jim talked to his friends; they knew even less than he did.

One day a patent attorney talked about a man, in the same city, who was an extremely successful entrepreneur. This man began as an individual inventor with one idea. He licensed it to a large company and was paid a handsome royalty. He then repeated his success and licensed several more inventions. This successful entrepreneur who we will call Norman, started his own company after licensing his early inventions, and manufactured and marketed his ideas himself. He lectured at business schools teaching students his secrets of new product development and marketing. He was pleased to share his knowledge with others because he had made many mistakes that he felt he could help others avoid.

Jim thought, "I must speak to Norman." He was convinced that this man could really help but wondered whether the successful entrepreneur would speak to him. The patent attorney gave him Norman's name and phone number.

That night, Jim was so excited that he could not sleep. He thought, "At last I can get answers to my questions!"

At 9:00 A.M. the next day, Jim phoned Norman, the successful entrepreneur, but could speak only with his secretary. Jim explained his dilemma and asked if Norman could spare even a couple minutes. Jim knew this man could help him.

It was apparent that he was not the first to ask Norman for help. The secretary indicated that Norman would be happy to speak with Jim since he enjoyed helping others. An appointment day and time was arranged. Jim was ecstatic that such a busy and successful man would take time to talk with him.

Jim arrived at Norman's office and was shown in. The office was beautiful with a view that overlooked the entire city. As soon as Jim entered, Norman came out from behind his massive desk to greet him. Their discussion began with a question that indicated Norman was not unfamiliar with Jim's concerns:

Norman: So you have a new idea and don't know what to do next? You are probably wondering if you should submit for a patent; if you should start your own company; or just license it to another company and collect royalties?

Jim (*amazed at the perceptiveness of this man*): How did you know? Did your secretary tell you about my situation?

Norman: She only briefly told me that you have a new idea and have several concerns. I see many people with new ideas and they usually have the same questions. Although their specific applications differ, they all generally have the same concerns. So don't feel like you are the only one with these problems.

Jim's relief was immediate. He was able to relax, thinking to himself, "At last, someone who understands!"

Norman: Tell me about your idea.

Jim: I would like to share my idea with you, except I am very concerned about telling others about it.

Norman: You are concerned that someone will steal your idea; I understand. We have a standard Non-Disclosure Agreement I'd be happy to sign for you.

With that, the successful entrepreneur signed the Non-Disclosure Agreement, (p. 5) and Jim began telling his story.

NON-DISCLOSURE AGREEMENT

I agree that, in consideration for access to information submitted to me by __(Inventor)__ , I will:

1. Keep all information relating to models, drawings, discussions, and printed materials in strict confidence.

2. Disclose this information solely to individuals who have signed a non-disclosure agreement with, or who have expressed written approval from, __(Inventor)__ to receive the information.

3. Not make any contact nor agreement with anyone else nor anyone outside my company on any idea submitted without prior written approval of __(Inventor)__ . Furthermore, I agree not to use, either directly or indirectly, any such information provided by __(Inventor)__ for our own benefit or for the benefit of any person, persons, firm, or corporation.

Understood and agreed this _____ day of _____ 19____ .

_____
(Signature)   (Date)

_____
(Printed Name)

_____
(Title)

_____
(Company)

_____
(Inventor's Name)

_____
(Inventor's Signature)   (Date)

Adapted from the Agreement used at the Institute for Research, Houston, Texas.

THE IDEA

Jim began to relate his story to Norman, starting with some background.

Jim: Three years ago, I saw my dentist for a check-up. He told me I was brushing my teeth incorrectly. He explained the proper way to brush was to start from the top of my gums and brush down. This will massage the gums and remove plaque build-up between the teeth.

Currently available toothbrushes did not seem to be designed to accomplish what the dentist had prescribed. After I left the dentist's office, and over the next several months, I gave some thought to this problem and devised a new toothbrush—the 'Scrub-n-Brush Toothbrush.' This innovation was designed to scrub the teeth and brush the gums in one easy motion.

I would like to market this invention but don't know what to do or how to go about doing it.

The successful entrepreneur started thinking back to the time he had his first idea and how he had the same concerns that Jim was expressing. He remembered all the mistakes he made at the beginning; and once he became successful, he developed a step-by-step procedure for invention marketing to help others in similar circumstances. Using his procedure, others would not have to make the same mistakes.

Norman (*turning to Jim*): Marketing your own idea takes tremendous perseverance, persistence, and sacrifice. If it were easy, everyone would be doing it. (*Then he looked right into the young man's eyes.*) Are you willing to devote yourself, for at least the next couple years, to seeing your idea become a reality?

I'd like you to think about that question. Go home and give it some thought, at least overnight. Call me when you are comfortable with your answer. Now is the easiest time to back out. Once you have begun the process and invested your time, money, and effort, it is not as easy to quit.

As Jim was leaving, he must have looked bewildered because Norman's secretary asked him if everything was alright.

Jim: Is he always so direct?

Secretary: Usually, initially so many people come to him with an idea and just want to follow the "yellow brick road" to the pot of gold. He wants to be sure they understand that it takes perseverance, persistence . . .

Jim (*interrupting*): and sacrifice. He just told me about that.

Secretary: Then I'm sure he also told you to think about it for awhile before you ask him for help. He does not want to waste his time nor your time and money. If you have any questions, please feel free to call me. I'd be happy to help you if I can.

That night Jim could not sleep. "If it is as difficult as they say, do I really want to do it?" he thought. He gave it more thought the following day. Jim discussed his dilemma with his friends and family, but the decision had to be his alone. He called Norman and told him that he was willing to make the commitment. The successful entrepreneur congratulated him and invited him to return so that they could discuss their strategy.

The next day on his way to Norman's office, Jim was very apprehensive and nervous. No longer was he so cocky. He was beginning to put his dream into perspective and realizing that if his invention is going to become a reality, he must dedicate himself to diligence and hard work.

When he arrived, the secretary greeted him and showed him into Norman's office.

Norman: OK, you have made your decision. It will take hard work, and we will no longer dwell on that. Our job now is to see about commercializing your idea. We can go over the step-by-step process my company uses to market our new products. This process has taken us over 10 years to develop and has proven to be quite effective.

With that, Norman pulled out a very old, tattered book titled *Invention Commercialization.*

2

Log Book

The successful entrepreneur continued, "The first place to start is to properly document your idea in an invention notebook. Keeping an up-to-date, witnessed logbook can not be overemphasized. A well-documented, dated, and witnessed invention record can provide substantial legal protection and will greatly reduce the possibility of someone stealing your idea. However, a specific format must be followed. He stood up, went to one of his cabinets, and took out a bound invention log book and gave it to the young man.

Norman (*handing the book to Jim*): This is now yours. Use it to record your present and future ideas.

The young man opened the book and noticed that all the pages were numbered and asked why?

Norman: This ensures that all the entries are made in chronological order. A spiral notebook is NOT acceptable. The pages may not be loose or removable without detection; a loose leaf notebook therefore would also not be acceptable.

Good records are admissible as legal evidence to establish the date of conception of your idea. A well-documented idea greatly reduces the risk of someone stealing your invention. For every one of your new product ideas, the following format should be used to enter your idea into your log book. (*Opening the log book, he reviews the first pages.*)

You will need to:

▶ Date each page.
▶ State the problem clearly.
▶ Explain the current state of the art.
▶ State your solution in sufficient length to explain your invention.

▶ Draw or sketch your idea, labeling important components.

▶ Sign each page.

▶ Obtain the signatures of two witnesses (not family or friends).

The entry must be able to stand alone. In other words, a third party should be able to understand your invention without additional explanation. In addition, two disinterested parties (witnesses) must sign that they actually understand the entry. Their signatures accomplish two purposes: (1) They can testify that you had this idea, and (2) a record date is specified.

This is the format we use for witnessing our own new concepts. The following statement should appear on each page of your Log Book:

FORMAT FOR WITNESS SIGNATURE

I have read and understand this idea. We are not co-inventors and we agree to keep this disclosure confidential.

_____ _____ (Signature) Date: _____ , 19____ .
(Print Name)

_____ _____ (Signature) Date: _____ , 19____ .
(Print Name)

Other Log Book guidelines include:

▶ Blank spaces or pages should be noted with a large 'X' inscribed on them.

▶ *Never* alter an entry. *Never* remove or add pages.

▶ If additional entries are required at a later date, write "Further entries appear on page xx of this book."

▶ All entries, drawings, and signatures must be written in indelible ink.

▶ Each experiment should be recorded with an explanation of what was done and the results achieved. This must be done even if the experiment was a failure. In fact, if the test failed, it might have even greater significance.

▶ Photographs, models, charts, specimens, etc., may be attached to the log book pages (if possible). They also should be signed, dated, and witnessed either on the item itself or on a permanent tag attached to the item.

Everything should be recorded in your log book. Each time you make an idea modification, discuss your idea with someone, buy supplies to build a model, perform library research, log it into your notebook. If you want to buy a log book, the best one that is publically available is offered through The Innovation Institute. You can obtain their *Idea Log* by sending a check for $21.50 to: The Innovation Institute, P.O. Box 48390, Niles, IL 60648. In addition to the log book, you will also receive instructions and examples of log book entries.

"Now," said the entrepreneur, "go home and try documenting your idea in your log book. We can meet tomorrow to review it and proceed to the next step."

As the young man was leaving, he felt pretty good. The secretary asked him how it went and Jim responded, "So far, great; I'll see you tomorrow."

The next day, Jim returned with the following entry in his Log Book.

Scrub 'n Brush Toothbrush

PROBLEM: Present toothbrushes do not both clean teeth and scrub gums.

SOLUTION: A brush that combines long bristles for cleaning gums AND short bristles for cleaning the tops of teeth.

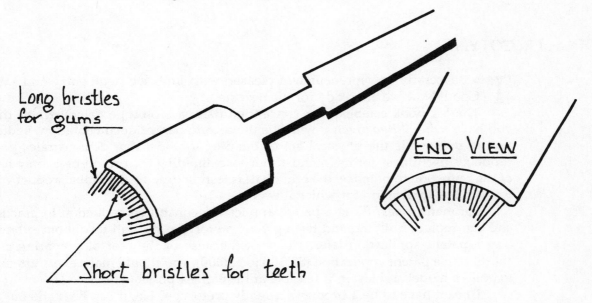

Long bristles for gums

END VIEW

Short bristles for teeth

I have read and now understand this idea. I am not a co-inventor and agree to keep this material confidential.

Print: _____ Signature: _____ Date: _____

Print: _____ Signature: _____ Date: _____

INVENTOR'S SIGNATURE ___Jim White___ DATE 1/1/89

This idea was suggested by Dr. Abe Ochstein.

3

Documentation

ROUGH PROTOTYPE

The successful entrepreneur was pleased with Jim's log book entry and said, "Good! Now we are ready for the next step."

The log book establishes a conception date; a prototype demonstrates that you have *reduced it to practice* which is the second part of documentation. Reduction to practice is the physical act of building a model that demonstrates your product's usefulness for its intended purpose. Building the prototype is only half of the reduction to practice; the other half is testing to show that your product will work in the application for which it was intended.

For many ideas, filing a patent application constitutes reduction to practice and can replace building and testing your prototype. We will talk about submitting a patent application later. However, because of the cost of preparing and submitting a patent application ($2,500 to $5,000), you should make every attempt to build a model and test it, if feasible at the earliest possible time.

Does it have to be a production-ready prototype? No, it can be made out of cardboard, toothpicks and erasers or another material as long as it *demonstrates the basic principles* of your invention, and that your innovation will work for its intended purpose. Now I'd like you to try to build a rough prototype yourself. You will be surprised what you can do with balsa wood, styrofoam, erasers, toothpicks, glue, and your imagination.

The young man left and could not wait to try his hand at making a model. He found some cast-off styrofoam at a television appliance store, and he bought a couple toothbrushes at the grocery store.

He used the styrofoam for the base of the toothbrush. He then cut the bristles into different lengths from the toothbrushes and embedded them into the styrofoam for the bristles. When he was finished, he looked at it and wasn't pleased. He made another, and another, until he finally satisfied himself.

He called Norman and told him that he had completed the prototype. The successful entrepreneur invited him to return and to show his model.

When they met, Norman said that while it would not win any contests for aesthetics, the model does demonstrate the principles of the invention. He also recommended tagging the model with the date and taking a picture of it and dating the picture so Jim would have a permanent record.

"Follow me and let's test it," Norman said, leading the way to the restroom. Norman actually put some toothpaste on the prototype and tried it. They returned to the office and Jim was instructed to make another entry in his log book describing the test that had been performed, who participated, the results achieved, the date the test was performed, and the date of the entry into the log book. Then an unrelated, disinterested party must sign and date the entry. This is very important; the inventor's word alone is not sufficient.

Jim: Why did you tell me this was going to be so difficult? It really isn't; so far, it is a lot of fun.

Norman was disappointed in the young man. Jim was intelligent and talented, however he did not realize that this was only the beginning of a long, obstacle-ridden journey. The successful entrepreneur wondered to himself if Jim would get disillusioned and quit like so many had done before or if he would endure and persevere.

Norman: I hope it will continue to be easy for you. Before we move on to the next step, you should be aware that you are required to work with *diligence* to build and test your idea. The U.S. Patent Office has found that unexcused delays, as little as one week, can show lack of diligence, which may invalidate your patent. Delays due to illness, material unavailability, and similar uncontrollable delays are allowed. It is therefore very important that you document weekly all your efforts in your log book, including materials purchased, modifications, tests performed, etc.

INVENTION DESCRIPTION

Proper, *thorough* description is the next task. For all new ideas, we use the following Confidential Invention Record. It helps accomplish several objectives. First, the detailed description forces us to think the idea through and to analyze other issues such as existing and anticipated competition, perceived consumer need, and technical feasibility. Second, it presents the invention in a form that others, such as potential licensees, can easily understand when the time comes for licensing. Such description is also vital to patent attorneys when you are ready to submit a patent application and will reduce the cost for preparing the patent application.

You must *be objective and accurate* when filling out the form. When you are objective and accurate, the chances of your making money on your invention and the likelihood of commercialization are greatly increased.

The Confidential Invention Record is fairly straightforward. However, one portion that may give you some trouble is determining the *sales potential* of your invention. Calculating demand is very important both for you as well as for potential licensees. Licensees or investors want to know what the sales opportunities are for your invention.

To determine the sales potential of your invention, you may need help from several sources. One of the most direct and productive is to contact the trade associations for your industry. Ask them:

▶ If they know the market size of your invention.

▶ If they know of other similar products on the market and what their approximate annual sales are.

Perhaps some of the more important questions you will want to ask are:

▶ Who else, or what other organizations, should be contacted for this information?

▶ Where would they go themselves if they needed this information?

The successful entrepreneur then handed the young man the following sources list:

SOURCES FOR LOCATING TRADE ASSOCIATIONS

▶ *Directory of European Associations*
Gale Research Co.
2200 Book Tower
Detroit, MI 48226.
(Over 7000 entries on associations in every nation of eastern and western Europe.)

▶ *Encyclopedia of Associations*
Gale Research Co.
2200 Book Tower
Detroit, MI 48226.
(Over 16,000 national and regional associations, their addresses, contact person, and number of members.)

▶ *Encyclopedia of Associations* Vol. 1
National Organization of the United States. Biennial. 14th ed.
Gale Research Co.
2200 Book Tower
Detroit, MI 48226.
(Trade, business, professional, labor, scientific, educational, fraternal, and social organizations of the United States.)

▶ *National Trade and Professional Associations of the United States*, 1984
Klein Publications, Inc.
Box 8503

Coral Springs, FL 33065.
(4500 national associations, executives, addresses, number of members.)

▶ *National Trade and Professional Associations of the United States*
Columbia Books, Inc.
Suite 300
917 15th St., NW
Washington, DC 20005.
(Approximately 4300 national associations, addresses, executives, number of members.)

If you are unable to obtain the information by contacting the above organizations, reference librarians at public and university libraries can be extremely helpful. Many libraries have computer access to a multitude of sources. Moreover, librarians, for a small fee ranging from $5 to $30, may be able to perform a search to help you get the needed information. Such searches can provide you with a list of journal articles, books, dissertations, technical reports, and government publications. Frequently, a brief summary of the article is provided so you can identify which references are of particular interest. These searches are usually not limited to books and magazines at that particular library.

Some of the computer databases that will be of particular interest for you at this stage include:

▶ *ABI/Inform:* Contains general information on banking, finance, labor relations, and sales management. Business and related international journals are included.

▶ *F & S Index:* Covers domestic and international companies, products, and industry information including new products, technical developments, and forecasts of companies' sales and profits. Publications included are business, financial and trade journals, plus bank letters.

▶ *Predicasts:* Lists a series of databases containing statistical data on time series and forecasts for products, industries, and demographics.

The young man asked, "Are these searches difficult to perform or could I do them myself?"

Norman responded, "All you need is a personal computer with a modem. You can do the search yourself, and it really is not that difficult. If you are interested, you should contact *Dialog Information Services, Inc.* They provide access to many different databases. They will even tell you how to perform the searches yourself. With Dialog's system, you could do computer trademark searches for $25 to $50. You may perform patent searches. In addition to the particular search fee, there is a $25 per year membership charge. Their address is:

Dialog Information Services, Inc.
3460 Hillview Avenue
Palo Alto, CA 94304
Phone: (800)-334-2564 or (415)-858-2700

"Take this copy of our Invention Record form," Norman continued. "Fill it out as accurately and objectively as possible. The more truthful and thorough you are, the greater the chances of your idea becoming a success."

Remember, if a dispute should arise between you and another inventor regarding who owns the same or a similar idea, the one to prevail is usually the person who had the idea first with the most complete records, including the date of conception; date that a prototype was built; results of testing (reduction to practice); and witnessed by a disinterested, unrelated party.

If an individual was the first to conceive an idea, but did not actively pursue building a prototype, he will lose to a second party who had *the same idea* after, but diligently acted to reduce it to practice by either building and testing a model or by submitting a patent application.

With that, the successful entrepreneur handed Jim the Invention Record form and said, "You may find this step a bit more difficult. Now you are on your own. Give me a call after you have completed the record, and I'd be happy to review it with you."

The young man was startled at how quickly things had begun to move. He stood up and thanked Norman and left.

As Jim left the successful entrepreneur's office, he felt very alone. He also was excited to try his hand at the challenge before him. He read the Invention Record. It was quite extensive. Most of the questions he could answer without too much difficulty, however, others would require additional research.

On pages 18–26 is a blank copy of the Invention Record, then there is a copy as filled out by Jim for his invention.

After Jim finished the Invention Record, he found only one question that gave him trouble—the market potential.

He thought, "Sure, I could put down millions—and I certainly hope for that—but let's see if I can be a little more accurate."

The next day the young man went to the main public library and began his search. He talked to Bill the reference librarian.

Jim: I am trying to find the market size for a new toothbrush. Where is the best place to start?

Bill: We have many sources you can check yourself; however, we also offer a computerized search. The cost ranges between $20 to $35 and will provide you with lists of journals, articles, books, dissertations, technical reports, and government publications applicable to your area of interest. Also included in the search is a brief summary of the article. Consequently if you find an article of particular interest, you can request the full article and read it in greater depth. Furthermore, the search is not limited to the books and magazines in this library.

Jim: That sounds fantastic! I never knew such a service was available.

Bill: Most large public and university libraries offer the service, and we have found it can be a great help while saving time. We have several computer databases, as well as lists of information. A computer database is just a term for a depository of information stored on a computer. It can be just about any type of information from magazine articles, books, and so on. We have compiled an information sheet of the databases we have found to be the most useful; here it is. (Hands Jim the following list.)

COMPUTER INFORMATION SEARCHES

▸ *Dissertation Abstracts On-Line:* Provides broad subject, title, and author access to all dissertations accepted for doctoral degrees granted by U.S. educational institutions and some non-U.S. institutions. Multidisciplinary subject coverage includes the humanities, sciences, and engineering.

▸ *National Technical Information Service:* Provides cross-disciplinary coverage primarily of federal government-sponsored technical reports and other government analyses prepared by government agencies or their contractors and grantees. Examples of topics included are: Environmental Pollution Control, Energy Conversion, Technology Transfer, Behavioral/Societal Problems, and Urban Planning.

Business/Management

▸ *ABI/Inform:* Stresses general sciences applicable to many types of business and industries such as banking, finance, labor relations, and sales management. Business and related international journals are covered, too.

▸ *F & S Index:* Covers domestic and international companies, products, and industries, including corporate acquisitions and mergers, new products, technological developments, sociopolitical factors, and forecasts of companies' sales and profits. Information is retrievable for countries and industries by company name, industry (SIC code), and subject.

Bill continued, "I think the best place for us to start is in *Business/Management.*"

After searching, he printed out the following:

824989 *Drug Merch 82/09 P22–24 Dentifrice manufacturers have been battling for brand dominance among Canadian consumers, who currently buy 90% from Crest, Colgate, Aquafresh and Macleans. Heavy consumer and retail promotions emphasizing the importance of having a toothpaste the children will enjoy using have won gels a 40% share. The overnight success of Johnson & Johnson's reach angled toothbrush, launched with a $500,000 TV ad campaign in an extensive sampling program in 1979, has made it clear that Canadian consumers can be persuaded to buy unconventional oral hygiene products. Increased health-consciousness has displaced cosmetic concerns with Canadian consumers who have proved willing to try specialty products that contribute to oral hygiene. Market trends, including the leadership of food stores in dentifrices and oral antiseptics are reviewed. Prospects for brand dominance in toothbrushes, a $16 mil/yr. market that has been growing at 14% yr., and dental floss, which is poised for growth from its current $4.38 million sales floor, are studied.*

CONFIDENTIAL INVENTION RECORD

Invention Title: _____

Date: _____

Inventor(s): _____

Address: _____

_____

_____

Inventor's Signature _____ Date _____

We have read and understand this invention record. We are not co-inventors and agree to keep this confidential.

Witness (Print name): _____

Signature: _____

Date: _____

Witness (Print name): _____

Signature: _____

Date: _____

Accuracy and objectivity are of paramount importance. Sources for all figures and/or estimates should be listed.

Sources: Battelle Memorial Institute, University of Wisconsin, University of Oregon.

I. DISCLOSURE

COMPLETE THIS AS SOON AS POSSIBLE. IT WILL HELP ESTABLISH A CONCEPTION DATE OF YOUR IDEA. Give a *Detailed* description of your invention. Include the size of the device, materials, uses, and so forth. Describe your invention in both technical and nontechnical manner.

Date invention was first conceived: _____

Date invention was first described or shown to others: _____

Who were these people? (name, address, employer):

_____

_____

Date of first sketch or drawing: _____

Date of first photo: _____

Date of first written description: _____

Has the invention been used commercially, sold, or offered for sale?
_____ No _____ Yes Date: _____

Has a prototype been built?
_____ No _____ Yes Date: _____

Future/past date when the invention will be/was likely to go on sale, sold, used publicly, or described in a printed publication:

_____

Was the invention disclosed nonconfidentially to others?
_____ No _____ Yes Date: _____

NOTARY SEAL

State of _____ County of _____ on

this _____ day of _____, 19_____, before me,

_____ Notary Public, personally

appeared _____

Notary's Signature: _____

Notary Public in and for the State of _____.

County of _____.

My commission expires _____.

II. DETAILED DRAWING

Sketch idea in detail labeling all important components.

III. CURRENT STATE OF THE ART

    A. State the problem and describe present method(s), if any, of solving the problem this invention addresses; list references, if possible.

    B. Disadvantages: Describe disadvantages of currently available alternative methods, products, or ideas:

IV. INVENTION DESCRIPTION

    A. Principles: Explain how it works.

    B. Novel Aspects: Describe any significantly different features of this product or idea.

C. Advantages: What are the advantages of this invention over anything similar? Do not say there is nothing similar.

D. Disadvantages: Explain the biggest problem or weakness of this product or process? Be honest and objective.

E. Alternatives: Describe alternative methods of construction, operation, or use.

F. Market Potential: Describe the sales, market potential, and the target market (who will buy the product). Also document how the sales potential information was obtained, (magazine, newspaper, trade organization, census data, etc.).

V. DEVELOPMENT STATUS

A. I currently have . . .

_____ Idea only

_____ Rough sketches and/or diagrams

_____ Finished, working drawings

_____ Photographs

B. Prototype availability:

_____ None at this time

_____ Functional model or prototype—Date built _____

_____ Market-ready prototype

C. Design modifications: What additional changes in the design have you considered?

_____

_____

_____

D. Were any government grants employed in the development of this? _____ No _____ Yes (If yes, give details.)

_____

_____

_____

E. Were any facilities, other than yours, used in the development of this invention?

_____ No _____ Yes (If yes, give details. What, where, and why did you use them?)

_____

_____

_____

_____

VI. LEGAL PROTECTION

A. I currently have . . .

_____ No protection

_____ Disclosure Document. Date _____

_____ Patent with U.S. Patent Office. Date _____

_____ Patent has been applied for. Date _____

VII. PRODUCT TESTING

A. Tests which have been conducted include:

_____ None

_____ User testing. Date _____

_____ Functional testing. Date _____

_____ Market testing. Date _____

_____ Product safety testing. Date _____

VIII. MARKET INFORMATION

A. Projected Market: Who will use your invention? List users in order of importance, i.e., the first is the most important.

1. _____

2. _____

3. _____

B. Customer Commitment: Have you secured any commitments from customers to buy your invention? If yes, supply details including actual unit volume or dollar amount?

_____

_____

_____

IX. PRODUCT COST

_____ I have made no attempt to gather cost information.

_____ Estimated product costs:

Materials $_____ Date of estimate _____

Source: _____

Labor $_____ Date of estimate _____

Source: _____

Manufacturing Equipment

Cost of dies, molds, etc. $_____

Date of Estimate _____

Source: _____

I estimate the amount of time that has been spent on the development of this idea to be: _____

Since date: _____

The amount of money spent, to date, on the development of this idea is approximately: _____

X. CONSUMER ACCEPTANCE:

I have planned for, or have developed . . .

_____ User instructions

_____ Packaging design

_____ Display advertising

_____ None of these

I have completed the above . . .

_____ With professional assistance

_____ On my own (supply details)

_____

_____

_____

CONFIDENTIAL INVENTION RECORD

Invention Title: *The Scrub-n-Brush Toothbrush*

Date: *January 1, 19—*

Inventor(s): *Mr. Jim White*

Address: *4451 La Salle, Chicago, IL 60601*

Inventor's Signature _____*Jim White*_____ Date ___1/1/--___

We have read and understand this invention record. We are not co-inventors and agree to keep this confidential.

Witness (Print name): _____

Signature: _____

Date: _____

Witness (Print name): _____

Signature: _____

Date: _____

I. DISCLOSURE

COMPLETE THIS AS SOON AS POSSIBLE. IT WILL HELP ESTABLISH A CONCEPTION DATE OF YOUR IDEA. Give a *Detailed* description of your invention. Include the size of the device, materials, uses, and so forth. Describe your invention in both technical and nontechnical manner.

Date invention was first conceived: _____ *12/18/86* _____

Date invention was first described or shown to others: _*12/20/86*_

Who were these people? (name, address, employer):
*Friends, Dave Johnson and Bill Thomas, Chicago, IL*
_____

Date of first sketch or drawing: _____ *7/3/87* _____

Date of first photo: _____ *10/15/87* _____

Date of first written description: _*7/3/87 (very brief description)*_

Has the invention been used commercially, sold, or offered for sale?
_√_ No _____ Yes Date: _____

Has a prototype been built?
_√_ No _____ Yes Date: _____

Future/past date when the invention will be/was likely to go on sale, sold, used publicly, or described in a printed publication:
_____

Was the invention disclosed nonconfidentially to others?
_____ No _√_ Yes Date: _*12/21/88*_

NOTARY SEAL

State of _____ County of _____ on

this _____ day of _____, 19_____, before me,

_____ Notary Public, personally

appeared _____

Notary's Signature: _____

Notary Public in and for the State of _____.

County of _____.

My commission expires _____.

II. DETAILED DRAWING

Sketch idea in detail labeling all important components.

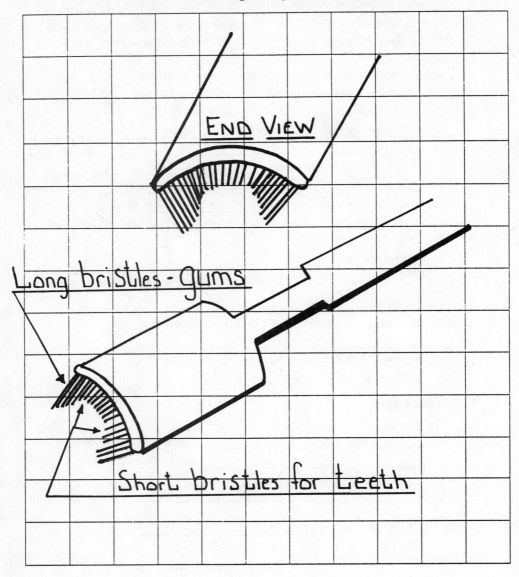

END VIEW

Long bristles - gums

Short bristles for teeth

III. CURRENT STATE OF THE ART

A. State the problem and describe present method(s), if any, of solving the problem this invention addresses; list references, if possible.

In order to brush ones' teeth properly, one needs to brush back-and-forth across the tops of the teeth. To clean the face surfaces, an up-and-down method is needed. Also the inside surfaces of the teeth require up-and-down strokes. Another, different stroke, is required to massage the gums. Many people will not take the time to complete all four. Therefore, the teeth are prone to cavity and disease.

B. Disadvantages: Describe disadvantages of currently available alternative methods, products, or ideas:

Current techniques require four different strokes to clean ones' teeth. Most people will use one or two different strokes to clean the teeth and will be far less diligent about cleaning the back surfaces of the teeth or massaging the gums.

IV. INVENTION DESCRIPTION

A. Principles: Explain how it works.

The principle of the Scrub-n-Brush toothbrush is to have angled brush bristles that enable the toothbrush to clean the teeth and massage the gums simultaneously.

B. Novel Aspects: Describe any significantly different features of this product or idea.

The angled side bristles not only massage the gums but also clean the teeth around the gums. This area is very difficult to clean with currently available brushes.

C. Advantages: What are the advantages of this invention over anything similar? Do not say there is nothing similar.

Simultaneous ability to:
1. *Clean tops of teeth.*
2. *Clean sides of teeth.*
3. *Massage the gums.*
4. *Clean around teeth at the gum line.*

D. Disadvantages: Explain the biggest problem or weakness of this product or process? Be honest and objective.

The side bristles may irritate the gums. These side bristles need to be made out of a softer, less irritating material.

E. Alternatives: Describe alternative methods of construction, operation, or use.

1) The side bristles could have variable angle settings to enable the brush to clean the gums at any given spot.

2) Adjustable head sizes to accommodate differing teeth sizes from adults' to childrens'.

F. Market Potential: Describe the sales, market potential, and the target market (who will buy the product). Also document how the sales potential information was obtained, (magazine, newspaper, trade organization, census data, etc.).

V. DEVELOPMENT STATUS

A. I currently have . . .
___√___ Idea only
_____ Rough sketches and/or diagrams
_____ Finished, working drawings
_____ Photographs

B. Prototype availability:
___√___ None at this time
_____ Functional model or prototype—Date built _____
_____ Market-ready prototype

C. Design modifications: What additional changes in the design have you considered?

Putting the toothpaste in the handle to automatically feed
into the bristles. _____

_____

D. Were any government grants employed in the development of this? ___√___ No _____ Yes (If yes, give details.)

_____

_____

_____

E. Were any facilities, other than yours, used in the development of this invention?
___√___ No _____ Yes (If yes, give details. What, where, and why did you use them?)

_____

_____

_____

_____

VI. LEGAL PROTECTION

A. I currently have . . .

___√___ No protection

_____ Disclosure Document. Date _____

_____ Patent with U.S. Patent Office. Date _____

_____ Patent has been applied for. Date _____

VII. PRODUCT TESTING

A. Tests which have been conducted include:

___√___ None

_____ User testing. Date _____

_____ Functional testing. Date _____

_____ Market testing. Date _____

_____ Product safety testing. Date _____

VIII. MARKET INFORMATION

A. Projected Market: Who will use your invention? List users in order of importance, i.e., the first is the most important.

1. *Adults—Higher educated* _____

2. *Adults—General* _____

3. *Kids* _____

B. Customer Commitment: Have you secured any commitments from customers to buy your invention? If yes, supply details including actual unit volume or dollar amount?

_____ *No* _____

_____

_____

IX. PRODUCT COST

__√___ I have made no attempt to gather cost information.

_____ Estimated product costs:

Materials $_____ Date of estimate _____

Source: _____

Labor $_____ Date of estimate _____

Source: _____

Manufacturing Equipment

Cost of dies, molds, etc. $_____

Date of Estimate _____

Source: _____

I estimate the amount of time that has been spent on the development of this idea to be: ____*90 hours*_____

Since date: ____*12/18/86*_____

The amount of money spent, to date, on the development of this idea is approximately: ____*$100.00*_____

X. CONSUMER ACCEPTANCE:

I have planned for, or have developed . . .

_____ User instructions

_____ Packaging design

_____ Display advertising

__√___ None of these

I have completed the above . . .

_____ With professional assistance

_____ On my own (supply details)

_____

_____

_____

Jim: It is nice to know what the Canadian market potential is, but I am primarily interested in the U.S. market.

Bill: You may want to check a couple of sources yourself. I would recommend that you look at the following books:

▶ *Predicasts F & S Index*

▶ *Statistical Abstracts of the U.S.A.*

▶ *Standard & Poor's Industry Surveys*

▶ *U.S. Industrial Outlook: Department of Commerce*

Also, you can call the trade association in your industry and ask them for market or other information. The best way to locate the trade association in your area is to get the book, *National Trade and Professional Associations of the United States*. That should get you started.

Jim: Yes, thank you (beginning his research).

Starting with *Predicasts F&S Index*, he found that the SIC number for toothbrushes, indexed in the front of the book, was 3991321 and noted that it listed the following magazine article:

D & C Inc. 2/00/87 p. 70

However, this did not appear to be what he was looking for. He asked for further assistance.

Bill: There are two other places we can look. Both are computer databases, one is offered through Dialog Information Systems, and the other is Lexis offered through Mead Data Center. These databases are collections of many business articles. However there will be a charge.

Jim: How much?

Bill: It should be approximately $50 for either one. It may be less if we can quickly find what we need.

Jim: OK, let's give it a try.

Bill: Let's start with Dialog. The first step is to write out your search before using any database; these computer databases are expensive and we do not want to spend more time on-line (using the database) than we have to. Now, we want to know the market share of toothbrushes. When we begin our search on-line our search command for Dialog will be:

s toothbrush?(5n)market and United()States

This instructs the computer to search (s) for *toothbrush* or *toothbrushes* or *toothbrushing*, and the word *market* must be within five words of toothbrush ('n' means near), in an article and the words *United States* must also appear either in the article or in the title.

You could do this at home; all you need is a computer and a modem (built-in telephone) which allows you to phone the computer database.

The first step is to dial the access phone number and *log-on* (obtain access to the database) using your user password that Dialog supplies to you.

Bill: (logging on) OK, we are now on-line. We want to begin our search in database number 16 which is PTS Prompt.

Bill then typed the following:

? b 16

The computer responded with (computer responses are in **bold**, Bill's input in *italics*):

File 16: Prompt
? s toothbrush?(5n)market and United()States
Processing. . . .
    238 Toothbrush?
    261923 Market
    17 Toothbrush?(5n)Market
    834703 United States
S1 15 toothbrush?(5n)market and United()States

Bill: This means that there are 15 articles that meet all our criterion. Let's take a brief look at them. He then typed:

? t S1/2/1–15

This instructs the computer to print Set 1 in format 2, which is a one sentence summary of the article, and to list citations 1 through 15.

The computer listed all 15 citations and two caught Bill's attention. These were citation 9 and 10. He then typed:

? t S1/5/9–10

This tells the computer to print out articles 9 and 10 in format 5 which gives a more detailed summary of the articles.

The computer responded with:

1/5/9
1542347
    TOOTHBRUSHES   Toothbrush market share by
retail outlet. 1986 (%). Chain Drug Review: Report for
the Chain Drug Store Industry. January 5, 1987 p. 12

Supermarket	**30**
Chain drugstores	**29**
Food/drug combos	**17**
Discounters	**15**
Independent drugstores	**9**
Total sales ($ mil)	**245**

1/5/10
1225403
Marketing briefs: Colgate Palmolive.
Soap/Cosmetics/Chemical Specialties July 1985 p. 22
      Colgate-Palmolive has introduced its Colgate Plus diamond-headed toothbrush that offers better access to back teeth. The toothbrush market is now worth $225 million.

Jim: That is exactly what I wanted! How much do I owe you?

Bill: The total search cost for this search comes to $19.52. Before we quit, let's try the database offered through Mead. I won't charge you for this search, it's for your information in case you want to do this again in the future.

Jim: Thank you very much.

Bill then performed a search using Mead's database and printed the following:

ADWEEK, April 18, 1988: Sunstar's acquired John O. Butler Company of Chicago, which gives Sunstar a foot in the door in the $265 million-a-year toothbrush market.

Bill: The cost for this search is $24.00. I think now you can be confident with the estimates of the market share because we have confirmed it through three different sources. You can perform the searches yourself by contacting either Dialog Information Services, 3460 Hillview Avenue, Palo Alto, CA 94304, (415) 858-4098 or outside California 1-800-334-2564, or by contacting Mead Data Center, 9443 Springboro Pike, P.O. Box 93, Dayton, OH 45401, (513) 865-6800 or outside Ohio 1-800-227-4908.

Jim paid Bill and returned to his desk and thought, "I could say that the market for my Scrub-n-Brush is approximately $250 million but a large portion of that market is very difficult to reach. It would be very difficult to try to sell my product to all the 'mom-and-pop' corner drugstores. I think that only the major chains would be accessible to me because of my limited resources. This market represents 29 percent of $245 million, or $71 million. Of that market, perhaps there are 10 major chains, and maybe I could sell 3 percent of them. This would mean that the market for my product would be about $2 million ($71 × .03). Since toothbrushes sell for about $1.29, the volume would be 1,500,000 units."

It was now closing time at the library, and the young man was feeling pretty good at having solved his problem. He went back to the librarian and thanked him for all the help.

Several days passed before the young man was ready to return to see the successful entrepreneur with his completed Invention Record form.

They met, and Norman read through the Confidential Invention Record and asked, "How did you calculate the market potential?"

The young man explained how helpful the reference librarian had been and how they found the market figures using the computer. "It took me all day, eight full hours, at the library."

The successful entrepreneur was pleased that Jim had the perseverance to meet the challenge. "He will need all of that perseverance and determination in the next steps," thought Norman.

Norman: The completed Invention Record will not only help you document and evaluate your idea, it will also assist you in marketing your invention when the time comes.

Jim: Now what's the next step?

Norman: The next step is to get you some legal protection against someone stealing your idea. We can do this in one of three ways:

1. Have two witnesses sign your invention log book and your Invention Record, then have the signatures notarized on your Invention Record.

2. Submit a Document Disclosure Form to the U.S. Patent Office.

3. Submit a patent application.

Since preparing and submitting a patent application will cost you over $2000, we will begin with the first two options; These cost much less.

The successful entrepreneur called in his secretary, and they both signed the young man's log book and Invention Record. Norman then told Jim to have the signatures notarized, available at most banks.

Norman: (continued) After you have your Invention Record notarized, we will send a copy of it to the U.S. Patent Office to be included under their Document Disclosure Program. Basically, this program, for a fee of $6.00, will hold your Record confidentially in their files for two years. Although the Document Disclosure Program does not give you any patent protection, it does help establish a conception date for your invention. This can be useful if you do not have anyone you trust to sign your log book. This Program can be valuable if someone else submits a patent application before you do but after you have submitted a Document Disclosure.

Jim: So the Document Disclosure, with my own records, gives me extra protection?

Norman: That's correct. However, you will need to send the Patent Office a cover letter along with your Invention Record, explaining your desire to have this information kept under the Document Disclosure Program. You can use the form letter we have that our own, new product engineers use. Include two copies of the letter so that the Patent Office can return one for your records. Also enclose a self-addressed stamped envelope.

You should be aware that you can be excluded from obtaining a patent if you have publicly disclosed your invention, in a printed publication, or offered it for sale more than one year prior to submitting a patent application. Even if you are awarded a patent and you publicly offered your innovation for sale over one year prior to applying for a patent, your patent may be found invalid. If you confidentially disclose your idea to others, the one-year clock does not start. Also, while it is true that you have a one-year grace period for a U.S. patent; a public disclosure *any time* before filing a foreign patent application invalidates most foreign patents. If you think your product has international sales potential, and many do, talk to a patent attorney to find out about various, cost-effective ways to obtain patents in foreign countries. Your attorney can also tell you more specifically when your one-year clock starts to tick.

The successful entrepreneur gave the young man the document on page 41.

Warning from the Patent Office

The two-year retention period should not be considered a grace period during which the inventor can wait to file his or her patent application without possible loss of benefits. It must be recognized that in establishing priority of an invention, the inventor must also be diligent in developing the invention. He or she cannot just submit for the Disclosure Document and do nothing else.

Inventors are also reminded that any public use or sale in the United States or publication of the invention anywhere in the world more than one year prior to the filing of a patent application on that invention will prohibit the granting of a patent.

If the inventor is not familiar with what is considered to be "diligence in completing the invention" or "reduction to practice" under the patent law or if he/she has other questions about patent matters, the Patent and Trademark Office advises him/her to consult an attorney or agent registered to practice before the Patent and Trademark Office. *The Directory of Registered Patent Attorneys and Agents Arranged by States and Counties* is available from the Superintendent of Documents, U.S. Government Printing Office, Washington, DC 20402. Patent attorneys and agents may be found in the telephone directories of most major cities. Also, many large cities have associations of patent attorneys which may be helpful.

DISCLOSURE DOCUMENT DEPOSIT

SUBJECT:
FOR: (INVENTOR'S NAME)

FOR OFFICE USE ONLY
DATE DEPOSITED:
DEPOSIT NUMBER:

Commissioner of Patents and Trademarks
Washington, D.C. 20231

To the Commissioner of Patents and Trademarks:

The undersigned, being the inventor of the disclosed invention, requests
that the enclosed papers be accepted under the Disclosure Document
Program, and that they be preserved for a period of two years.

The $6.00 fee is enclosed check #
Mail receipt to:

_____

_____

_____

_____
(Signature)

_____
(Print)

_____
(Date)

Enclosures:
Drawing Enclosures _____ page/s
Description Enclosures _____ page/s
(1) Self addressed envelope
(1) Duplicate copy of this letter

DISCLOSURE DOCUMENT DEPOSIT

SUBJECT: *The scrub-n-Brush Toothbrush*
FOR: *Mr. Abe Order*

FOR OFFICE USE ONLY
DATE DEPOSITED:
DEPOSIT NUMBER:

Commissioner of Patents and Trademarks
Washington, D.C. 20231

To the Commissioner of Patents and Trademarks:

The undersigned, being the inventor of the disclosed invention, requests that the enclosed papers be accepted under the Disclosure Document Program, and that they be preserved for a period of two years.

The $6.00 fee is enclosed check # *1244*
Mail receipt to:

Mr. Jim White

451 La Salle Avenue

Chicago, IL 60601

Jim White
(Signature)

Jim White
(Print)

2/3/--
(Date)

Enclosures:
Drawing Enclosures __1__ page/s
Description Enclosures __9__ page/s
(1) Self addressed envelope
(1) Duplicate copy of this letter

4

Evaluation

INVENTION EVALUATION

The successful entrepreneur continued his discussion with Jim.

Norman: Before you invest all your time and money in your new idea, let's take an objective look at your invention and evaluate its potential. We do that at our company by completing a New Product Evaluation. We ask the development engineer to fill it out; then we ask an "expert" to complete one. This procedure enables us to assess the commercial potential and feasibility before investing substantial resources in the idea.

Answer each question by checking the appropriate blank. We can do it together if you prefer, but we must make a conscientious effort to be frank and honest when answering each question.

Jim, together with Norman, filled out the New Product Evaluation Form.

When the New Product Evaluation Form was complete, Norman instructed Jim to appraise his Scrub-n-Brush.

Norman: After you have finished evaluating each aspect of the questionnaire, transfer your answers onto the Profile Chart. We should be able to more closely determine the prospects of success for your product.

Norman: (reviewing the chart) It appears pretty good. Your product seems especially strong in most areas except in marketing. Before we make a go/no-go assessment, let's get an "expert" to complete a similar chart. This will give us an independent opinion of your invention. Do you know an expert in the field?

Jim: What do you mean "expert"?

Norman: An individual who works in the field with intimate knowledge of the needs and constraints of the customers.

Jim: Well, I know an orthodontist. Would he be OK?

Norman: Yes. Ask him to answer the questions on the New Product Evaluation
          Form and fill in the Expert Evaluation Profile Chart. Once he has com-
          pleted that, give me a call and we can get back together and discuss this
          further.

When the orthodontist had completed his evaluation, he filled out the Expert
Evaluation Profile Chart (page 63).

The successful entrepreneur looked at Jim's chart and compared it to the
expert's Profile.

Norman: Several discrepancies surfaced. We first look to see if there are any −2s
          or +2s for the Critical Aspects. This tells us if the product is particularly
          good or bad in specific areas. Then we compare both charts to try to
          determine why differences were recorded between the Expert's and
          Individual's Charts. (turning to the young man) Why do you think there
          was a difference in "Market Penetration"? Your opinion was 2 to 4 years
          but the expert said it would take 5 to 10 years.

Jim: I asked him that question, and he said that it will take several years to
          make people aware that this product exists. Then it will take several
          years to get dentists to recommend it to patients.

Norman: Oh, I see. Then why did you say promotion was not needed, but your
          expert said extensive advertising was needed?

Jim: He said it was similar to the market penetration question. It would take
          extensive promotion to make people aware that the product is available.

Norman: That sounds reasonable. Let's take a look at each Profile Chart. Yours
          has more positive answers; it tilts to the right. However, the expert's
          chart is fairly evenly distributed—more neutral.

Jim: What does that mean?

Norman: It means that we may continue developing and marketing the product,
          but you should neither sell your house nor spend your kids' education
          money just yet.

The young man became depressed and felt rejected.

Norman: Now these differences are not uncommon. In fact, usually the Expert
          takes a more negative posture. We are only concerned with responses
          that are extremely positive or negative. In this instance, there are not
          significant numbers of either. So let's continue with the next step, unless
          you would like to quit?

NEW PRODUCT EVALUATION*

Title: _____

Inventor(s): _____

Address: _____

Date: _____

*This evaluation is a digest of forms and procedures used by: Monsanto Chemical Company, General Electric Company, Pittsburgh Steel, The University of Wisconsin, The University of Oregon, and Baylor University.

For each question, check the one answer that most accurately applies.

A. Critical Aspects

1. NEED: People perceive their need for this invention as being:
   _____ (−2) Very low. Most people are unaware a problem exists.
   _____ (−1) Low. Some people feel a problem exists.
   _____ (0) Do not know.
   _____ (+1) Moderate. Most people feel a problem exists.
   _____ (+2) High. Most people feel a problem exists and think this invention would solve the problem.

2. SALES: Estimated annual sales are likely to be:
   _____ (−2) Less than $500,000
   _____ (−1) $500,000–$1 million
   _____ (0) Do not know
   _____ (+1) $1 million–$10 million
   _____ (+2) Greater than $10 million

3. FUNCTIONAL FEASIBILITY: Will this invention do what it was intended to do?
   _____ (−2) No. The concept cannot be made to work.
   _____ (−1) Yes. But major engineering changes might be needed.
   _____ (0) Do not know.
   _____ (+1) Yes. But minor changes might be needed.
   _____ (+2) It will work without any engineering modifications.

4. PROFITABILITY: How likely is the anticipated revenue from the invention able to cover anticipated costs like manufacturing, advertising, and selling?
   _____ (−2) Might not cover any of the relevant costs
   _____ (−1) Might cover some of the costs
   _____ (0) Do not know
   _____ (+1) Might cover all costs and provide some profit
   _____ (+2) Will cover all costs and provide substantial profit

5. COMPETITION: Existing competition for this invention appears to be:
   _____ (−2) Substantial—several directly competitive products exist
   _____ (−1) Moderate—several somewhat competitive products
   _____ (0) Do not know
   _____ (+1) Low—one or two somewhat competitive products
   _____ (+2) No competitive products known

6. PRODUCT DIFFERENTIATION: Compared to substitutes and/or competing products or processes, the function of this innovation might be perceived as:

_____ (−2) Inferior to other products
_____ (−1) Similar to other products
_____ (0) Do not know
_____ (+1) Superior to other products
_____ (+2) Far superior to other products

7. PRODUCTION FEASIBILITY: With regard to equipment or technological requirements, this idea might:

_____ (−2) Be impossible to produce
_____ (−1) Be difficult to produce
_____ (0) Do not know
_____ (+1) Have minor problems in production
_____ (+2) Have no problems in production

8. MARKET PENETRATION: The time to reach targeted yearly sales volume would be:

_____ (−2) More than 10 years
_____ (−1) 5 to 10 years
_____ (0) Do not know
_____ (+1) 2 to 4 years
_____ (+2) Less than 2 years

B. Financial and Legal Aspects

9. PAYBACK: The time required to recover initial investment (production molds, etc.) is likely to be:

_____ (−2) Over 10 years
_____ (−1) 3 to 10 years
_____ (0) Do not know
_____ (+1) 1 to 3 years
_____ (+2) Less than 1 year

10. PROTECTION: The prospects for patent, copyright, or other legal protection appears to be:

_____ (−2) None. No legal protection possible
_____ (−1) Limited legal protection possible
_____ (0) Do not know
_____ (+1) Patent protection possible
_____ (+2) Can definitely be patented with broad coverage

C. Product Aspects

11. VISIBILITY: The advantages and benefits of this product might appear to customers to be:

_____ (−2) Very obscure. Cannot determine the advantages

_____ (−1) Obscure. Requires explanation

_____ (0) Do not know

_____ (+1) Noticeable. Advantages are apparent to some customers

_____ (+2) Very visible. Advantages and benefits are obvious to everyone

12. DURABILITY: Compared to competing or substitute products or processes, the durability of this product is likely to be perceived as:

_____ (−2) Inferior

_____ (−1) Similar

_____ (0) Do not know

_____ (+1) Superior

_____ (+2) Far superior

13. SOCIETAL: The benefit to society from this invention might:

_____ (−2) Have a large negative effect

_____ (−1) Have some or moderate negative effect

_____ (0) Do not know

_____ (+1) Have a positive effect

_____ (+2) Have a strong positive effect on society

14. REGULATIONS: In terms of present laws and regulations, this invention:

_____ (−2) Might not comply

_____ (−1) Might require major changes to comply

_____ (0) Do not know

_____ (+1) Might require minor changes

_____ (+2) Complies without any changes

15. ENVIRONMENT: In terms of pollution and litter, use of this product might:

_____ (−2) Violate environmental regulations or have dangerous environmental consequences

_____ (−1) Have some negative effect on the environment

_____ (0) Do not know

_____ (+1) Have no effect

_____ (+2) Have positive effect on environment

16. SAFETY: Considering potential safety hazards, the use of this innovation might be:

_____ (−2) Very unsafe when used as intended
_____ (−1) Relatively unsafe
_____ (0) Do not know
_____ (+1) Safe when used as intended
_____ (+2) Very safe under all conditions including misuse

17. TRAINING: The amount of training or education required for correct use of the invention is likely to be:

_____ (−2) Extensive
_____ (−1) Considerable
_____ (0) Do not know
_____ (+1) Little
_____ (+2) None

18. PRODUCT DEPENDENCE: The degree to which the sale or use of this product depends on other products or processes is:

_____ (−2) High. Invention is only usable in conjunction with other product(s)
_____ (−1) Moderate. Invention is contingent upon sales of another product(s)
_____ (0) Do not know
_____ (+1) Low. Invention is slightly dependent on other product(s)
_____ (+2) None. Invention requires no other products to be useful

19. COMPATIBILITY: To be able to use this product in conjunction with other existing products, the other products may have to be:

_____ (−2) Significantly altered
_____ (−1) Slightly altered
_____ (0) Do not know
_____ (+1) Alteration not needed
_____ (+2) Product is independent of all other products

20. PRODUCT LIFE: The total sales life of this invention is likely to be:

_____ (−2) 1 to 3 years
_____ (−1) 3 to 5 years
_____ (0) Do not know
_____ (+1) 5 to 10 years
_____ (+2) More than 10 years

21. PRODUCT EXPANSION: The potential for this product to develop into additional products (more styles, price ranges, quality levels) is:

_____ (−2) Very limited. Single product only
_____ (−1) Limited. Additional products possible but unlikely
_____ (0) Do not know
_____ (+1) Moderate. Additional products likely
_____ (+2) High. New product spin-offs likely with applications to several different markets

D. Engineering and Production Aspects

22. DEVELOPMENT STAGE: This invention is in the following stage of development:

_____ (−2) Idea phase. Drawings only
_____ (−1) Rough prototype stage
_____ (0) Do not know
_____ (+1) Final prototype phase—after field test
_____ (+2) Market-ready prototype completed

23. INVESTMENT: The amount of money necessary to bring this invention to a market-ready stage might be:

_____ (−2) Excessive. May not be recoverable
_____ (−1) Heavy. Probably recoverable
_____ (0) Do not know
_____ (+1) Moderate. Recoverable within five years
_____ (+2) Low. Recoverable within two years

24. RESEARCH AND DEVELOPMENT: The research and development necessary to reach the production stage might be:

_____ (−2) Extremely involved and complex
_____ (−1) Moderately complex
_____ (0) Do not know
_____ (+1) Relatively easy
_____ (+2) Very simple

25. RAW MATERIALS: The availability of raw materials necessary to produce this invention appears to be:

_____ (−2) Very low. Extremely difficult and costly
_____ (−1) Low. Limited availability
_____ (0) Do not know
_____ (+1) Moderate. Readily available
_____ (+2) High. Both available and inexpensive

26. QUALITY CONTROL: The quality control required to produce this invention is likely to be:

_____ (−2) Very strict. Precise fit required, no tolerance acceptable
_____ (−1) Semi-strict. Close fit required
_____ (0) Do not know
_____ (+1) Moderate. Allowance for error
_____ (+2) Low. High margin for errors

27. SERVICE: The cost and difficulty of servicing this product might be:

_____ (−2) Very high. Requires frequent servicing and spare parts
_____ (−1) High. Requires periodic servicing and parts
_____ (0) Do not know
_____ (+1) Moderate. Infrequent need for servicing and parts
_____ (+2) Low. Will require little or no parts and service

E. Marketing Aspects

28. MARKET POTENTIAL: The total market for products similar to the invention might be:

_____ (−2) Very small. Very specialized or restricted market
_____ (−1) Small. Regional market
_____ (0) Do not know
_____ (+1) Medium. Limited national market
_____ (+2) Large. Broad national or international potential

29. MARKET ACCEPTANCE: With today's attitudes, this product's chances of being accepted by consumers is likely to be:

_____ (−2) Very low. People do not want to change
_____ (−1) Low. Some resistance
_____ (0) Do not know
_____ (+1) Moderate. No conflict
_____ (+2) High. Readily accepted

30. PRICE: This invention would be priced:

_____ (−2) Higher than competition with less or equal quality
_____ (−1) Higher than competition with higher quality
_____ (0) Do not know
_____ (+1) Similar in price but higher quality
_____ (+2) Lower price and higher quality

31. **CUSTOMER COMMITMENT:** Have you been able to sell or obtain commitments from customers to buy, make, or use the invention?

_____ (−2) Have had no customer inquiries

_____ (−1) Have had some customer inquiries

_____ (0) Do not know

_____ (+1) Have sold product in limited quantities

_____ (+2) Have sold substantial quantities ($10,000 or more)

32. **POTENTIAL COMPETITION:** The expected reaction from current competition or the competition from new entrants to this innovation is likely to be:

_____ (−2) Very high. Short lead time

_____ (−1) High. Relatively short lead time

_____ (0) Do not know

_____ (+1) Moderate. Product lead time is relatively long

_____ (+2) Low. Strong chance to gain large market shares

33. **DISTRIBUTION:** The anticipated cost and difficulty of establishing sales and distribution channels are likely to be:

_____ (−2) Very high. Requires specialized and dedicated sales force

_____ (−1) Medium. Distributor can handle product with other lines

_____ (0) Do not know

_____ (+1) Low. Trade show exposure is sufficient

_____ (+2) Very low. Product sells itself with just point of purchase displays

34. **DEMAND STABILITY:** The cyclical demand is likely to be:

_____ (−2) Highly unstable. Severe, unpredictable fluctuations

_____ (−1) Unstable. Moderate fluctuations

_____ (0) Do not know

_____ (+1) Stable. Modest variations that can be accurately predicted

_____ (−2) Highly stable. Steady demand

35. **DEMAND TREND:** The market demand for products similar to this invention appears to be:

_____ (−2) Declining. Potentially obsolete soon

_____ (−1) Steady. Demand expected to remain constant

_____ (0) Do not know

_____ (+1) Growing slowly. Modest growth

_____ (+2) Rapidly expanding. Significant growth potential

36. **PROMOTION:** The advertising or promotion for this invention is likely to be:

_____ (−2) Extensive. Advertising and promotion needed

_____ (−1) Appreciable. Advertising and promotion required

_____ (0) Do not know

_____ (+1) Little. Advertising and promotion required

_____ (+2) No promotion needed

INVENTION EVALUATION
PROFILE CHART

CRITICAL ASPECTS

MINUS		PLUS		
-2	-1	0	+1	+2
					NEED
					SALES
					FUNCTIONALITY
					PROFITABILITY
					COMPETITION
					DIFFERENTIATION
					PRODUCTION FEASIBILITY
					MARKET PENETRATION

PRODUCT NAME: _____

DATE: _____

OTHER ASPECTS

MINUS		PLUS		
-2	-1	0	+1	+2
PAYBACK				
PROTECTION				
VISIBILITY				
DURABILITY				
SOCIETAL				
REGULATIONS				
ENVIRONMENTAL				
SAFETY				
TRAINING				
DEPENDENCE				
COMPATIBILITY				
PRODUCT LIFE				
EXPANSION				
DEVELOPMENT				
INVESTMENT				
R & D				
RAW MATERIALS				
QUALITY				
SERVICE				
POTENTIAL				
ACCEPTANCE				
PRICE				
COMMITMENT				
POTENTIAL COMPETITION				
DISTRIBUTION				
STABILITY				
TREND				
PROMOTION				

Modified from: John H. Harris, "New Product Profile Chart," Chemtech, September 1976.

NEW PRODUCT EVALUATION*

Title: *Scrub-n-Brush Toothbrush*

Inventor(s): *Jim White*

Address:

Date: *January 2, 1989*

*This evaluation is a digest of forms and procedures used by: Monsanto Chemical Company, General Electric Company, Pittsburgh Steel, The University of Wisconsin, The University of Oregon, and Baylor University.

For each question, check the one answer that most accurately applies.

A. Critical Aspects

1. NEED: People perceive their need for this invention as being:
_____ (−2) Very low. Most people are unaware a problem exists.
_____ (−1) Low. Some people feel a problem exists.
__√__ (0)   Do not know.
_____ (+1) Moderate. Most people feel a problem exists.
_____ (+2) High. Most people feel a problem exists and think this invention would solve the problem.

2. SALES: Estimated annual sales are likely to be:
_____ (−2) Less than $500,000
_____ (−1) $500,000–$1 million
_____ (0)   Do not know
__√__ (+1) $1 million–$10 million
_____ (+2) Greater than $10 million

3. FUNCTIONAL FEASIBILITY: Will this invention do what it was intended to do?
_____ (−2) No. The concept cannot be made to work.
_____ (−1) Yes. But major engineering changes might be needed.
_____ (0)   Do not know.
_____ (+1) Yes. But minor changes might be needed.
__√__ (+2) It will work without any engineering modifications.

4. PROFITABILITY: How likely is the anticipated revenue from the invention able to cover anticipated costs like manufacturing, advertising, and selling?
_____ (−2) Might not cover any of the relevant costs
_____ (−1) Might cover some of the costs
__√__ (0)   Do not know
_____ (+1) Might cover all costs and provide some profit
_____ (+2) Will cover all costs and provide substantial profit

5. COMPETITION: Existing competition for this invention appears to be:
_____ (−2) Substantial—several directly competitive products exist
__√__ (−1) Moderate—several somewhat competitive products
_____ (0)   Do not know
_____ (+1) Low—one or two somewhat competitive products
_____ (+2) No competitive products known

6. PRODUCT DIFFERENTIATION: Compared to substitutes and/ or competing products or processes, the function of this innovation might be perceived as:

_____ (−2) Inferior to other products
_____ (−1) Similar to other products
_____ (0) Do not know
_____ (+1) Superior to other products
___√___ (+2) Far superior to other products

7. PRODUCTION FEASIBILITY: With regard to equipment or technological requirements, this idea might:

_____ (−2) Be impossible to produce
_____ (−1) Be difficult to produce
_____ (0) Do not know
_____ (+1) Have minor problems in production
___√___ (+2) Have no problems in production

8. MARKET PENETRATION: The time to reach targeted yearly sales volume would be:

_____ (−2) More than 10 years
_____ (−1) 5 to 10 years
_____ (0) Do not know
___√___ (+1) 2 to 4 years
_____ (+2) Less than 2 years

B. Financial and Legal Aspects

9. PAYBACK: The time required to recover initial investment (production molds, etc.) is likely to be:

_____ (−2) Over 10 years
_____ (−1) 3 to 10 years
_____ (0) Do not know
___√___ (+1) 1 to 3 years
_____ (+2) Less than 1 year

10. PROTECTION: The prospects for patent, copyright, or other legal protection appears to be:

_____ (−2) None. No legal protection possible
_____ (−1) Limited legal protection possible
_____ (0) Do not know
___√___ (+1) Patent protection possible
_____ (+2) Can definitely be patented with broad coverage

C. Product Aspects

11. VISIBILITY: The advantages and benefits of this product might appear to customers to be:

_____ (−2) Very obscure. Cannot determine the advantages

_____ (−1) Obscure. Requires explanation

_____ (0) Do not know

_____ (+1) Noticeable. Advantages are apparent to some customers

__√__ (+2) Very visible. Advantages and benefits are obvious to everyone

12. DURABILITY: Compared to competing or substitute products or processes, the durability of this product is likely to be perceived as:

_____ (−2) Inferior

__√__ (−1) Similar

_____ (0) Do not know

_____ (+1) Superior

_____ (+2) Far superior

13. SOCIETAL: The benefit to society from this invention might:

_____ (−2) Have a large negative effect

_____ (−1) Have some or moderate negative effect

_____ (0) Do not know

__√__ (+1) Have a positive effect

_____ (+2) Have a strong positive effect on society

14. REGULATIONS: In terms of present laws and regulations, this invention:

_____ (−2) Might not comply

_____ (−1) Might require major changes to comply

_____ (0) Do not know

_____ (+1) Might require minor changes

__√__ (+2) Complies without any changes

15. ENVIRONMENT: In terms of pollution and litter, use of this product might:

_____ (−2) Violate environmental regulations or have dangerous environmental consequences

_____ (−1) Have some negative effect on the environment

_____ (0) Do not know

__√__ (+1) Have no effect

_____ (+2) Have positive effect on environment

16. SAFETY: Considering potential safety hazards, the use of this innovation might be:

_____ (−2) Very unsafe when used as intended

_____ (−1) Relatively unsafe

_____ (0) Do not know

__√__ (+1) Safe when used as intended

_____ (+2) Very safe under all conditions including misuse

17. TRAINING: The amount of training or education required for correct use of the invention is likely to be:

_____ (−2) Extensive

_____ (−1) Considerable

_____ (0) Do not know

__√__ (+1) Little

_____ (+2) None

18. PRODUCT DEPENDENCE: The degree to which the sale or use of this product depends on other products or processes is:

_____ (−2) High. Invention is only usable in conjunction with other product(s)

_____ (−1) Moderate. Invention is contingent upon sales of another product(s)

_____ (0) Do not know

__√__ (+1) Low. Invention is slightly dependent on other product(s)

_____ (+2) None. Invention requires no other products to be useful

19. COMPATIBILITY: To be able to use this product in conjunction with other existing products, the other products may have to be:

_____ (−2) Significantly altered

_____ (−1) Slightly altered

_____ (0) Do not know

__√__ (+1) Alteration not needed

_____ (+2) Product is independent of all other products

20. PRODUCT LIFE: The total sales life of this invention is likely to be:

_____ (−2) 1 to 3 years

_____ (−1) 3 to 5 years

_____ (0) Do not know

__√__ (+1) 5 to 10 years

_____ (+2) More than 10 years

21. PRODUCT EXPANSION: The potential for this product to develop into additional products (more styles, price ranges, quality levels) is:

_____ (−2) Very limited. Single product only
__✓__ (−1) Limited. Additional products possible but unlikely
_____ (0)   Do not know
_____ (+1) Moderate. Additional products likely
_____ (+2) High. New product spin-offs likely with applications to several different markets

D. Engineering and Production Aspects

22. DEVELOPMENT STAGE: This invention is in the following stage of development:

_____ (−2) Idea phase. Drawings only
__✓__ (−1) Rough prototype stage
_____ (0)   Do not know
_____ (+1) Final prototype phase—after field test
_____ (+2) Market-ready prototype completed

23. INVESTMENT: The amount of money necessary to bring this invention to a market-ready stage might be:

_____ (−2) Excessive. May not be recoverable
_____ (−1) Heavy. Probably recoverable
_____ (0)   Do not know
_____ (+1) Moderate. Recoverable within five years
__✓__ (+2) Low. Recoverable within two years

24. RESEARCH AND DEVELOPMENT: The research and development necessary to reach the production stage might be:

_____ (−2) Extremely involved and complex
_____ (−1) Moderately complex
_____ (0)   Do not know
_____ (+1) Relatively easy
__✓__ (+2) Very simple

25. RAW MATERIALS: The availability of raw materials necessary to produce this invention appears to be:

_____ (−2) Very low. Extremely difficult and costly
_____ (−1) Low. Limited availability
_____ (0)   Do not know
_____ (+1) Moderate. Readily available
__✓__ (+2) High. Both available and inexpensive

26. QUALITY CONTROL: The quality control required to produce this invention is likely to be:

_____ (−2) Very strict. Precise fit required, no tolerance acceptable

_____ (−1) Semi-strict. Close fit required

_____ (0) Do not know

_____ (+1) Moderate. Allowance for error

__√__ (+2) Low. High margin for errors

27. SERVICE: The cost and difficulty of servicing this product might be:

_____ (−2) Very high. Requires frequent servicing and spare parts

_____ (−1) High. Requires periodic servicing and parts

_____ (0) Do not know

_____ (+1) Moderate. Infrequent need for servicing and parts

__√__ (+2) Low. Will require little or no parts and service

E. Marketing Aspects

28. MARKET POTENTIAL: The total market for products similar to the invention might be:

_____ (−2) Very small. Very specialized or restricted market

_____ (−1) Small. Regional market

_____ (0) Do not know

_____ (+1) Medium. Limited national market

__√__ (+2) Large. Broad national or international potential

29. MARKET ACCEPTANCE: With today's attitudes, this product's chances of being accepted by consumers is likely to be:

_____ (−2) Very low. People do not want to change

__√__ (−1) Low. Some resistance

_____ (0) Do not know

_____ (+1) Moderate. No conflict

_____ (+2) High. Readily accepted

30. PRICE: This invention would be priced:

_____ (−2) Higher than competition with less or equal quality

_____ (−1) Higher than competition with higher quality

__√__ (0) Do not know

_____ (+1) Similar in price but higher quality

_____ (+2) Lower price and higher quality

31. **CUSTOMER COMMITMENT:** Have you been able to sell or obtain commitments from customers to buy, make, or use the invention?

_____ (−2) Have had no customer inquiries

_____ (−1) Have had some customer inquiries

__√__ (0) Do not know

_____ (+1) Have sold product in limited quantities

_____ (+2) Have sold substantial quantities ($10,000 or more)

32. **POTENTIAL COMPETITION:** The expected reaction from current competition or the competition from new entrants to this innovation is likely to be:

_____ (−2) Very high. Short lead time

__√__ (−1) High. Relatively short lead time

_____ (0) Do not know

_____ (+1) Moderate. Product lead time is relatively long

_____ (+2) Low. Strong chance to gain large market shares

33. **DISTRIBUTION:** The anticipated cost and difficulty of establishing sales and distribution channels are likely to be:

_____ (−2) Very high. Requires specialized and dedicated sales force

__√__ (−1) Medium. Distributor can handle product with other lines

_____ (0) Do not know

_____ (+1) Low. Trade show exposure is sufficient

_____ (+2) Very low. Product sells itself with just point of purchase displays

34. **DEMAND STABILITY:** The cyclical demand is likely to be:

_____ (−2) Highly unstable. Severe, unpredictable fluctuations

_____ (−1) Unstable. Moderate fluctuations

_____ (0) Do not know

_____ (+1) Stable. Modest variations that can be accurately predicted

__√__ (+2) Highly stable. Steady demand

35. **DEMAND TREND:** The market demand for products similar to this invention appears to be:

_____ (−2) Declining. Potentially obsolete soon

__√__ (−1) Steady. Demand expected to remain constant

_____ (0) Do not know

_____ (+1) Growing slowly. Modest growth

_____ (+2) Rapidly expanding. Significant growth potential

36. **PROMOTION:** The advertising or promotion for this invention is likely to be:

_____ (−2) Extensive. Advertising and promotion needed

_____ (−1) Appreciable. Advertising and promotion required

_____ (0) Do not know

_____ (+1) Little. Advertising and promotion required

__√__ (+2) No promotion needed

INVENTION EVALUATION PROFILE CHART

CRITICAL ASPECTS

MINUS			PLUS		
-2	-1	0	+1	+2	
		■			NEED
			■		SALES
				■	FUNCTIONALITY
	■				PROFITABILITY
■					COMPETITION
				■	DIFFERENTIATION
				■	PRODUCTION FEASIBILITY
			■		MARKET PENETRATION

PRODUCT NAME: *Scrub-n-Brush*

DATE: *January 2, 1989*

OTHER ASPECTS

	MINUS			PLUS	
	-2	-1	0	+1	+2
PAYBACK				■	
PROTECTION		■			
VISIBILITY					■
DURABILITY	■				
SOCIETAL				■	
REGULATIONS					■
ENVIRONMENTAL				■	
SAFETY				■	
TRAINING				■	
DEPENDENCE				■	
COMPATIBILITY		■			
PRODUCT LIFE				■	
EXPANSION		■			
DEVELOPMENT		■			
INVESTMENT					■
R & D					■
RAW MATERIALS					■
QUALITY					■
SERVICE					■
POTENTIAL					■
ACCEPTANCE		■			
PRICE			■		
COMMITMENT			■		
POTENTIAL COMPETITION		■			
DISTRIBUTION		■			
STABILITY					■
TREND		■			
PROMOTION					■

INVENTION EVALUATION
PROFILE CHART

EXPERT'S EVALUATION

PRODUCT NAME: _____

CRITICAL ASPECTS

MINUS　　　　PLUS

-2	-1	0	+1	+2	
					NEED
					SALES
					FUNCTIONALITY
					PROFITABILITY
					COMPETITION
					DIFFERENTIATION
					PRODUCTION FEASIBILITY
					MARKET PENETRATION

OVERALL EVALUATION

In my opinion, the likelihood of this product being successful in the marketplace is (please circle scale next to appropriate number):

It definitely will not be successful — **0**

It probably will not be successful — **25**

It might be successful — **50**

It probably will be successful — **75**

It definitely will be successful — **100**

Print Name:_____

I agree to keep this information confidential:

Signature: _____　　Date: _____

OTHER ASPECTS

MINUS　　　　PLUS

	-2	-1	0	+1	+2
PAYBACK					
PROTECTION					
VISIBILITY					
DURABILITY					
SOCIETAL					
REGULATIONS					
ENVIRONMENTAL					
SAFETY					
TRAINING					
DEPENDENCE					
COMPATIBILITY					
PRODUCT LIFE					
EXPANSION					
DEVELOPMENT					
INVESTMENT					
R & D					
RAW MATERIALS					
QUALITY					
SERVICE					
POTENTIAL					
ACCEPTANCE					
PRICE					
COMMITMENT					
COMPETITION					
DISTRIBUTION					
STABILITY					
TREND					
PROMOTION					

INVENTION EVALUATION PROFILE CHART

EXPERT EVALUATION

PRODUCT NAME: *Scrub-n-Brush*

CRITICAL ASPECTS

	MINUS			PLUS	
	-2	-1	0	+1	+2
NEED		■			
SALES				■	
FUNCTIONALITY				■	
PROFITABILITY			■		
COMPETITION		■			
DIFFERENTIATION					■
PRODUCTION FEASIBILITY					■
MARKET PENETRATION		■			

OTHER ASPECTS

	MINUS			PLUS	
	-2	-1	0	+1	+2
PAYBACK			■		
PROTECTION			■		
VISIBILITY				■	
DURABILITY	■				
SOCIETAL				■	
REGULATIONS					■
ENVIRONMENTAL				■	
SAFETY				■	
TRAINING		■			
DEPENDENCE			■		
COMPATIBILITY				■	
PRODUCT LIFE		■			
EXPANSION		■			
DEVELOPMENT			■		
INVESTMENT			■		
R & D				■	
RAW MATERIALS				■	
QUALITY				■	
SERVICE				■	
POTENTIAL			■		
ACCEPTANCE		■			
PRICE			■		
COMMITMENT			■		
COMPETITION	■				
DISTRIBUTION	■				
STABILITY			■		
TREND		■			
PROMOTION	■				

OVERALL EVALUATION

In my opinion, the likelihood of this product being successful in the marketplace is (please circle scale next to appropriate number:

It definitely will not be successful	0
It probably will not be successful	25
It might be successful	(50)
It probably will be successful	75
It definitely will be successful.	100

Print Name: Dr. John Smith   **Date:** 2/5/19--

I agree to keep this information confidential:

Signature: *John Smith*   Date: 2/5/19--

5

Patent Search

The young man was not ready to quit. He said, "let's continue."

Norman: The next step is to complete a patent search to see if someone else has already patented your idea.

Jim: Isn't that expensive?

Norman: If you have a patent attorney or patent agent perform the search for you, the cost can range from $400 to $500, or more. However, you can do a preliminary search yourself at a nominal charge, usually under $50. If you plan to complete the search yourself, and I wholeheartedly encourage you to try, you will find the references you need at most major public libraries. Plan on spending a full 6- to 8-hour day in research; not only will you save money, but you also may run across some patents that will give you ideas for additional products or improvements. Performing the search yourself may not be as complete as having a patent agent in Washington do it for you, however, it will give you a first cut to see if someone has already patented your innovation or a similar one. When the time comes to submit a patent application, your preliminary search will assist your patent attorney in preparing the patent application. This will make the attorney's job easier and should save you money. Performing the search yourself can be fun as well as educational if you know what you are doing.

Jim: But I don't. Let me guess; you have developed a step-by-step patent search procedure?

Norman: Right! We have found that just about anyone can perform a patent search if he follows a sequential procedure. Ours is one that is easy to follow.

There are basically two places to perform a patent search:

▶ The Public Search Room
  U.S. Patent Office
  2221 Jefferson Davis Boulevard
  Arlington, VA
  The U.S. Patent Office is the best place, or

▶ One of the local Patent Depository Libraries

It is much easier to complete a search at the U.S. Patent Office, because the patents are filed by subject. So if you want to search "Toothbrushes," you could go to the bin for toothbrushes; and most of the relevant patents would be there. On the other hand, Patent Depository Libraries file the patents according to patent *number*, not by *subject*, making your chore more difficult and time consuming. Following is a list of Patent Depository Libraries:

Patent Depository Libraries

ALABAMA
Auburn University Library
Auburn University
Auburn, AL 36849

Birmingham Public Library
2100 Park Place
Birmingham, AL 35203

ARIZONA
Arizona State University Library
Tempe, AZ 85287

CALIFORNIA
Los Angeles Public Library
630 West Fifth Street
Los Angeles, CA 90071

California State Library
Library Courts Building
Sacramento, CA 95809

San Diego Public Library
202 C Street
San Diego, CA 92101

Patent Information Clearinghouse
Sunnyvale Public Library
665 West Olive Avenue
Sunnyvale, CA 94806

COLORADO
Denver Public Library
3840 York Street
Denver, CO 80205

DELAWARE
University of Delaware Library
Newark, DE 19711

GEORGIA
Georgia Institute of Technology
Price Gilbert Memorial Library
Atlanta, GA

IDAHO
University of Idaho Library
Moscow, ID 83843

ILLINOIS
Chicago Public Library
400 N. Frankin
Chicago, IL 60602

Illinois State Library
Centennial Building
Springfield, IL 62756

INDIANA
Indianapolis Public Library
40 E. St. Clair Street
Indianapolis, IN 46206

LOUISIANA
Louisiana State University
Troy H. Middleton Library
Baton Rouge, LA 70803

MARYLAND
University of Maryland Library
University of Maryland
College Park, MD 20742

MASSACHUSETTS
Boston Public Library
Copley Square
Boston, MA 02117

MICHIGAN
The University of Michigan
818 Harlan
Hatcher Library–South
Ann Arbor, MI 48109

Detroit Public Library
5201 Woodward Avenue
Detroit, MI 48202

MINNESOTA
Minneapolis Public Library
300 Nicollet Mall
Minneapolis, MN 55401

MISSOURI
Linda Hall Library
5109 Cherry Street
Kansas City, MO 64110

St. Louis Public Library
1301 Olive Street
St. Louis, MO 63103

MONTANA
Montana College of Mineral Science
and Technology
Butte, MT 59701

NEBRASKA
University of Nebraska
Lincoln Library
Lincoln, NB 68588

NEVADA
University of Nevada–Reno
Reno, NV 89557

NEW HAMPSHIRE
University of New Hampshire
The University Library
Durham, NH 03824

NEW JERSEY
Newark Public Library
5 Washington Street
Newark, NJ 07101

NEW MEXICO
The University of New Mexico
General Library
Albuquerque, NM 87131

NEW YORK
The New York State Library
Cultural Education Center
Albany, NY 12230

Buffalo and Erie County Public Library
Lafayette Square
Buffalo, NY 14203

The New York Public Library
521 West 43rd Street
New York, NY 10036

NORTH CAROLINA
North Carolina State University
The D.H. Hill Library
Raleigh, NC 27650

OHIO
Public Library of Cincinnati
800 Vine Street
Cincinnati, OH 45202

Cleveland Public Library
325 Superior Avenue
Cleveland, OH 44114

Ohio State University Library
1858 Neil Avenue Mall
Columbus, OH 43210

Toledo Public Library
325 Michigan Street
Toledo, OH 43624

OKLAHOMA
Oklahoma State University Library
Stillwater, OK 74078

PENNSYLVANIA
Alliance College
Cambridge Springs, PA 16403

The Franklin Institute Library
20th Street & Parkway
Philadelphia, PA 19103

Carnegie Library of Pittsburgh
4400 Forbes Avenue
Pittsburgh, PA 15217

Pennsylvania State University
Pattee Library
University Park, PA 16802

RHODE ISLAND
Providence Public Library
150 Empire Street
Providence, RI 02903

SOUTH CAROLINA
Medical University of South Carolina
171 Ashley Avenue
Charleston, SC 29425

TENNESSEE
Memphis Public Library
1850 Peabody Avenue
Memphis, TN 38104

TEXAS
The University of Texas at Austin
The General Libraries
Austin, TX 78712

Texas A&M University
Sterling C. Evans Library
College Station, TX 77843-5000

Dallas Public Library
1515 Young Street
Dallas, TX 75201

Rice University
The Fondren Library
Houston, TX 77251-1892

WASHINGTON
University of Washington
Suzzallo Library
Seattle, WA 98195

WISCONSIN
University of Wisconsin
Kurt F. Wendt Engineering Library
215 North Randall Avenue
Madison, WI 53706

Milwaukee Public Library
814 West Wisconsin Avenue
Milwaukee, WI 53233

PERFORMING THE PATENT SEARCH

Outline

The basic procedure for performing a patent search is as follows:

▶ Identify into which "classification" your invention falls, such as brushes, cleaning instruments, etc.

▶ Get a listing of patents in that classification(s).

▶ Briefly check the patents cited to see which ones, if any, are relevant.

▶ Review the patents that appear to be similar.

▶ Make copies of the patents that appear similar.

▶ Fill out the search report.

In order to perform your search, the following government publications will be helpful:

1. *Index to Classification* —to determine the class and subclass of your product

2. *Manual of Classification* —to locate a more specific detailed subclass

3. *Classification Definition* —to check whether your class/subclass is correct

4. *U.S. Patent Classification–Subclass Listing* —to get a listing of patent numbers in each class/subclass

5. *Official Gazette* —to review a patent's brief picture and one paragraph summary to see if it is relevant to your product

"Wait a minute! Norman stopped, "Instead of my telling you how to do this, I know the 'searcher' at the downtown library, let's see if he can help you."

The successful entrepreneur picked up the phone, dialed the library, and asked for the Patent Search Room. When the connection was completed, the successful entrepreneur was able to make an appointment for Jim with an associate who worked in the Search Room. He turned to the young man and said, "OK, you're all set. Tom is a friend of mine and is an extremely knowledgeable searcher. He works in the Search Room at the library, and he can help you get started and answer any questions you may have. Good-bye and good hunting."

When the young man got to the main library he found Tom. The young man asked, "How do you know Norman?"

Tom: Many years ago, when the successful entrepreneur was just starting, he used to come here frequently. He would be waiting outside the library before we would open at 8:30 A.M. and would stay until closing at 5:30 P.M. Over the years, he has made many searches and has become quite proficient at it; look at him now. Did you know he has over 100 patents?

Jim: No, I didn't.

Tom: Since those early days, he has sent many others over here, but most of them get discouraged and quit. It really takes a special individual to see an idea through to reality. It takes . . .

Jim: Perseverance and persistence. (breaking in) I know. The successful entrepreneur has already given me that lecture.

Tom: OK, let's get started. I've put these books here for you to use. They are really all you'll need to complete your search. I'll get you set up and then you can continue.

Jim: OK.

Tom: The first thing we do is get the classification number of your patent. What is your idea?

Jim: It's a toothbrush.

Tom: To get the classification number, we look at the *Index to Classification*. We look under "Tooth" and "Teeth." Notice there is a listing for "Brushes." It cites *Class 15, Subclass 167A* (page 70).

Because there might be several different subclasses which further break down "Brushes," we will try to clarify the subject further. To do this, we need the *Manual of Classifications* (page 71).

These categories are listed numerically according to subclasses. The *Manual of Classifications* is used in conjunction with the *Index to Classification* to check selected classes and locate other ones that are closely related.

We can see that "Subclass 167" has subcategories: R and A. These represent further breakdowns of the subclasses. Before checking each patent in each subclass, let's first see if we are on the right track. We do this by using the *Classification Definitions*. This book further defines products within different subclasses (page 72).

We can see that under "Class 15 Subclass 167" it says, *Implements of the brush or broom type especially adapted for cleaning the teeth or nails. It also cites Subclasses 132 and 401;* however, these are not relevant to your product, therefore you need not research those two.

Now we try to get a list of the patents in Class 15, Subclass 167, A and R. First, let's start with 167A. To get a listing of patents in this class and

MANUAL OF CLASSIFICATIONS

CLASS 15   BRUSHING, SCRUBBING AND GENERAL CLEANING

	IMPLEMENTS	179	...Rotary
	.Eraser	180	....Disk
	..Including handling means	181	....Laminated
	...Which is pencil sheath or casing	182	....Spiral bristle mount
	....Including advancing means for	183	....Tuft-holding bar
	erasive body	184	..Housings
430	.....Axially adjustable sleeve	185	..Pivoted
431	....Including enclosure for base of	186	..Individual-bristle mount
	erasive body	187	...Integral
432	.....Multi-partite handling means	188	...Rubber
433	...Including advancing means for erasive	189	..Stitched and wire bound
	body	190	..Tuft fasteners
434	...Directly adjustable erasive body	191 R	..Tuft socket
435	.Penpoint or penholder	191 A	....Fountain
436	..Including projectable and retractable	192	...Cemented
	penpoint	193	...Plastic mass
437	..With means supporting or stabilizing	194	...Detachable tuft
	implement in use	195	...Folded tuft
438	..Including manually adjustable gripping	196	...Drawn work
	or releasing means for penpoint	197	...Metal bristle
439	...Pivoted or arcuately movable	198	.....Rotary
440	....About axis of penholder	199	....Retaining wire
441	...Including opposed, relatively axially	200	...Metal bristle
	movable gripping members	201	...Movable tuft section
442	...And ejector	202	....Detachable
443	..Penholder shaped to receive or engage	203	....Folding
	hand or finger	204	....With core
444	..Penholder includes specific penpoint	205	....Folded tuft
	retaining means	206	..Twisted bristle holder
445	..Specific penpoint	207	..Wire wound
446	...Specific material	208	.Fabric
447	...Bifurcate	209 R	.Wipers, daubers, and polishers
141 R	.Beaters	209 B	....Scourers
141 A	...Rotary	209 C	....Fibrous mass
142	.Grids and combs	209 D	......With handle
143 R	.Handles	209 E	....Powder puff
143 A	...For portable machine	210 R	...Special work
143 B	...Variable length	210 A	.....Venetian blind
144 R	..Adjustable	210 B	.....Rod or wire
144 A	....Universally	210.5	...Graining implements
144 B	....Telescopic type	211	...Hollow-ware cleaners
145	..Detachable	212	......Expansible
146	.Holders, brush and broom	213	......Rotary
147 R	.Holders, mop	214	....Lens cleaners
147 A	...Non-clamped	215	....Mats
147 B	...Frame attached cloth	216	.....Combined
147 C	...Both jaws movable	217	.....Tuft carrying
147 D	...With shaker	218	....Razor cleaners
148	..Convertible	218.1	....Cutlery cleaners
149	..Expansible	219	....Wall-paper cleaners
150	...Pivoted jaw	220 R	...Window cleaners
151	...Sliding jaw	220 A	......Magnetic
152	...Lever operated	221	...Collection chamber
153	...Screw operated	222	...End grip
154	..Spring wire and runner	223	..Work face with exposed laminae
159 R	.Brushes and brooms	224	....Channeled
159 A	...Bristle configuration or composition	225	....Coil
160	..Special work		....Laminated
161	...Boot cleaners	226	....Strands
162	...Flue cleaners	227	..Mitts, cots, and shoes
163	....Suspension	228	..Mops and heads
164	...Hollow-ware cleaners	229 R	....Strands
165	....Collapsible	229 A	......Implement handle non-rotatable
166	...Stripping	229 AC	........Cloth sheath type head
167 R	...Tooth and nail brushes	229 AP	........Pocket type head
167 A	.....Toothbrush, work enveloping	229 AW	........Twisted wire frame
167 B	....Nail brush	229 B	......Implement handle rotatable
168	..Bridles	229 BC	........Cloth sheath type head
169	...Adjustable	229 BP	........Pocket type head
170	...Straw supported	229 BW	........Twisted wire frame
171	...Heads and casings	230	....Rotary
172	...Adjustable head	230.1	....With cooling means
173	...Axial clamp	230.11	....Roller with handle
174	...Bands	230.12	....Adhesively bound parts
175	...Braces, caps, and shields	230.13	....Coil wound
176	...Detachable head	230.14	....Sectored disc or cylinder
177	...Lateral clamp	230.15	....Stitched laminates
178	....Pivoted jaw	230.16	....Interrupted work engaging surface

112, 216, and 217.

SEARCH CLASS:

401, Coating Implements with Material Supply, subclass 39 for a device including a brush for cleaning shoes combined with an applying brush and material supply (polish) therefor.

162. Implements of the brush or broom type especially adapted for cleaning chimney-flues or stove-flues.

　　(1)　Note. See this class, subclasses 104.03+, 163, 242, 243 and 249.

　　(2)　Note. See Class 126, Stoves and Furnaces, subclass 16.

163. Implements of the brush or broom type especially adapted for cleaning chimney or other flues and so suspended that they may be drawn up and let down in the flue.

　　(1)　Note. See this class, subclasses 243 and 249.

164. Implements of the brush or broom type especially adapted for the cleaning of hollow ware.

SEARCH THIS CLASS, SUBCLASS:

71, 180, 211 and 502, for other hollow ware cleaners.

165. Implements of the brush or broom type especially adapted for cleaning hollow ware and which are collapsible for entrance through the narrow mouth of such ware and expansible after entrance.

SEARCH THIS CLASS, SUBCLASS:

72 and 212.

SEARCH CLASS:

29, Metal Working, subclasses 110+ particularly subclasses 113, 117 and 126 for expansible rolls per se not elsewhere classifiable and see the Notes thereto for other rolls and combinations involving rolls.

166. Implements of the brush or broom type especially adapted for applying coloring or other matter in stripe form or for lettering goods with distinguishing marks or addresses.

SEARCH THIS CLASS, SUBCLASS:

246+, and especially subclass 248 for striping attachments.

503, for fluid pavement and floor markers.

560, for implements with material supply having a work surface or member engaging guide.

167. Implements of the brush or broom type especially adapted for cleaning the teeth or nails of the user or another.

SEARCH CLASS:

132, Toilet, subclass 84 for a toilet kit including a tooth brush and an additional part or device particularly useful for a toilet function (e.g., comb, mirror).

401, Coating Implements with Material Supply, subclasses 118+ for a toilet kit consisting of a supply of toothpaste and a toothbrush separate from the supply; and subclasses 268+ for a toothbrush having a supply of toothpaste contained therein, (e.g., having a toothpaste reservoir in the handle and means to feed the toothpaste to the bristles).

168. Devices embracing the bristles or fibers of implements of the brush or broom type in such manner as to prevent undue spreading, breaking, or wear thereof.

　　(1)　Note. See this class, subclasses 169, 170 and 248.

169. Devices embracing the bristles or fibers of implements of the brush or broom type in such manner as to prevent undue spreading, breaking, or wear thereof and which are adjustable lengthwise of the implement as wear occurs to expose a fresh portion of the implement for use.

170. Devices embracing the material constituting the working face of implements of the brush or broom type to prevent undue spreading, breaking, or wear thereof and which are supported or carried by said material.

171. Miscellaneous brush or broom heads and casings therefor. These relate in general to means not otherwise provided for to connect the elements of the material forming the

subclass, we refer to the *U.S. Patent Classification–Subclass Listing*. We can see there are 91 patents listed (page 74).

Now comes the fun part. Can you guess what you have to do?

Jim: Look each one up?

Tom: That's right. You look up each patent number in the *Official Gazette Volumes*. Not only will there be a brief synopsis of the patent, but you will also find a picture as well. Once you find a relevant patent, make note of it; I can pull it out for you. You then make copies of those patents you feel are closely related to your idea.

Another tip is that once you find a patent that's similar to yours, make a copy of all the patents cited on that patent as *prior art*. The patent examiner has done some of your work for you. You can use the Searcher's Worksheet Form we use while conducting our own search. It will help you record and keep track of the scope of your search.

Also, the "D" in front of a patent number signifies it is a "Design Patent." This is a patent based primarily on the invention's design or shape. An example of a design patent would be a Raggedy Ann or Raggedy Andy doll. The shape or decoration of the doll is what is unique. You should check the "D" patents as well.

I think you can proceed on your own. You should start with the *Official Gazette*. Any questions?

Jim: No.

Tom: OK, I will be here if you need me.

Jim: Thank you.

Tom: Oh, one more thought. If you do this again in the future and cannot determine the class and subclass you need, the U.S. Patent Office will do it for you if you fill out the following sample form and send it to the Commissioner of Patents and Trademarks. Do not be overly specific, because this is not kept confidential. In other words, try not to disclose any confidential information (page 75).

To simplify matters, you can use this Patent Search Flow Chart that the successful entrepreneur prepared to assist his people in searching. It is so good, we give a copy to everyone doing a search here. Hopefully, it will help you, too (page 77).

The young man began his search in the *Official Gazette*. He was surprised by the many ideas regarding toothbrushes he found; one was the Chewing Toothbrush (page 79).

However none was similar to his Scrub-n-Brush Toothbrush. He then came across the abstract of the *Twin Toothbrush #3,953,907* and he requested a copy of the patent (page 80).

After reviewing this abstract, the young man realized that although this toothbrush had some similarities to his Scrub-n-Brush, this one addressed a different problem from his idea. So he continued checking. He discovered patent #4,223,417. (See pp. 81–88.)

U.S. PATENT CLASSIFICATION - SUBCLASS LISTING

* 165	* 166	* 167A	167B	* 167R
3,750,214X	2,631,325X	1,599,339	2,283,123	D 196,635X
3,810,334X	2,644,186X	1,616,484	3,966,335X	D 223,651X
3,992,745X	2,662,240X	1,668,385	4,255,826X	RE 16,869U
4,057,871X	2,736,051X	1,679,946	4,420,853X	RE 19,006U
4,393,535X	2,750,616X	1,707,118X	4,454,622	RE 21,197U
4,446,880X	2,810,148X	1,709,262	4,479,277X	RE 22,938
4,562,608X	2,837,757X	1,727,497	4,480,351X	RE 23,975U
	2,853,731X	1,748,895	4,572,689X	2,976U
166	2,907,061X	1,776,312		18,653
	2,936,474X	1,818,146U	167R	26,629
133,088	2,985,902	1,818,840X		28,794
169,906	3,099,029X	1,830,995	D 25,518U	29,419
293,075X	3,114,166X	1,854,264	D 28,523U	43,597
328,426	3,172,140	1,868,368	D 28,527X	54,604
332,392	3,330,253U	1,908,509	D 29,219U	74,560
367,895X	3,333,289U	1,911,973U	D 58,445U	92,298X
377,846	3,337,894	1,950,300X	D 63,608U	140,429
441,012X	3,341,879X	1,967,783U	D 71,286U	158,099
445,158	3,401,418	2,066,241	D 85,112U	164,353
454,755X	3,455,788X	2,077,392	D 88,805U	306,776
467,046X	3,462,789	2,090,663	D 89,299U	323,305X
517,868U	3,611,469X	2,093,383	D 90,106U	335,345
776,329X	3,636,581	2,120,604	D 92,616U	361,806
857,239	3,722,019X	2,140,294	D 94,303U	380,080U
1,004,438	3,930,278	2,214,404U	D 95,405U	407,115X
1,260,189	4,237,579	2,237,694	D 96,599U	430,909X
1,424,416X		2,244,615	D 96,749U	445,683X
1,491,625X	167A	2,257,709X	D 98,042U	461,661
1,584,687X		2,263,360	D 99,364U	467,046X
1,689,855	D 48,666U	2,283,686U	D 100,124U	552,114
1,697,756	D 136,632U	2,284,200X	D 100,558U	560,663
1,714,397	D 141,562U	2,306,264X	D 107,228U	561,995U
1,744,577	D 196,635U	2,528,992	D 109,472U	569,870X
1,882,535	D 258,143X	2,588,601	D 110,186U	669,402
1,915,893	44,997X	2,682,066X	D 113,743U	670,481U
1,927,962	48,666X	2,701,380	D 116,272U	741,722X
1,931,848X	229,823	2,771,624	D 120,345U	758,109
1,946,260	348,508U	3,065,479	D 121,437U	758,764U
1,954,260	569,870	3,067,447	D 121,506U	760,047
1,968,062U	680,365	3,087,183X	D 121,539U	796,980U
2,042,315X	715,263	3,109,192U	D 123,254U	800,422U
2,078,193	741,722	3,640,291U	D 127,983U	803,995
2,116,406	864,054	3,677,264X	D 133,542U	805,733U
2,116,407X	887,181	3,732,589X	D 136,156U	824,087U
2,175,587X	1,025,751	3,769,652	D 136,463U	827,965
2,184,602	1,091,291	3,874,084X	D 136,566U	828,393X
2,237,923	1,111,144	3,953,907	D 136,631U	835,709U
2,247,622X	1,118,156U	4,131,967	D 137,249U	846,900U
2,270,298X	1,133,930	4,137,593	D 137,641U	851,550U
2,289,136U	1,137,916	4,223,417X	D 138,640U	860,435
2,290,302	1,210,623	4,237,574	D 139,246U	860,527U
2,311,038X	1,225,955	4,317,463X	D 139,524U	860,840
2,467,570U	1,270,233	4,366,592X	D 140,438U	876,185
2,507,056X	1,353,780	4,382,309	D 142,917U	878,486U
2,525,100X	1,389,624	4,428,091	D 151,237U	890,143
2,532,110X	1,417,407	4,449,266	D 153,130U	914,501U
2,553,453U	1,421,199	4,486,914	D 162,941X	935,493X
2,558,191	1,492,660	4,493,125	D 163,707X	958,371
2,584,504	1,546,322X	4,498,209	D 165,248U	1,018,927
2,610,344	1,565,750	4,530,369X	D 187,976U	1,028,211

CLASS/SUBCLASS CLARIFICATION SAMPLE LETTER

Date:

Commissioner of Patents and Trademarks
Washington, D.C. 20231
Subject: _____(Invention Name)_____

Dear Sir:

Please let me know what subject area [class(es) and subclass(es)] cover my idea, which has certain features of structure, modes of operation, and intended uses which I have described on the attached page.

Please fill in the Class/Subclass on the blank provided and return one copy of this form to me in the enclosed, self-addressed stamped envelope.

This invention appears to be covered in Class _____ Subclass _____ .
Related Classes/Subclasses are: _____ .

Thank you for your help.

Sincerely,

Name
Address

Enclosures:
Self-addressed stamped envelope
2 Copies of this letter

SEARCHER'S WORKSHEET

INVENTION NAME:

INVENTOR(S):

DATE & LOCATION OF SEARCH:

INVENTION DESCRIPTION:

SEARCH CLASSIFICATIONS

Class/Subclass	Description	Comments

RELEVANT PATENTS

Patent Number	Title	Date	Class/Sub	Why Better/Worse?

Page ___ of ___

PATENT SEARCH FLOW CHART

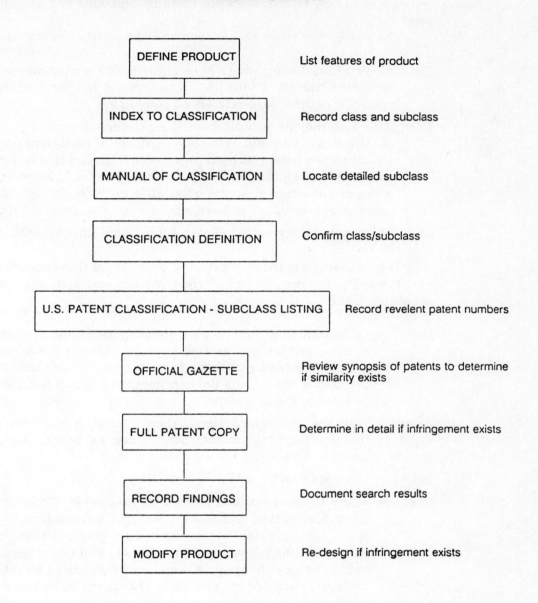

DEFINE PRODUCT	List features of product
INDEX TO CLASSIFICATION	Record class and subclass
MANUAL OF CLASSIFICATION	Locate detailed subclass
CLASSIFICATION DEFINITION	Confirm class/subclass
U.S. PATENT CLASSIFICATION - SUBCLASS LISTING	Record revelent patent numbers
OFFICIAL GAZETTE	Review synopsis of patents to determine if similarity exists
FULL PATENT COPY	Determine in detail if infringement exists
RECORD FINDINGS	Document search results
MODIFY PRODUCT	Re-design if infringement exists

"This patent looks very similar to mine," thought the young man. "What am I going to do? All this work for nothing. Someone has already patented *my* idea!"

The young man returned to Tom and told him what he had discovered.

Tom: I have a friend here doing a patent search. She is a patent attorney. It would be best to ask her. (With that, Tom brought Julie over to meet the young man. She reviewed the referenced patent.)

Julie: Although the one you discovered looks similar to your product, a review of the claims at the end of the patent, the most important part of the patent which gives a patent its legal protection, indicates that this patent covers a "mechanized" toothbrush with "movable bristles." However, your "Scrub-n-Brush Toothbrush" seems quite different than the mechanical one because your idea does not have movable bristles. Does it? You are OK.

Jim: Thank you. I am greatly relieved. I think I am finished with my search.

The following day the young man returned to see the successful entrepreneur. When Jim entered Norman's office, the successful entrepreneur asked how the search went.

Jim: Quite well. I had one concern about someone else's patent being similar to mine; but a friend of Tom, a patent attorney, reviewed it with me. I am now satisfied that there does not seem to have been a patent issued previously that covers the concept of the Scrub-n-Brush. I'm ready to proceed to the next step.

Norman: Wait one minute my friend. There are still a few more considerations that you must take into account. It may make your life easier the next time you have to perform a patent search.

Jim: What are they?

Norman: Many Patent Depository Libraries now offer "CASSIS" which stands for Classification and Search Support Information System. CASSIS is a computer database that can reduce your searching time by listing for you all the relevant patent numbers you might need without your having to look them up. A search can be done in minutes and usually without charge, or for a minimal charge normally less than $25.

Jim: That would have made my job much easier. Why didn't you tell me about CASSIS before?

Norman: Because, first you should know the manual procedure. Also, CASSIS is *not* a complete listing of all issued patents, only the more recent ones. CASSIS can search for key words in a patent as well as patents cited as references in other patents, such as *brushes, teeth,* or *toothbrush,* which will help you get started.

3,769,652
CHEWING TOOTHBRUSH
Corrado Rainer, 2 Via Brennero, Bolzano, Italy
Filed Nov. 30,1971, Ser. No. 203,309
Claims priority, application Italy, Nov. 30, 1970, 4901 A/70
Int. Cl. A46b 1/00, 9/02
U.S. Class 15-167A   2 Claims

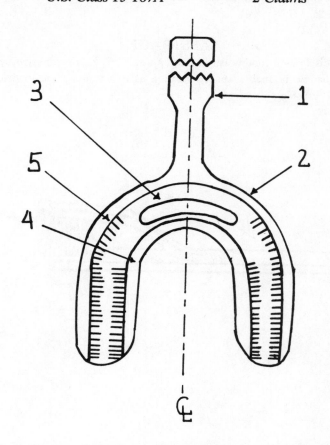

A chewing toothbrush comprising a handle having an arcuately shaped portion of resilient material at one end thereof, which is of a size shape to conform to the line of teeth of the user when the latter bites down onto the same. The said arcuate portion has upstanding flanges on its edges, which extend generally parallel to the lateral surfaces of the teeth, and projecting from said flanges toward the tooth surfaces are short bristles of soft elastomeric material, which scrub the surfaces and interstices of the teeth as the user chews on the device.

United States Patent [19]

Froidevaux

[1] **3,953,907**

[45] May 4, 1976

---

[54] TWIN TOOTHBRUSHES

[76] Inventor: Camille Henri Froidevaux, P.O. Box 63, Lookout Mountain, TN 37350

[22] Filed: Feb. 26, 1975

[21] Appl. No.: 553,221

ABSTRACT

This document discloses a toothbrush having opposed bristles rigidly separated from the bifurcated end of a handle in such a spaced relation as to accommodate teeth of different thicknesses for vertical brushing

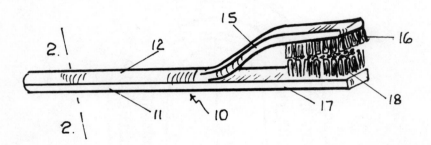

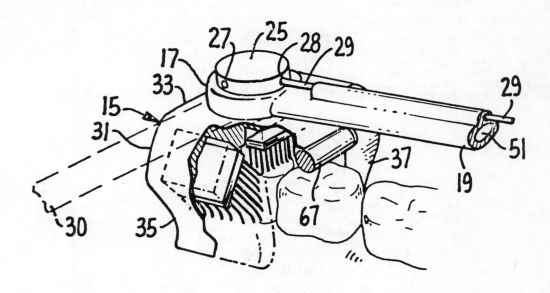

United States Patent [19]

Solow

[11] **4,223,417**

[45] **Sep. 23, 1980**

[54] **GLIDING, MECHANIZED TOOTHBRUSH**

[76] Inventor: Terry S. Solow, 410 Playa Blvd., La Selva Beach, Calif. 95076

[21] Appl. No.: 8,064

[22] Filed: Jan. 31, 1979

[51] Int. Cl.² A46B 13/02
[52] U.S. Cl. .... 15/22 R; 15/167 A; 128/62 A
[58] Field of Search .... 15/22 R, 22 A, 22 C 15/167 A; 128/62 A

[56] **References Cited**

U.S. PATENT DOCUMENTS

Re. 26,589	5/1969	Murey et al.	15/22 R
2,766,750	10/1956	Darcissac	128/62 A X
2,771,624	11/1956	Ripper	15/167 A
3,382,519	5/1968	Piggott	15/22 R
3,984,890	10/1976	Collis	15/22 R
4,137,593	2/1979	Porper	15/167 A

FOREIGN PATENT DOCUMENTS

2012815 9/1971 Fed. Rep. of Germany .... 128/62 A

Primary Examiner—Edward L. Roberts
Attorney, Agent, or Firm—Robert G. Slick

[57] **ABSTRACT**

A Gliding, Mechanized Toothbrush is provided wherein a small box-like member, called the head, having a handle thereon, encloses a pair of brushes adapted to brush both sides of a tooth at the same time. The bristles of these brushes extend at an angle to the sides of the teeth whereby these bristles also enter and clean the sulcus area and embrasures. In the preferred embodiment of this invention, additional brushes clean the biting surfaces of the teeth. A handle is used to pull the head along a row of teeth. Preferably, the head is mounted on a swivel so that the head can be turned relative to the handle, facilitating brushing teeth in various parts of the mouth.

18 Claims, 16 Drawing Figures

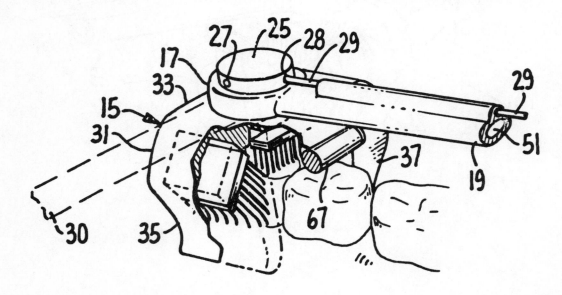

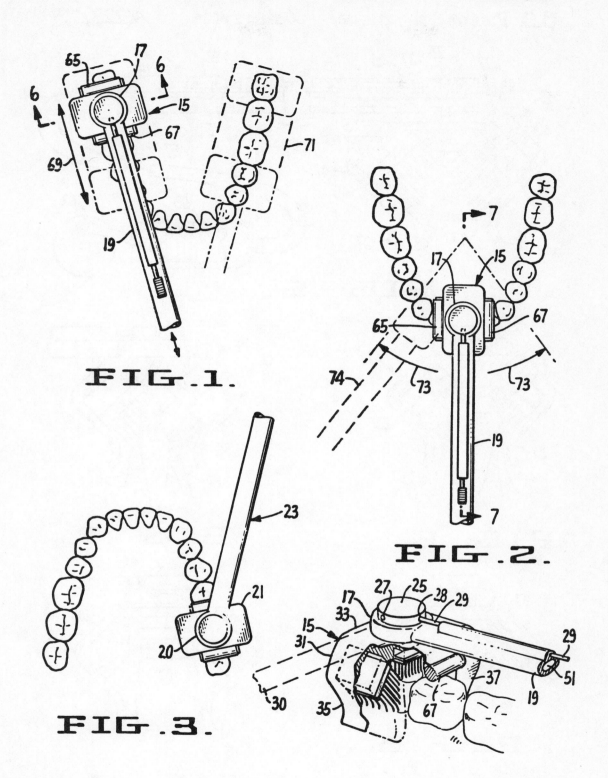

FIG.1.

FIG.2.

FIG.3.

FIG.4.

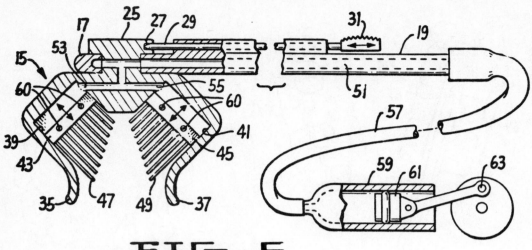

FIG .5.

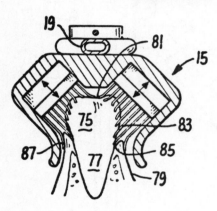

FIG .6.

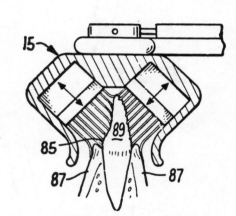

FIG .7.

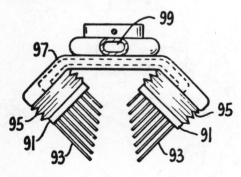

FIG .8.

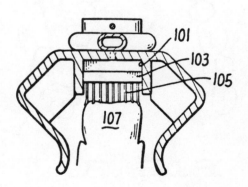

FIG .9.

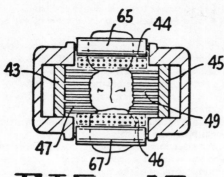

FIG .10.

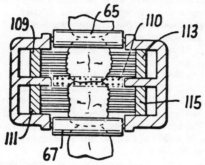

FIG .11.

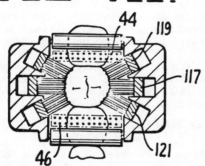

FIG .12.

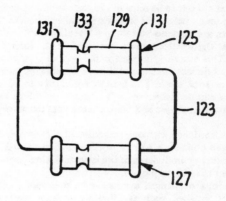

FIG .13.

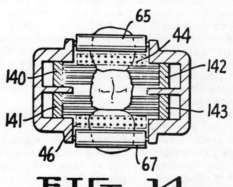

FIG .14.

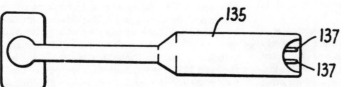

FIG .15.

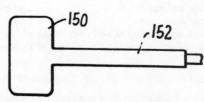

FIG .16.

GLIDING, MECHANIZED TOOTHBRUSH

SUMMARY OF THE INVENTION

The present invention relates to a gliding, mechanized toothbrush wherein the plurality of mechanically-driven brush elements are mounted in a head in such a manner that the brush elements can be passed over a row of teeth, brushing both sides of the tooth at the same time as well as the top of the tooth. The angle that the bristles of the brushes come down on each side of a tooth is chosen to be an acute angle, so that the bristles also enter and clean the sulcus area and embrasures. The brushes are made to vibrate in a "jackhammer" fashion so that the bristles vibrate back and forth along their axes. This vibratory mode for the bristles is important for the efficient cleaning of the sulcus areas, the embrasures and the teeth. The bristles are chosen to be soft, pliable and bendable, yet still resilient enough to clean accumulated plaque and not harm the gum tissues or the teeth.

In accordance with one embodiment of the invention, the head contains a pair of brushes and, in accordance with other embodiments of the invention, three or more brushes may be employed.

Various mechanical means can be employed to actuate the brushes, such as vibrating rods or strings or reciprocating cams or gears, but preferably this is accomplished by means of a flexible tube leading to a source of alternating vacuum and pressure.

The brushes proper are mounted in a head, and this head is preferably rotatably mounted on a handle. Thus, as is later explained in detail, the relative angular position of the head and handle in the preferred embodiment can be altered for various parts of the mouth. This may involve a free-moving swivel connection or a snap-type connection wherein a detent locks the head into either one of two positions with respect to the handle. Additional positions may also be incorporated.

In a less preferred embodiment, the handle is fixed relative to the head and is not rotatable.

The handle itself can also serve as the means for powering the brushes. For instance, the handle may be hollow and connected through a tube to an alternating source of vacuum and pressure for the purpose of actuating the brush elements.

The swivel arrangement wherein the head can turn with respect to the handle greatly facilitates the brushing operation as is later explained in detail. Preferably, the head has rollers or glides thereon which tend to guide the head over the row of teeth.

Thus, the primary object of the present invention is to provide a mechanized toothbrush having a relatively small, compact head wherein both sides and the top of a tooth are brushed at the same time by mechanical means and wherein the bristles also do a good cleaning job on the embrasures as well as entering and cleaning the sulcus area.

Various other features and advantages of the invention will be brought out in the balance of the specification.

BRIEF DESCRIPTION OF THE DRAWINGS

FIG. 1 is a plan view of a toothbrush embodying the present invention showing its use in brushing the molars and the bicuspids.

FIG. 2 is a view, similar to FIG. 1, showing the brush in use for brushing the incisors and the canines.

FIG. 3 is a plan view of another brush wherein the head is free to rotate with respect to the handle.

FIG. 4 is an enlarged perspective view of the brush head.

FIG. 5 is a side view, partially in section, showing one form of actuating mechanism for the brushes.

FIG. 6 is a sectional view on the line 6—6 of FIG. 1 showing the action of the brushes on a molar.

FIG. 7 is a sectional view showing the action of the brushes on an incisor.

FIG. 8 is a sectional view showing a bellows arrangement for driving the brushes.

FIG. 9 is a sectional view showing an embodiment of the invention wherein a separate brush is used for the top or biting surfaces of the teeth. To simplify the illustration, the side brushes are not shown.

FIG. 10 is a plan view in section of a brush head showing a pair of brushes whose bristles brush both sides of a tooth and two narrow brushes that brush the biting surfaces of the teeth.

FIG. 11 is a plan view in section wherein the side brushes are split into double pairs and the bristles of these brushes brush both sides of the teeth. In addition, a narrow brush brushes the tops of the teeth.

FIG. 12 is a plan view in section of a brush head wherein three sets of brushes are used on each side of a tooth for better cleaning action in the embrasures and sulcus. In addition, two narrow brushes brush the biting surfaces of the teeth.

FIG. 13 is a diagrammatic plan view showing an alternate form of guiding the roller.

FIG. 14 is a plan view in section wherein the side brushes are split into double pairs and the bristles of these brushes brush both sides of the teeth. In addition, two narrow brushes brush the biting surfaces of the teeth.

FIG. 15 is a plan view of an electrically motor-driven toothbrush having a built-in rechargeable battery.

FIG. 16 is a plan view of a brush wherein the relative positions of the head and handle are fixed.

DESCRIPTION OF THE PREFERRED EMBODIMENTS

Referring now to the drawings shown in FIGS. 1 and 2, the toothbrush of the present invention includes a head, generally designated 15, connected by a swivel arrangement 17 to a handle 19. In the preferred embodiments the head 15 can rotate with respect to the handle 19 via swivel 17 for reasons later brought out in detail; and in FIGS. 1, 2, 4 and 5, the relative position of the head and handle is held in a desired angular relationship by way of a detent means. This detent means is not mandatory and, in the embodiment shown in FIG. 3, the head 21 is free to rotate with respect to handle 23 via swivel 20 and the teeth themselves will guide the head 21 in the correct angular relationship as will be brought out later in detail.

In the preferred embodiment of this invention, it is desired to provide means for holding the head in either one of two positions, 90° apart in relation to the handle. FIG. 1 shows the head 15 perpendicular to handle 19 and FIG. 2 shows head 15 shifted 90° so that it is parallel to handle 19. FIG. 4 shows a perspective view showing handle 19 in a similar position to that shown in FIG. 1. Handle 30 (dashed lines) of FIG. 4 shows the other

3

90° position, similar to handle 19 versus body 15 of FIG. 2.

As best seen in FIGS. 4 and 5, head 15 is provided with a top cap 25, which mates with swivel 17. Cap 25 has two depressions 27 and 28 that are 90° apart. The handle 19 is provided with a detent pin 29, which can be moved in and out by means of handle 31, so that one can pull back on handle 31, turn the head 15 to a desired position, and push back on handle 31 to lock the head in a desired position with respect to the handle. Alternatively, the pin 29 could be spring-loaded, and the depressions 27 and 28 made shallow so that the head could be turned to a desired position, and the detent would then snap into one of the two depressions 27 or 28 and hold it in that position. Additional depressions may be provided at other angles if desired.

The head 15 has a casing 31 which includes the top 33 and sides 35 and 37 which extend downwardly so that the sides substantially encompass all the tooth and a portion of the gum. Within the head 15 are the individual brush elements and ordinarily two to eight brushes would be employed, depending on the required cost of manufacture and the desired speed and brushing efficiency of the final toothbrush design.

Various methods can be used for actuating the individual brush elements but a preferred method is a pneumatic method as is best seen in FIG. 5. Here the head 15 is shaped to provide two chamber walls 39 and 41 and each of the chambers has a piston forming a tight fit with the chamber walls and being adapted to move back and forth therein. Each of the pistons has a brush 43 and 45 attached to it by screws 60. Brushes 43 and 45 have bristle elements 47 and 49 firmly embedded. Brushes 43 and 45 are easily replaceable, via screws 60, by the user whenever wear or other reasons dictate.

Although it is not mandatory, the head 15 can be provided with rollers 65 and 67 shown in FIGS. 1 and 2 that maintain the head and its reciprocating brushes at a fixed height above the tops or biting surfaces of the teeth. Smooth gliding surfaces may be substituted for the rollers where lower manufacturing costs are required.

Referring to FIG. 5, handle 19 is hollow and has a passage 51 therein, and this leads to the passages 53 and 55 which connect passage 51 to the head space above the pistons 43 and 45. Passage 51 leads to a flexible tube 57 connected to a cylinder 59 having a piston 61 therein driven in the usual manner by the crank 63. With the arrangement shown, it is obvious that reciprocation of the piston 61 will result in alternating vacuum and air pressure in the space above the pistons 43 and 45, causing them to move up and down. Hydraulic pressure can be substituted for the pneumatic operation shown.

The arrangement shown in FIG. 3 can be the same except that here the detent or snap arrangement is missing so that the head can rotate freely with respect to the handle. This, in effect, makes the device self-centering.

The method of using the Gliding, Mechanized Toothbrush will now be described. One first turns the head 17 at right angles to the handle 19 as is shown in FIG. 1. As can be seen, the molars and bicuspids are in a substantially straight line. One places the brush over the molars, as is shown on the left hand side of FIG. 1, turns on the power, and then moves the brush back and forth over the molars and bicuspids as indicated by the arrow 69. One now moves the head to the opposite side of the dental arch, as is shown by dashed lines 71 on the right hand side of FIG. 1 and repeats the operation with these

4

molars and bicuspids. Now one inverts the brush and runs it over the upper molars and bicuspids of the upper dental arch in a similar manner.

One now rotates the head 15 (90°) so it is in line with the handle 19 as is shown in FIG. 2. The brush is placed over the incisors and moved back and forth through an arc covering the canines and the incisors as is indicated by the arrow 73. In a similar fashion, after the lower canines and incisors are cleaned, the toothbrush is turned over for cleaning the upper canines and incisors. Of course, if the embodiment shown in FIG. 3 is employed, it is not necessary to rotate head 21 manually but as the teeth are brushed, the head will naturally follow the contour of the teeth and rotate with respect to the handle 23 automatically.

The action of the toothbrush is shown on various types of teeth in FIGS. 6 and 7. In FIG. 6 a molar having a crown 75 and a root 77 bounded by gum 79 is shown and the head 15 has been rotated so that it is perpendicular to the handle 19, i.e. similar to that shown in FIG. 1. It will be seen that the bristles do a thorough job of brushing both the top flat surface 81, the sides 83, as well as the important sulcus area 85, and that the bristles also massage the gum as is shown at 87.

In FIG. 7, head 15 has been turned 90° so that it is now parallel to handle 19. This position is similar to that shown in FIG. 2 and is here shown brushing an incisor 89. As before, it will be seen that all of the surfaces of the tooth are thoroughly brushed including the sulcus 85. The gum 87 is gently massaged.

Various methods can be used to actuate the brush elements and another embodiment of the invention is shown in FIG. 8 wherein the backing 91 for the bristles 93 is connected by means of a bellows 95 to a head 97. Tube 99 leads to a source of alternating vacuum and pressure, driving the bristles as previously described.

Ordinarily, when trying to keep the toothbrush cost low, it will suffice to use only one pair of brushes with a brush on each side, since these bristles can be caused to clean even the top surface of a molar as is shown in FIG. 6 as well as the sides. However, it is more desirable to provide a third or top brush as is shown in FIG. 9 to clean the top surfaces of the teeth in a faster and more efficient manner. Here the side brushes are not illustrated since they are as previously described. This top brush may be chosen to be in the same plane as the side brushes and designed to reciprocate in-phase or 180° out-of-phase with these side brushes.

A simpler approach is to make this top brush narrow and place it so that it is not in the same plane with the side brushes. FIGS. 10, 11, 12 and 14 show this approach with the top brush shown singly (110) and in pairs (44 and 46). Being in different operating planes, any and all brushes can be shaped as desired without interfering with any other brush.

In forthcoming description of FIGS. 10, 11, 12 and 14, all side brushes when viewed in cross section have their bristles striking the tooth and sulcus areas at an acute angle to the tooth, similar to that shown in FIGS. 6 and 7.

FIG. 10 shows a sectional view through a brush head. It will be seen that bristles 47 and 49 of brushes 43 and 45 brush the sides of the molar as well as entering the embrasures between the teeth. Brushes 44 and 46 brush the tops or biting surfaces of the teeth.

FIG. 11 is a similar plan view showing another embodiment of the invention wherein pairs of brushes are used on each side of the teeth; thus, this Figure shows the brushes 109 and 111 on one side of the teeth, while brushes 113 and 115 are on the opposite side. A single brush 110 brushes the tops of the teeth. This embodiment is particularly effective in keeping the toothbrush centered over the teeth as a train is centered over the tracks if the pairs of brushes are driven alternately rather than in synchronism (i.e., 180° out of phase). This is so because there is much less leeway for the head to wander from the desired center position over the teeth because when brush pair 111 and 115 release their grab on the teeth, brushes 109 and 113 apply their grab, etc.

In FIG. 12, another embodiment of the invention is shown wherein a set of three brushes is used on each side of the teeth. This embodiment also shows that the brushes can be set at various angles around the tooth. Thus, looking at the brushes on one side, the brush 117 is set at the side of the tooth while the brushes 119 and 121 are set at an angle. This is particularly effective in entering the embrasures and sulcus areas. The brushes on the opposite side are obviously a mirror image and are not described in detail.

In FIG. 13, a diagrammatic view is shown of a head 123 having guiding rollers, generally designated 125 and 127. The guiding rollers have a central flat portion 129 which glides over the surfaces of the teeth, while the rims 131 on the rollers keep the rollers from sliding off the molars and bicuspids. The notches 133 in the rollers aid in centering the brush heads over the incisors and the canines.

FIG. 14 is another embodiment of the invention similar to FIG. 11 but with paired, top brushes versus a single top brush in FIG. 11. In this embodiment, side brushes 140, 141, 142 and 143 are employed with top brushes 44 and 46.

Although the Mechanical, Gliding Toothbrush of the present invention is preferably pneumatically operated, it is also possible to operate it in other manners. In the embodiment shown in FIG. 15, a handle 135 encloses a driving motor and rechargeable battery, and prongs 137 enable one to plug into an outlet for recharging the battery. Said motor could drive crank 63 of FIG. 5 where hollow handle 19 could attach directly to cylinder 59 so that the system of FIG. 5 is built into the outline of FIG. 15. Other well known reciprocating systems may be built into the outline of FIG. 15, such as vibrating rods and strings or reciprocating cams or gears (not shown).

Although it is preferred that the head be rotatable with respect to the handle, this is not strictly necessary. Thus, in FIG. 16, head 150 is fixed with respect to handle 152. In this case, the user would brush his molars and bicuspids as shown in FIG. 1. To brush the incisors and canines, the user simply would turn the toothbrush handle manually, thereby rotating the head into the proper position.

Ordinarily, it is not necessary to provide any means for adjusting the position of the piston-chambers or other means for holding the brushes, since usually sufficient movement or throw is imparted to the brushes to clean anything from the largest to the smallest tooth, as is shown in FIGS. 6 and 7. However, in some instances, it is desirable to provide for such an adjustment so that the brushes are set farther apart for a molar and closer together for a small tooth such as an incisor. This is easily achieved by means of a cam or gear arrangement, so that as the head is turned 90° relative to the handle, the piston-chambers are brought nearer or farther apart. Refer to FIGS. 1 and 2.

Although certain specific embodiments of the invention have been shown, these are for illustrative purposes only and many variations can be made of the structures shown without departing from the spirit of this invention.

I claim:

1. A mechanized toothbrush for cleaning both sides of a tooth simultaneously, said toothbrush having a housing adapted to be moved along a row of teeth comprising a head portion and a handle portion, said head portion containing a pair of brushes, each of said brushes being individually movable with respect to said head, said brushes having bristles set at an acute angle to the sides of the tooth, pointing toward the sulcus, said brushes being adapted to move toward and away from each other during vibration, said brushes being adapted to contact opposite sides of the tooth, and means to vibrate said brushes to contact and clean opposite sides of a tooth simultaneously.

2. The toothbrush of claim 1 where said head has glide means so that said head can be moved along a row of teeth.

3. The toothbrush of claim 2 wherein said head has rollers, said rollers being adapted to roll over the tops of the teeth.

4. The toothbrush of claim 3 wherein said rollers have lips at the edge thereof to prevent said rollers from sliding off the teeth.

5. The toothbrush of claim 3 wherein said rollers have notches therein, said notches locating said rollers over the incisors and bicuspids.

6. The structure of claim 2 wherein the brushes are caused to vibrate in a direction parallel to the bristles.

7. The toothbrush of claim 1 where there is connection means between said head and said handle, whereby the angle between the head and the handle can be altered.

8. The toothbrush of claim 1 having at least one additional brush adapted to clean the top or biting surface of a tooth, said brush being adapted to be movable in said head, said brush being adapted to move toward and away from the tooth top during vibration, said brush being adapted to contact the top of the tooth, and means to vibrate said brush to clean the top of the tooth.

9. The toothbrush of claim 1 having detent means between said head and said handle, whereby said head can be turned to a desired angle with respect to said handle and maintained in this desired angular relationship.

10. The toothbrush of claim 1 wherein the head has more than two brushes normally consisting of an equal number on each side of a tooth, said brushes being adapted to be driven in any selected phase relationship with each other.

11. The toothbrush of claim 10 wherein said brushes have bristles adapted to impinge on a tooth's surface at different selected angles for optimum cleaning and embrasure penetration.

12. The toothbrush of claim 11 wherein there is added at least one brush to clean the top of the tooth.

13. The toothbrush of claim 10 wherein there is added at least one brush to clean the top of the tooth.

14. The structure of claim 1 wherein the brushes are caused to vibrate in a plane parallel to the bristles.

15. The structure of claim 1 wherein said pair of brushes brush the sides and top of a tooth at the same time.

16. The structure of claim 15 where said head has glide means so that the head can be moved along a row of teeth.

17. The structure of claim 1 wherein the means to vibrate the bristles is pneumatic.

18. The structure of claim 1 wherein the means to vibrate the bristles is hydraulic.

* * * * *

The following libraries have CASSIS access available:

Birmingham, AL: Birmingham Public Library
Tempe, AZ: Arizona State University
Los Angeles, CA: Los Angeles Public Library
Sacramento, CA: California State Library
Sunnyvale, CA: Sunnyvale Public Library
Denver, CO: Denver Public Library
Newark, DE: University of Delaware
Atlanta, GA: Price Gilbert Memorial Library, Georgia Institute of Technology
Chicago, IL: Chicago Public Library
Baton Rouge, LA: Troy H. Middleton Library, Louisiana State University
Boston, MA: Boston Public Library
Detroit, MI: Detroit Public Library
Minneapolis, MN: Minneapolis Public Library
St. Louis, MO: St. Louis Public Library
Lincoln, NB: University of Nebraska-Lincoln Engineering Library
Durham, NH: University of New Hampshire Library
Newark, NJ: Newark Public Library
Albany, NY: New York State Library
Buffalo, NY: County Public Library
New York, NY: New York Public Library
Raleigh, NC: D.H. Hill Library North Carolina State University
Cincinnati, OH: Cincinnati and Hamilton County Public Library
Columbus, OH: Ohio State University Library
Toledo, OH: Toledo/Lucas County Public Library
Stillwater, OK: Oklahoma State University Library
Philadelphia, PA: Franklin Institute Library
Pittsburgh, PA: Carnegie Library of Pittsburgh
University Park, PA: Pattee Library, Pennsylvania State University
Providence, RI: Providence Public Library
Charleston, SC: Medical University of South Carolina
Memphis, TN: Memphis and Shelby County Public Library
Dallas, TX: Dallas Public Library
Houston, TX: The Fondren Library, Rice University
Seattle, WA: Engineering Library, University of Washington
Madison, WI: Kurt F. Wendt Engineering Library, University of Wisconsin
Milwaukee, WI: Milwaukee Public Library

Other companies offer computer searches somewhat similar to CASSIS. These include:

▶ Dialog Information Services, 3460 Hillview Avenue, Palo Alto, CA 94304, (415) 858-4098 or outside CA 1-800-334-2564 [Claims Database]

▶ Mead Data Center, 9443 Springboro Pike, P.O. Box 93, Dayton, OH 45401, (513) 865-6800 or outside OH 1-800-227-4908 [Lexpat]

▶ BRS Information Technologies, 555 E. Lancaster Avenue, St. Davis, PA 19087, (215) 254-0233 or outside PA 1-800-468-0908

▶ Permagon InfoLine, Inc., 1340 Old Chain Bridge Road, McLean, VA 22101, (703) 442-0900 or outside VA or Washington, DC 1-800-336-7575

Typical fees for their patent services are approximately $60 for a subject search, $15 for a list of up to 100 patent numbers in a given class, and $65 for searches by inventor's or a company's name.

You can obtain most of the information you need by doing your own patent search. And further, by using CASSIS, you need not spend the extra money to use these fee services if you live close to a Depository Library. Computer searches should only be used as a supplement to your own search, because the computer databases contain only the more recent patents, usually after 1965. Also, you can obtain copies of patents at the Patent Depository Libraries or request them directly from the U.S. Patent and Trademark Office for $1.50 each. You need only send a letter of request like the sample that follows.

SAMPLE PATENT COPY REQUEST LETTER

(Your Name)

(Your Address)

Date:

Commissioner of Patents and Trademarks

Washington, D.C. 20231

Subject: Patent Copies

Dear Sir:

Please send me one copy of each of the patents listed below:

Patent #	Inventor	Date

Enclosed is my check #_____ for $_____ ($1.50 per patent).

Your prompt attention to this request is greatly appreciated.

Thank you.

Respectfully,

(Your Signature)

6

Marketing Research

We may now leave the product development phase and concentrate on marketing. We cannot benefit from any good idea unless we can find a way to market the product. Therefore we need to focus our attention on sales and marketing issues; we need to ask ourselves:

1. Will people buy my product?
2. Who would most likely be my customer? Who and where is my target market?
3. How much will people pay for my product?
4. Where would they be most likely to buy my product?
5. How can I get my product where people will buy it?
6. How do people perceive my product compared to other, competitive products on the market (cheaper vs. more expensive, better vs. inferior)?

Resources for printed materials on the characteristics and dynamics of an industry are:

▶ *Standard and Poor's Industry Surveys* Analyzes industry's leaders, trends and historical information.

▶ *U.S. Industrial Outlook* Published by the Department of Commerce annually, details trends and forecasts for over 200 industries.

▶ *U.S. Economic Census* Compiled every five years by the U.S. government. This report will assist in identifying and quantifying potential markets and market share data. There are separate sections for: retail trades, service industries, wholesale trades and manufacturing. Information available includes: sales, payroll, number of employees, establishment size, and number of companies.

▶ *Predicasts Basebook* Arranged by Standard Industrial Classifications (SIC) lists sales, consumption, and growth rate by industry.

We can find some answers to these questions and learn a great deal more about your product and the current competitive situation if we conduct a preliminary market study.

Such a study involves asking people appropriate questions that will give an indication of what others think of your product and how it compares to others like it on the market.

A market study is more than asking a friend or relative whether or not he or she thinks your idea is a good one. A valid market study involves asking independent, unrelated people a series of questions.

The general *New Product Questionnaire* (pp. 94–100) was designed for that purpose. You can omit questions that do not apply and insert questions you think are more appropriate.

Answers to these questions are extremely important when developing marketing strategies. There are several ways to administer a market study. You can ask friends and relatives what they think of your idea. You can go to where people congregate, such as airports, grocery stores, shopping malls, and so on, and ask people some questions concerning the product. You may also conduct meetings with 6 to 10 people (focus groups) who are familiar with this field and brainstorm to shed new light on your market study. You may also, in the process discover some new problems or opportunities previously unknown.

The study can also be used as a sales tool when you are ready to license or sell your product. It can be very useful in explaining to a potential licensee that your market survey has determined that people are willing to pay, say 50 percent more for your product over the competition.

Determining the size of a reasonable survey sample is a complex question. The answer depends on many factors including target market, market size, diversity of customers, and so on. However, 25 to 30 potential customers should be sufficient to get an adequate understanding of peoples' needs and concerns. *As a word of warning, after you describe your idea in a printed publication, publicly use it or place your product on sale, you have one year to apply for a patent.* However, in many foreign countries, once you publicly disclose your idea you may not be able to submit for a patent. If you feel your product has international potential, you should consult a patent attorney; he or she will be able to advise you on the laws of specific countries.

INDEPENDENT EVALUATIONS

Another method for determining the marketability and sales potential of your product is to have an independent organization evaluate it for you. Doing so accomplishes two purposes, it:

1. Gives a general indication of the likelihood of success of your idea

2. Provides an analysis performed by an independent third party which can be used later as a sales tool. It would be helpful to be able to say, for example, that the University of Wisconsin gave my idea a 75 percent or 85 percent likelihood of success.

NEW PRODUCT QUESTIONNAIRE

Title:

Inventor(s):

Address:

Date:

I agree to keep all information disclosed to me regarding ____(new product)____ confidential and will neither use, directly nor indirectly, any such information provided to me for my own benefit or for the benefit of any person, firm, or corporation.

_____
(Signature)

_____
(Date)

_____
(Name of Respondent)

_____
(Job Title/Company Affiliation)

_____
(Address)

_____
(City)   (State)   (Zip)

_____
(Phone Number)

A. General Information

1. Approximately how many similar products do you currently own or use per month? [Check one answer that most closely applies.]

    _____ 0

    _____ 1–5

    _____ 6–10

    _____ 11–25

    _____ Over 25

2. What reasons are important to you in determining which (old product) you buy?

    _____

    _____

    _____

3. How often do you presently buy more or another (old product)?

    _____

    _____

    _____

4. For what reasons do you determine when it is time to buy more (old product)?

    _____

    _____

    _____

5. What other brand or types of (old product) do you currently buy?

    _____

    _____

    _____

6. Which one do you like best? Why?

    _____

    _____

    _____

7. Do you feel that the currently available methods of performing this function have any problems (if yes, please explain)?

_____
_____
_____

8. Approximately how much did you pay for your current model? Was it worth the cost?

_____
_____
_____

9. What features or characteristics do you especially like concerning your currently used product?

_____
_____
_____

10. What features or characteristics do you especially dislike concerning the product you currently use?

_____
_____
_____

11. If you could design such a product, how would you change it?

_____
_____
_____

B. New Product Information

12. How would you benefit from using this new product?
_____ Would greatly simplify things
_____ Would help me a little
_____ Not much difference
_____ Would hinder performance

13. Are the special features on this new product important?

_____ Extremely important

_____ Important

_____ Neither important nor unimportant

_____ Definitely not important

14. How important would you rate the following characteristics for this new product (5 = Very Important, 1 = Not Important)?

_____ Appearance

_____ Ease of use

_____ Durability

_____ Maintenance required

_____ Price

15. What are the key attributes (i.e., essentials) that this product must have for you?

_____

_____

_____

16. What do you think the advantages of this new product are?

_____

_____

_____

17. What do you think the disadvantages of this new product are?

_____

_____

_____

18. How would you overcome the disadvantages (shortcomings)?

_____

_____

_____

19. What won't this product do that you would like it to do?

_____

_____

_____

20. What product or products would this product replace for you?

_____

_____

_____

21. When or where would you use this product?

_____

_____

_____

22. What would cause you to stop using this product?

_____

_____

_____

23. Of what material do you think this product should be made? Why?

_____

_____

_____

24. How long would you expect this product reasonably to last?

_____

_____

_____

25. Would you need or want various sizes, colors, or quality levels of this product (Please explain)?

_____

_____

_____

26. How would you prefer this product to be packaged? Why?

_____

_____

_____

27. Where would you most likely buy this product?

    _____
    _____
    _____

28. Where would be the most convenient place for you to buy this product?

    _____
    _____
    _____

29. How would you describe the person who would most likely use this product (young/old, more affluent/less affluent, male/female, etc.)?

    _____
    _____
    _____

30. Considering everything you know about this new product, which statement best describes how much you like or dislike it?
    _____ Like it extremely well
    _____ Like it moderately
    _____ Neither like nor dislike it
    _____ Dislike it

31. Which of these statements best describes how interested you would be in buying this new product or process?
    _____ I definitely would buy it.
    _____ I probably would buy it.
    _____ I might try it.
    _____ I definitely would not buy it.

32. How much extra would you pay for this product over current products?
    _____ -0-
    _____ 10% more
    _____ 20% more
    _____ 50% more
    _____ over 70% more
    _____ Other

33. What price would you consider fair for this new product?

    $ _____ each _____

34. How many of these new products would you buy at the above price?

    Per month? _____

    Per year? _____

35. How many of these new products would you purchase at one time?

    _____

36. What additional products would you like to see offered along with this new product (Accessories, etc.)?

    _____

    _____

    _____

37. Other Comments:

    _____

    _____

    _____

    _____

    _____

    _____

    _____

    _____

    _____

The cost for such an evaluation may be $150 to $250 and it should conclude with a summary of findings and a section such as, "Likelihood of Success." Although the evaluation may seem to answer questions as to the potential of your invention, you should remember that the people performing the evaluation on your idea usually are not experts in your specific industry or application. They may not know, for instance, that using the competitor's product may result in user injury in a particular application and that yours would not. Do not expect 99 or 100 percent rating. Only 1 percent of all the inventions submitted to the University of Wisconsin for evaluation received a score of 50 percent to 100 percent out of a possible score of 100.

If you are interested in having an evaluation performed, you can write or call the following organizations to find out specifically what they can do for you and how much they charge.

Organizations That Will Do Evaluations and Provide Assistance

The University of Kansas
Center for Research, Inc.
2291 Irving Hill Road Campus
West Lawrence, KS 66045
Provides general assistance for small businesses.

Massachusetts Institute of Technology
Innovation Center
Room 33-111
Cambridge, MA 02139
Emphasizes idea evaluation and start up problem assessment. Students are heavily
    involved in this Center's programs.

University of Utah
Utah Innovation Center
417 Wakara Way
Salt Lake City, UT 84112
Completes general evaluations on new products.

Center for Private Enterprise and Entrepreneurship
Hankamer School of Business, Suite 308
Baylor University
Waco, TX 76703

University of Wisconsin
Wisconsin Innovation Service Center
402 McCutchan
Whitewater, WI 53190
Performs an extensive preliminary commercial feasibility analysis for under $150.

Illinois State University
Technology Commercialization Center
Novey Hall 401L
Normal, IL 61761
Provides general assistance for small businesses.

California State University at Fresno
Bureau of Business Research and Service
Fresno, CA 93740
Conducts research on small business problems. Provides consulting services for
    small businesses.

Center for New Business Executives
Innovation Center
P.O. Box 12793
Research Triangle Park, NC 27709
An independent, state-affiliated organization, closely associated with the University of North Carolina. Provides training and management assistance to new and potential entrepreneurs.

University of New Mexico
Technical Applications Center
Albuquerque, NM 87131
Provides general assistance to small businesses.

George Washington University
Innovation Information Center
2130 H Street, NW
Washington, DC 20052
Provides general information on inventions and searches.

Jackson State University
Bureau of Business and Economic Research 1400 J.R. Lynch Street
Jackson, MS 39217
Performs management consulting services for small businesses.

University of Illinois
Bureau of Economic and Business Research
408 David Kinley Hall
Urbana, IL 61801
Publishes information for small businesses management.

Stanford University
Innovation Center
Stanford, CA 94305
Provides development assistance and technical advice to inventors.

Carnegie-Mellon University
Center for Entrepreneurial Development
4516 Henry Street
Pittsburgh, PA 15213
National Science Foundation (NSF) sponsored Center.

Government Evaluation Centers

Office of National Bureau of Standards
Institute of Applied Technology
Office of Energy-Related Inventions (OERI)
Department of Commerce
Washington, DC 20234
Evaluates and assists in developing energy **and** nonenergy related inventions (nonnuclear). In 1989, this organization was given the expanded role to handle nonenergy related inventions as well.

Science and Technology Division
Congressional Library
Washington, DC 20234
Researches written requests in 2 to 3 weeks, usually without charge.

Inventors' Associations

There are many inventors' associations and organizations that can provide a variety of services including workshops, counseling, networking, and news letters. Sometimes it helps to be able to talk with others who have faced and have overcome the same problems you face or faced.

Keep in mind that while many agencies, universities, independent companies, governmental organizations, and acquaintances may be of help to you in your quest to develop and market your new product, try to have your *Non-Disclosure Agreement* SIGNED *BEFORE* you disclose your ideas. This is for two reasons. First, signing an agreement decreases the probability of theft of your invention and second, confidential disclosure will *not* start your one year clock to submit a patent application. (See p. 5.)

Some of the better known inventor associations are:

ALABAMA
Alabama Inventors Association
3409 Fountain Circle
Montgomery, AL 36116

ARKANSAS
Arkansas Inventors Congress, Inc.
One State Capital Mall
Little Rock, AR 72201
Contact: Morris Jenkins

CALIFORNIA
Inventors Workshop International
    Education Foundation
3537 Old Conejo Road, Suite 120
Newbury, CA 91320
Contact: Alan Tratner, Executive Director
One of the larger inventor organizations,
    operating throughout the U.S.A.
    Members total over 16,000, with
    14 chapters in California. Contact
    them for their chapter located
    near you.

National Inventors Foundation
345 W. Cypress Street
Glendale, CA 91204
Contact: Ted De Boer, Executive Director

National Congress of Inventor
    Organizations
214 Rheem Blvd.
Moraga, CA 94556
Contact: Norman Parrish, President
This organization has chapters throughout
    the country.

Inventors of California
215 Rheem Blvd.
Moraga, CA 94556
Contact: Norman Parrish, President

Inventors' Assistance League
345 West Cypress
Glendale, CA 91204

Inventors' Council of California
250 Vernon Street
Oakland, CA 94610

California Inventors' Council
P.O. Box 2036
Sunnyvale, CA 94087

Inventors' Resource Center
P.O. Box 5105
Berkeley, CA 94705

Technology Transfer Society
11720 West Pico Boulevard
Los Angeles, CA 90064

Silicon Valley Entrepreneurs Club, Inc.
TECHMART Building, Suite 360
5201 Great America Parkway
Santa Clara, CA 95054
Contact: Robert Hansens

COLORADO
Affiliated Inventors Foundation, Inc.
501 Iowa Avenue
Colorado Springs, CO 80909-4799
Contact: John Farady, Executive Director
A national organization with chapters in
    30 states.

Governor's High Tech Cabinet Council
3271 S. Clay
Englewood, CO 80110
Contact: Stephen Andrade

National Inventors Cooperative
    Association
P.O. Box 6585
Denver, CO 80206

CONNECTICUT
Inventors Association of Connecticut
9 Sylvan Road South
Westport, CT 06880
Contact: Murray Schiffman

FLORIDA

Society of American Inventors
505 E. Jackson Street, Suite 204
Tampa, FL 33602
Contact: Donald Hinst, President

Tampa Bay Inventor's Council
805 W. 118th Avenue
Tampa, FL 33612
Contact: F. MacNeill MacKay

Florida Entrepreneurship Program
Bureau of Business Assistance
Division of Economic Development
Florida Department of Commerce
107 W. Gaines Street, Room G-26
Tallahasse, FL 32399-2000
Contact: Mary Hagerman

The Inventors Club
Route 11, Box 379
Pensacola, FL 32514
Contact: Bill Bowman

Society for Inventors and Entrepreneurs
306 Georgetown Drive
Casselberry, FL 32707
Contact: Frank Dumont

Central Florida Inventors Club
4849 Victory Drive
Orlando, FL 32808

Central Florida Inventors Council
4855 Big Oaks Lane
Orlando, FL 32806
Contact: Dr. David Flinchbaugh

Innovation Group
Innovative Products Group
2325 Ulmerton Road, Suite 16
Clearwater, FL 33520
Contact: George Feldcamp, Vice President

Palm Beach Society of American Inventors
P.O. Box 26
Palm Beach, FL 33480
Contact: Robert White

GEORGIA

Inventors Club of America
P.O. Box 450261
Atlanta, GA 30345
Contact: Alexander Marinaccio, President

Inventor Associates of Georgia
637 Linwood Avenue, NE
Atlanta, GA 30306

Patent Assistance Program
Georgia Institute of Technology
Atlanta, GA 30332-0999
Contact: Jean Kirkland, Patent Librarian

Inventors Association of Georgia
241 Freyer Drive NE
Marietta, GA 30060
Contact: Hal Stribling

HAWAII

Inventors' Council of Hawaii
P.O. Box 27844
Honolulu, HI 96827
Contact: George Lee

Statewide Strategy for High Technology
    Growth
High Technology Development
    Corporation
220 South King Street, Suite 840
Honolulu, HI 96813
Contact: William Bass, Jr.

ILLINOIS

Inventors' Council of Chicago
53 W. Jackson, Suite 1041
Chicago, IL 60604
Contact: Don Moyer, President
This is a very active club in Chicago
    with over 3500 members, and
    provides invention evaluations free of
    charge.

Illinois Business Innovation Fund
Illinois Department of Commerce and
    Community Affairs
100 W. Randolph Street, Suite 3-400
Chicago, IL 60601
Contact: Dick LeGrand, Finance Manager

Chicago High Tech Association
20 N. Wacker Drive, Suite 1929
Chicago, IL 60606
Contact: Sheridan Turner, Executive
    Director

Illinois Commercialization Center
Hovey Hall
Illinois State University
Normal, IL 61761-7127
Contact: Jerry Abner, Director

Technology Commercialization Program
University of Illinois at Chicago
815 W. Van Buren Street
Chicago, IL 60607
Contact: Dr. L. Barry Barrington

INDIANA

Indiana Inventors Association, Inc.
612 Ironwood Drive
Plainfield, IN 46168
Contact: Randall Redelman, President

The Inventors and Entrepreneurs Society
of Indiana, Inc.
P.O. Box 2224
Hammond, IN 46323
Contact: Daniel Yovich

International Association of Professional
Inventors
Route 1, Box 1074
Shirley, IN 47384

International Association of Professional
Inventors
Route 10, 4412 Greenhill Way
Anderson, IN 46011
Contact: Jack Banther

International Association of Professional
Inventors
818 Westminster
Kokomo, IN 46901

KANSAS
Kansas Technology Enterprise Center
400 SW 8th Street
Topeka, KS 66603
Contact: William Brundage, President

KENTUCKY
Alternative Energy Development
Program
Division of Alternative Energy
Development
Kentucky Energy Cabinet
P.O. Box 11888
Lexington, KY 40578-1916
Contact: John Stapleton, Director

Center for Entrepreneurship
School of Business
University of Louisville
Louisville, KY 40292
Contact: Lou Dickie, Director

LOUISIANA
Louisiana Innovation Program
Louisiana Department of Commerce
P.O. Box 94185
Baton Rouge, LA 70804
Contact: Regis Allison

MASSACHUSETTS
Inventors Association of New England
P.O. Box 325
Lexington, MA 02173
Contact: Donald Job

Innovation Invention Network
132 Sterling Street
West Boylston, MA 01583

Innovation Invention Network
13 Benjamin Road
Worcester, MA 01602
Contact: Andrew Stidsen

MARYLAND
Systems Engineering Center
University of Maryland
College Park, MD 20740
Contact: Charles Heller

MICHIGAN
Inventors Council of Michigan
2200 Bonisteel Blvd.
Ann Arbor, MI 48109
Contact: J. Downs Herold, Chairman

MINNESOTA
Minnesota Inventors Congress
P.O. Box 71
Redwood Falls, MN 56283-0071
Contact: Penny Becker

Minnesota Project Innovation, Inc.
1107 Hazeltine Blvd.
Chaska, MN 55318
Contact: James Swiderski

Midwest Inventors' Society
P.O. Box 335
St. Cloud, MN 56301

Inventors and Technology Transfer
Society
P.O. Box 14775
Minneapolis, MN 55414

Society of Minnesota Inventors
20231 Basalt Street, NW
Anoka, MN 55303
Contact: Paul Paris

Inventors Education Network
P.O. Box 14775
Minneapolis, MN
Contact: Marge Braddock

MISSOURI
Inventors Association of St. Louis
P.O. Box 16544
St. Louis, MO 63105
Contact: Roberta Toole, Executive
Director

Columbia Venture Club
Missouri Ingenuity, Inc.
T-16 Research Park
Columbia, MO 65211
Contact: Dr. Bruce Maier, Executive
Director

MISSISSIPPI

Mississippi Research and Development
Center
3825 Ridgewood Road
Jackson, MS 39211-6453
Contact: R.W. Parkin

Confederacy of Mississippi Inventors
1415 Post Road
Clinton, MS 39056

Confederacy of Mississippi Inventors
4759 Nailor Road
Vicksburg, MS 39180
Contact: Rudy Paine

Mississippi Society of Scientists and
Inventors
P.O. Box 2244
Jackson, MS 39205

Mississippi Inventors Workshop
4729 Kings Highway
Jackson, MS 39206
Contact: Karl Rabe, President

Gulf Coast Breeder
109 E. Scenic Drive
Pass Christian, MS 39571
Contact: Frank Wilem Jr., President

NEBRASKA

Lincoln Inventors Association
P.O. Box 94666
Lincoln, NE 68509
Contact: Steve Williams

Omaha Inventors Club
U.S. Small Business Administration
11145 Mill Valley Road
Omaha, NE 68145
Contact: Bob Simon

Kearney Inventors Association
Kearney Development Council
2001 Avenue A, Box 607
Kearney, NE 68847
Contact: Steve Buttress, President

NEVADA

Nevada Innovation and Technology
Council
1755 E. Plum Lane, Suite 152
Reno, NV 89502

NEW JERSEY

National Society of Inventors
539 Laurel Place
South Orange, NJ

American Society of Inventors
402 Cynwyd Drive
Absecon, NJ 08201

NEW YORK

New York Society of Professional
Inventors
SUNY at Farmingdale
Lupton Hall
Farmingdale, NY 11735
Contact: J.E. Manuel

Innovative Design Fund, Inc.
866 United Nations Plaza
New York, NY 10017

Center for Technology Transfer
SUNY-College at Oswego
209 Park Hall
Oswego, NY 13126
Contact: Harry Hawkins, Director

NORTH CAROLINA

North Carolina Technology Development
Authority
4216 Dobbs Building
430 N. Salisbury Street
Raleigh, NC 27611

NORTH DAKOTA

Innovation Institute
Box 429
Larimore, ND 58215
Contact: Dr. Jerry Udell

OHIO

Ohio's Thomas Edison Program's Seed
Development Fund
Ohio Department of Development
65 E. State Street, Suite 200
Columbus, OH 43266-0330
Contact: Devon Streit

Ohio Department of Development
Division of Technological Development
30 E. Broad Street
P.O. Box 1001
Columbus, OH 43266-0101
Contact: Annette Burgess

Inventors Club of Greater Cincinnati
18 Gambier Circle
Cincinnati, OH 45218
Contact: William Selenke

Inventors Council of Dayton
140 E. Monument Avenue
Dayton, OH 45402
Contact: Leonard Smith

Columbus Inventors Association
2480 East Avenue
Columbus, OH 43202
Contact: Tim Nyros

OKLAHOMA
Oklahoma Inventors Congress
P.O. Box 75635
Oklahoma City, OK 73147
Contact: Ken Addison, Jr.

Invention Development Society
8502A SW 8th Street
Oklahoma City, OK 73128
Contact: William Enter, Sr.

OREGON
Western Inventors Council
P.O. Box 3288
Eugene, OR 97403

Western Inventors Council
E.E. Easton School of Business
Oregon State University
Corvallis, OR 97331

PENNSYLVANIA
American Society of Inventors
P.O. Box 58426
Philadelphia, PA 19102-8426
Contact: Henry Skillman

American Society of Inventors
545 Hughes Road
King of Prussia, PA 19406

American Society of Inventors
1710 Fidelity Building
123 South Broad Street
Philadelphia, PA 19109

TENNESSEE
Tennessee Inventors Association
P.O. Box 11225
Knoxville, TN 37939-1225
Contact: Martin Skinner

Appalachian Inventors Group
P.O. Box 388
Oak Ridge, TN 37830

Tennessee Inventors Association
1116 Weisgarber
Knoxville, TN 37919

TEXAS
Technology Business Development
Texas Engineering Experiment Station
Texas A&M University
310 Wisenbaker Engineering Research
  Center
College Station, TX 77843-3369
Contact: Gail Kelly

Texas Innovation Information Network
  System
INFOMART
P.O. Box 471
1950 Stemmons Freeway
Dallas, TX 75207
Contact: John Rodman

Texas Inventors Association
4000 Rock Creek Drive, Suite 100
Dallas, TX 75204
Contact: Tom Workman, President

UTAH
Utah Technology Finance Corporation
419 Wakara Way, Suite 215
Salt Lake City, UT 84108
Contact: Brant Cannon, Executive Director

Intermountain Society of Inventors &
  Designers
P.O. Box 1056
Tooele, UT 84074
Contact: Edward DeVore

WASHINGTON
Innovators International Project
P.O. Box 4636
Rolling Bay, WA 98061
Contact: Paul von Minden

Inventors' Association of Washington, Inc.
P.O. Box 1725
Bellevue, WA 98009

Northwest Inventors Association
723 East Highland Drive
Arlington, WA 98223

WISCONSIN
Midwest Inventors Group
P.O. Box 1
Chippewa Falls, WI 54729
Contact: Steve Henry

Sources for many of the organizations listed were from Argonne National Laboratory's Study of Innovative Programs for Inventors, Environmental Systems Division, Mail Stop 362-2B, Argonne, IL 60439, Contact: Marty Bernard, Dated March, 1988.

There are also several governmental organizations that can help you, frequently at no charge or with only nominal charge. The following are worth contacting:

Government Organizations

National Innovation Workshops (NIW)
Office of Energy Related Inventions
National Institute of Standards and Technology
Gaithersburg, MD 20899
NIWs are seminars given six times per year in different cities. Subjects include: Patents, Licensing, Estimating the Value of Your Invention, Marketing, Invention Documentation, Raising Money, Starting Your Own Business, and Sources for Assistance. Contact this office to inquire the time and place of the NIWs. These workshops are an excellent way to economically learn about commercializing your invention.

SCORE (Service Corps of Retired Executives)
U.S. Small Business Administration
1441 L Street, NW, Room 100
Washington, DC 20416
(400 chapters throughout the United States)
SCORE is an excellent organization that can put you in touch with retired business executives who can counsel you on a variety of questions, from helping you identify the best channel of distribution, to assisting you raise money.

NASA
Technology Utilization Program
P.O. Box 8756
Baltimore, MD 21240

Army Materials and Mechanics Research Center
Watertown, MA 02172

Office for Promoting Technical Innovation
New Jersey Department of Labor and Industry
Labor and Industry Building
Trenton, NJ 08625

National Technical Information Center
Springfield, VA 22161

Office of Energy Related Inventions
National Bureau of Standards
Gaithersburg, MD 20899
For inventions in the energy related field.

Other Sources of Assistance

Center for Innovation
P.O. Box 3809
Butte, MT 59701
Emphasizes new products and inventions related to energy, agriculture, and mining.

Golden State Energy Center
Building 1055
Fort Cronkhite
Sausalito, CA 94965
Emphasizes San Francisco based firms dealing with renewable energy products. The Center works closely with the Department of Energy as well as other federal and state agencies.

University of Pennsylvania
Small Business Development Center
The Wharton School
W-178 Dietrich Hall
Philadelphia, PA 19104

The Small Business Administration's Division of Management Assistance, 1441 L Street, NW, Washington, DC 20410, 1-800-368-5855 sponsors nationwide assistance programs, the Small Business Development Center Program (SBDC), for small businesses. There are approximately 500 universities and colleges participating in this program. Usually a university graduate student or faculty advisor will provide on-site management counseling. The following organizations are the lead SBDCs in each state. Contact the one listed in your state to get the name of your local SBDC.

University of Alabama at Birmingham
Small Business Development Center
901 15th Street, South
Building 4, Room 150
Birmingham, AL 35294
Contact: Vernon Nabors

Anchorage Community College
Small Business Development Center
430 West 7th Avenue, Suite 115
Anchorage, AK 99501
Contact: Mike Buller

University of Arkansas at Little Rock
Small Business Development Center
100 South Main, Suite 401
Little Rock, AR 72201
Contact: Paul McGinnis

Colorado Community College
Occupational Education System
Small Business Development Center
1391 North Speer Blvd., Suite 600
Denver, CO 80204
Contact: Richard Wilson

University of Connecticut
Small Business Development Center
School of Business
Box U-41, Room 422
366 Fairfield Road
Storrs, CT 06226
Contact: John O'Connor

University of Delaware
Small Business Development Center
Purnell Hall, Suite 005
Newark, DE 19716
Contact: Helene Butler

Howard University
District of Columbia Small Business Development Center
6th and Fairmount Street, NW
Room 128
Washington, DC 20059
Contact: Nancy Flake

University of West Florida
Small Business Development Center
College of Business
Building 8
Pensacola, FL 32514
Contact: Donald Clause

University of Georgia
North Regional Small Business Development Center
Chicopee Complex
1180 East Broad Street
Athens, GA 30602
Contact: George St. Germain

Boise State University
College of Business
Idaho Small Business Development
  Center
Control Center
1910 University Drive
Boise, ID 83725
Contact: Ronold Hall

Illinois Department of Commerce and
  Community Affairs
Illinois Small Business Development
  Center
620 East Adams Street, 5th Floor
Springfield, IL 62701
Contact: Jeff Mitchell

Indiana Economic Development
  Council
Indiana Chamber of Commerce
Small Business Development Center
One North Capitol, Suite 200
Indianapolis, IN 46204
Contact: Steve Thrash

Iowa State University
Small Business Development Center
College of Business
Chamberlynn Building
137 Lynn Avenue
Ames, IA 50010
Contact: Robert Parker

Wichita State University
Small Business Development Center
College of Business
Campus Box 48
021 Clinton Hall
Wichita, KS 67208
Contact: Mary Jenkins

University of Kentucky
Central Kentucky Small Business
  Development Center
18 Porter Building
Lexington, KY 40506-0205
Contact: Bill Morley

Northeast Louisiana University
Small Business Development Center
College of Business
700 University Avenue
Monroe, LA 71209
Contact: Paul Dunn

University of Southern Maine
Small Business Development Center
246 Deering Avenue
Portland, ME 04102
Contact: Robert Hird

University of Massachusetts
Small Business Development Center
205 School of Management
Amherst, MA 01003
Contact: John Ciccarelli

Wayne State University
Small Business Development Center
2727 Second Avenue
Detroit, MI 48201
Contact: Raymond Genick

College of St. Thomas
Small Business Development Center
23 Blair Avenue
St. Paul, MN 55103
Contact: Tom Trutna

University of Mississippi
Small Business Development Center
School of Business
3825 Ridgewood Road
Jackson, MS 39211
Contact: Robert Smith

St. Louis University
Small Business Development Center
O'Neil Hall-100
3674 Lindell Blvd.
St. Louis, MO 63108
Contact: Virginia Campbell

Montana Department of Commerce
Small Business Development Center
1424 Ninth Avenue
Helena, MT 59620
Contact: Carol Daly

University of New Hampshire
Small Business Development Center
370 Commercial Street
Manchester, NH 03103
Contact: James Bean

Rutgers University at Newark
Small Business Development Center
3rd Floor Ackerson Hall
180 University Street
Newark, NJ 07102
Contact: Lee Merel

Upstate New York Small Business
  Development Center
State University of New York
SUNY Plaza, S-523
Albany, NY 12246
Contact: James L. King

University of North Carolina
Small Business Development Center
Research Triangle Park Area
820 Clay Street
Raleigh, NC 27605
Contact: Marcus C. King

North Dakota Economic Development
    Commission
Small Business Development Center
Liberty Memorial Building
Capitol Grounds
Bismarck, ND 58505
Contact: Terry Stallman

Ohio Department of Development
Small Business Development Center
30 East Broad Street
P.O. Box 1001
Columbus, OH 43215
Contact: Jack Brown

Southeastern Oklahoma State University
Small Business Development Center
517 West University
Station A, Box 4194
Durant, OK 74701
Contact: Lloyd Miller

University of Pennsylvania
The Wharton School
Pennsylvania Small Business
    Development Center
3201 Steinberg-Dietrich Hall/CC
Philadelphia, PA 19104
Contact: Susan Garber

University of Puerto Rico
Small Business Development Center
Box 5253 College Station
Mayaguez, PR 00709
Contact: Jose M. Romaguera

Bryant College
Small Business Development Center
Douglas Pike, Route 7
Smithfield, RI 02917
Contact: Douglas Jobling

University of South Carolina
Small Business Development Center
College of Business Administration
Columbia, SC 29208
Contact: Albert Sidney Britt III

University of South Dakota
Small Business Development Center
School of Business
414 East Clark
Vermillion, SD 57069
Contact: Anne Shank-Volk

Memphis State University
Small Business Development Center
320 South Dudley Street
Memphis, TN 38104
Contact: Edgar R. Cole

Dallas County Community College
Small Business Development Center
302 North Market, Third Floor
Dallas, TX 75202-3299
Contact: Norbert R. Dettman

University of Houston
Small Business Development Center
University Park
401 Louisiana Street, 8th Floor
Houston, TX 77002
Contact: Jon P. Goodman

Texas Tech University
Northwestern Texas Small Business
    Development Center
2005 Broadway
Lubbock, TX 79401
Contact: Ted Cadou

University of Texas at San Antonio
Small Business Development Center
Center for Economic Development
Hemisphere Plaza Building #448
San Antonio, TX 78205-0660
Contact: Henry Travieso

University of Vermont
Extension Service
Small Business Development
Morrill Hall
Burlington, VT 05405
Contact: Norris Elliott

University of the Virgin Islands
Small Business Development Center
Grand Hotel Building, Annex B, Box 1087
St. Thomas, U.S. Virgin Islands 00801
Contact: Solomon S. Kabuka

Washington State University
Small Business Development Center
441 Todd Hall
Pullman, WA 99164-4740
Contact: Lyle M. Anderson

Governor's Office of Community and
Industrial Development
Small Business Development Center
1115 Virginia Street, East
Charleston, WV 25310
Contact: Warren Bush

University of Wisconsin
Small Business Development Center
79 Bascom
Madison, WI 53706
Contact: Bill Pinkovitz

Wyoming Small Business Development
  Center
Casper Community College
130 North Ash, Suite A
Casper, WY 82601
Contact: McRay C. Bryant

Another good way to get knowledgeable people to evaluate your invention is to attend industry trade shows and show manufacturers and manufacturers' representatives your rough prototype or photos (after they sign the *Non-Disclosure Agreement*). Ask them what they think. You can also ask them who they think would be the best company to approach for licensing your product. You can find trade shows in your industry by checking:

The 1986 Exhibits Schedule, Copyright 1986, by *Successful Meeting Magazine,* New York, NY.

Trade Shows and Professional Exhibits Directory, Copyright 1985, Gale Research Company, Detroit, MI.

7

Building a Prototype

After you have completed both your patent search and your market research, you should have a good "feel" whether your new product is designed correctly. In other words, do people seem to like your idea the way it is? Would they prefer that you change the color, style, or shape? Answers to these questions should have surfaced after you have completed the previous exercises.

Your patent search also should have given you additional ideas about your product. Before you have your near-production prototype built, be sure that you have incorporated all the information that you have gained into modifying your prototype. Expect the cost to range between $500 to $10,000, or more, depending on the complexity of the model to be built.

After you have completed the previous steps, you should have an intuitive feeling about whether your idea has market potential and whether it is worth your investing in it. Now you basically have two options. The first is to license your idea to another company; and the second is to start your own company and sell the product yourself.

A potential licensee will want to show your product to its customers for their reaction before making a commitment to you. If you want to sell your product yourself, having a finished model will enable you to show it to prospective buyers and to take orders before a manufacturer goes into full production.

PROTOTYPE DEVELOPMENT

Developing an idea or rough prototype into an aesthetically pleasing product ready for production can be extremely costly. Fortunately, many firms specialize in industrial design. They can help you.

Industrial designers are concerned with appearance as well as other factors such as function, ease of use, ease of manufacture, and product performance. You may need to use an industrial designer if you are unable to complete the design yourself. However, industrial designers are not cheap. Costs are broken down into phases, such as initial drawings, rough prototype, re-work drawings, and production-ready prototype. The cost can range from $1,000 to $10,000 for each phase. You can see how important it is to use the designer sparingly. Therefore, you may want to do the actual work yourself, using designers as consultants to check your work and give you pointers. The latter option will greatly reduce your cost, because the contracted services might then be limited to just a couple of hours on each phase. Your cost might be held closer to $500 per phase.

However, I must repeat a note of caution: Always try to get a *Non-Disclosure Agreement* signed first. This is a good rule to follow throughout the development process.

If you should decide to seek help from a design house, the best approach is to list all of your conditions and expectations at the outset. In this way, each party knows what to expect from the other. It may not solve all your problems, but it will greatly reduce surprises and disappointments.

Even with the best and most comprehensive contract, remember, this project will not run itself. You should expect to meet at least once per month, with the developer to:

▶ Make sure they are working on your project and making progress.

▶ Ascertain whether they are on the meeting your terms regarding the goals, restraints, and budgets.

▶ Revise and modify the design as necessary.

▶ Schedule another meeting and agree what should be accomplished in the interim.

Industrial designers and model builders are listed in the Yellow Pages of phone directories of major cities. Finding a competent designer or model builder is more difficult. Query each prospect:

▶ When was your company established?

▶ What areas or industries are your specialties?

▶ On what projects have you worked previously?

▶ Who are some of your clients?

▶ What are your capabilities (wood shop, paint booths, machining equipment)?

▶ How many square feet is your facility?

▶ How many employees do you have?

▶ How many engineers are on your staff?

▶ Do you utilize computers in the design process? (Computer help reduce costs when drawing modifications are needed.)

▶ Supply us with references of three recent customers for which you produced prototypes from design through production-ready samples.

When you call the references, you should ask:

▶ What did XYZ Design Company do for you?

▶ Were you satisfied with their work?

▶ What did you most like about their service?

▶ On a scale 1 to 10 (10 being fantastic), how would you rate them?

▶ If lower than 10, why?

▶ Were their costs as you expected?

▶ What could you have done to reduce costs?

▶ Would you use XYZ Co. again? Why? Why not?

▶ How would you use their services differently in the future?

Answers to these questions should give you better insight into your designers' areas of proficiency and whether you are compatible with them.

MODEL BUILDING

The following companies build prototypes and models (they are listed alphbetically by state):

Southern Cast Products, Inc.
P.O. Box 2126
Jonesboro, AR 72403
(Aluminum Products)

Quality Plus Industry, Inc.
1563 West 130 Street
Gardena, CA 90249

Scale Models Unlimited
111 Independence
Menlo Park, CA 94026
(Architectural Models)

Keck-Craig, Inc.
245 Fair Oaks Avenue
South Pasadena, CA 91030

P & F Metals
301 S. Broadway
Turlock, CA 95380
(Food Processing Equipment)

Bond's Custom Manufacturing, Inc.
12555 West 52nd Avenue
Arvada, CA 80002

Moore Special Tool Company
P.O. Box 4088
Bridgeport, CT 06607

Central Machine Products, Inc.
2709 B N.E. 20th Way
Gainsville, FL 32609

Model Builders, Inc
6155 S. Oak Park Avenue
Chicago, IL 60638

Pentagon Pattern & Engineering Company
400 N. May
Chicago, IL 60622

Courtesy Manufacturing Company
1300 Prah Boulevard
Elk Grove Village, IL 62241

Precision Enterprises, Inc.
999 Main Street, Suite 203-A
Glen Ellyn, IL 60137
(Custom Plastic Fabrication)

Anderson Tool & Engineering Company
P.O. Box 1118
Anderson, IN 46015

Metal Spinners, Inc.
1025 S. Wayne Street
Angola, IN 46703
(Metal Spinning diameters to 180 inches)

Midwest Metal Spinning Inc.
1335 9th Street
Bedford, IN 47421

Boyer Machine & Tool Company, Inc.
1080 S. Gladstone
P.O. Box 422
Columbus, IN 47202

The Erler Group
5651 S. Harding Street
Indianapolis, IN 46217
(Molded Plastics, Injection Molds, and
     Products)

New Castle Engineering, Inc.
555 North 12th Street
New Castle, IN 47362

Indiana Tool & Manufacturing Co., Inc.
P.O. Box 399
13141 6th Road
Plymouth, IN 46563

Garvin Brothers, Inc.
P.O. Box 3716
South Bend, IN 46619

Doerfer Engineering
201 Washington Street
Department M
Cedar Falls, IA 50613

Porcelain Metals, Corporation
13th & Burnett Streets
Louisville, KY 40210
(Porcelain, Metals, Enameling,
     Machining)

Lion Tool & Die Company, Inc.
607 Marigny Street
New Orleans, LA 70117

Pan-Tec, Inc.
12 Republic Road
Billerica, MA 01821

Engineer Dynamics Corporation
120 Steadman Street
Lowell, MA 01851

Everett Pattern & Manufacturing, Inc.
194 S. Main Street
Route 114
Middleton, MA 01949
(Wood, Metal, Plastic)

Snyder Machine Company, Inc.
190 Walnut Street
Saugus, MA 01906

Keen Machine Company
74 Maple Street
Stoneham, MA 02180

Versatile Manufacturing Company
8061 Marsh Road
Algonac, MI 48001

Allen Pattern of Michigan
200 McGrath Place
Battle Creek, MI 49017

Alform Inc.
2699 John Daly Avenue
Inkster, MI 48141

Mid American Products, Inc.
1603 Wildwood Avenue
P.O. Box 983
Jackson, MI 49204

Allmand Association, Inc.
12001 Levan Rd
Livonia, MI 48150
(Zinc Alloys, Epoxy Squeeze Molds, Die
     Casting)

Barum Brothers Fibre Company
P.O. Box 9085
Livonia, MI 48151

Dunham Mold & Prototype
13191 Wayne Road
Livonia, MI 48150

Avlodynamic Corporation of America
29380 Stephenson Highway
Madison Heights, MI 48071

Aero Detroit, Inc.
1100 E. Mandoline
Madison Heights, MI 48071

Paramount Boring & Machine Company
15255 Eleven Mile Road
Oak Park, MI 48237

Huron Plastics Inc.
1219 Fred Moore Highway
P.O. Box 195
St. Clair, MI 48079

D & F Corporation
42455 Merrill
Sterling Heights, MI 48078
(Wood Dies)

W.K. Industries, Inc.
6119 E. 15 Mile Road
Sterling Heights, MI 48078

Delta Model & Mold Company
1360 Big Beaver
Troy, MI 48083

Structural/Kinematics
950 Maplelawn Drive
Troy, MI 48084
(Product Design & Testing Using
     Computer Modeling)

Modern Engineering Services
     Company
28150 Dequindre Road
Warren, MI 48092

Mid-City Precision, Inc.
7430 Oxford Street
Minneapolis, MN 55426

Hansman Industries, Inc.
10860 N. 60th Street
Stillwater, MN 55082

Micro Precision, Inc.
P.O. Box 815
Sunapee, NH 03782

Des Champs Laboratories, Inc.
P.O. Box 440
17 Farinella Drive
East Hanover, NJ 07936

Joule, Inc.
1245 Route 1 South
Edison, NJ 08818
(Engineering, Design, Feasibility Studies,
 Prototypes)

Precision Forms, Inc.
Route 23 South
P.O. Box 788
Butler, NJ 07405

Structural Foam Plastics, Inc.
P.O. Box 5208
North Branch, NJ 08876

Endicott Machine & Tool Co., Inc.
100 Delaware Avenue
Endicott, NY 13760

Mercury Aircraft, Inc.
Wheeler at Lake
Hammondsport, NY 14840

Production Previews, Inc.
29 East 21st Street
New York, NY 10010

Therm, Inc.
Hudson Street Ext.
P.O. Box 220
Ithaca, NY 14851

Stock Model Parts Division
Designatronics, Inc.
2101 Jericho
New Hyde Park, NY 11040

Carter Tool Corporation
606 Hague Street
Rochester, NY 14606

Newbook Machine Corporation
1974 Mechanic Street
Silver Creek, NY 14136

Belcan Engineering Corporation
10200 Anderson Way
Cincinnati, OH 45242

Teledyne Efficient Industries
5514 Old Brecksville Road at
 Route 21
Cleveland, OH 44131

Defiance Metal Products Company
P.O. Box Drawer 447
Defiance, OH 43512

GDA Technical Models
255 Industrial Drive,
Franklin, OH 45005

Modern Tool Division
Libbey Owens Ford
911 Matzinger Road
Toledo, OH 43612

Berks Engineering Company
6th & Chestnut
Reading, PA 19611

HMS Associates Company
2425 Maryland Road
Willow Grove, PA 19090

Numaco Plastic Box Inc.
82 Boyde Avenue
East Providence, RI 02914
(Plastic Molds)

Bel Air Tool Corporation
111 Byfield Street
Warwick, RI 02888

Smoak Manufacturing Co., Inc.
Department M
P.O. Box 749
Orangeburg, SC 29116

Applied Engineering, Inc.
1900 East Highway 50
Yankton, SD 57078

Artech Corporation
2901-H Telstar Court
Falls Church, VA 22042

Design & Production Inc.
7110 Rainwater Road
Lorton, VA 22079

DEI-East Inc.
703 Middle Ground Road
Newport News, VA 23606
(Wind Tunnel Research)

Sail Engineering
P.O. Box 17036
Richmond, VA 23226

Medalist Steel Products
2400 W. Cornell
Milwaukee, WI 53209

Remember, you do not have to do everything that has been suggested. You should select only those portions you think are most appropriate to your application.

The next step is to have your product tested, preferably by an independent testing laboratory. Using an independent laboratory is important for two reasons:

1. To ensure that your product performs as you intended
2. To provide impartial, unbiased performance results

To have "verification" that your product has been tested by an independent laboratory and proven to be (some percent) longer lasting than the competitor, or (some percent) safer, stronger, or more durable adds credibility to your product. This authentication can be useful when marketing your product.

Locating a testing laboratory is not difficult. The telephone Yellow Pages are one source and the following two directories can provide you with a list of testing facilities that should be able to conduct your performance tests. You can also call the American Council of Independent Laboratories in Washington, DC, to get the names of laboratories near you; their phone number is (202) 877-5872.

▶ *Directory of Testing Laboratories*, American Society for Testing and Materials, 1916 Race Street, Philadelphia, PA 19103

▶ *Directory of the American Council of Independent Laboratories*, 1725 K Street N.W., Washington, DC 20006

After you have selected a facility, be sure to ask for references and ask their references questions similar to those for the product development companies that we talked about before. Also, inquire how the testing facility plans to test your product. You may want to try to test your product yourself first so there won't be any surprises when an independent laboratory tests your innovation.

Before proceeding, consider whether you would rather license your product to another company or whether you prefer to manufacture and sell your products yourself.

The decision depends on several considerations, including what resources you have (how much money); how complex your product is; if you want to run your own company or if you want to sell your product to someone else and let them do all the work and you collect a royalty on each one they sell.

Finding companies who are willing or eager to license someone else's idea is not easy and starting your own manufacturing facility complex, costly, and time consuming. You have to be prepared to consider hiring personnel, obtaining financing, acquiring a plant and manufacturing equipment, training salesmen, and so on. As you can see, both options have definite advantages and disadvantages. Consider the basics of both options, then you can make your decision.

SAMPLE PROTOTYPE DEVELOPMENT LETTER

(Your Letterhead)

Mr. (Manufacturer's name and address)

Subject: Product Development Agreement

Dear Mr. _____ :

This proposal is pursuant to our conversation on (date) at (location), regarding your development work for our (it sounds more professional to use "our" vs. "my") (name of product), U.S. Patent number _____ (if available). The work required is to develop our (product or prototype) into an aesthetically pleasing looking, reliable product that will enable the user to:

1.
2.
3. etc.

Our goal is for it to be able to __(list goals)__ , and we hope to sell this item for under $ (sell price) . Its manufactured cost should be under $_____ (one-half to one-fourth of your selling cost). The restraints are:

1. [Sizes, colors, etc.]
2.
3. etc.

You and your firm agree that, in consideration for access to information submitted to (manufacturer's name) or its employees, you will:

▶ Keep all information relating to models, drawings, discussions, and printed material in strict confidence within your company.

▶ Disclose this information solely to individuals who have signed a *Non-Disclosure Agreement* with (your company) or to those who have written approval from (your company) to receive said information.

▶ Not make any contact or agreement with anyone outside your company on any idea submitted without prior written approval from (your company). Furthermore, you agree not to use, directly or indirectly, any such information provided by (your company) for your own benefit or for the benefit of any person, firm, or corporation.

▶ (Your company) agrees to pay you at the rate of $_____ per hour for shop and technical labor, and $_____ per hour for engineering time.

▶ Materials are to be billed at cost plus <u>(normally 30 to 50%)</u>. However, in no case is the monthly charge to exceed $\$$_____, or the total project work to exceed $\$$_____ unless agreed by written mutual consent. Work may be terminated at our option with two weeks advance notice provided all charges within the cost limitation as set forth herein are paid.

Although this agreement was made in the hope of a mutually satisfactory conclusion of this project—one where the criteria set forth would be met, it is hereby understood that no guarantee on the developer's part other than to provide his/her best efforts is made or given.

Agreed:

By:

_____
(your company)

_____
(your signature)   Date

Manufacturer

_____
Signature (authorized officer)   Date

_____
Print name

_____
Title

_____
Company name

8

Marketing
Your Idea

There are basically four steps in the licensing process:

1. Locating a licensee
2. Evaluating that licensee
3. Negotiating and signing an agreement
4. Collecting the royalties

On the surface, although the procedure appears simple and straightforward, it is not. However, if you have completed the *Expert Evaluation*, the *Patent Search*, the *Market Study*, and the prototype phases, you will find licensing much easier. It is like a painting project. If you do the preparation correctly, the actual painting is easy.

However, you need to keep your expectations in perspective. Many inventors expect royalties of 50 percent or more. Such a high percentage is not realistic, and unless the new product is based on significant new and innovative technology, unreasonable expectations will ensure failure in trying to attract a potential licensee. A good rule of thumb is to expect a 3 to 8 percent royalty rate based on the selling price. That price, computed at the manufacturer's selling price, excluding charges such as sales commissions, freight, taxes, and customer discounts.

The royalty that you receive depends on several factors:

▶ What the stage of development of your idea is? Is it only a rough concept or has the production model been completed? Have you submitted a patent application? Has a patent been awarded? Have you built a production-ready prototype? Has your product been field tested, and what were the results of the field testing?

▶ What is the profit potential and profit margin of the innovation? If a licensee can only mark-up your product 10 percent don't expect to receive 5 percent royalty.

▶ What is the scope of legal protection? Is the technology know-how, trade secret, single patent, or multiple patents with broad scope?

▶ How distinct is your innovation? Are there similar products currently in the market?

▶ What is the market potential? Does your innovation have limited local potential or broad international appeal?

▶ Does your licensee currently have major share in your market or does it want to expand into a new market?

▶ Does the licensee want to increase its product line or is it a manufacturer that wants to enter this market for the first time?

▶ What is the value to the licensee for your innovation? Will it enable them to use currently idle equipment, stabilize their sales fluctuations, or compliment a current product or product line?

▶ Is it an exclusive or nonexclusive agreement? Will you try to sell others your innovation or does only one company have rights to sell your product?

▶ How much training is involved for the licensee to manufacture and sell the innovation?

▶ Is there potential for derivatives or follow-on products?

▶ Are there product liability concerns?

The more familiar you are with these factors and the better you are able to address these concerns, the greater are your chances of getting higher royalties.

Keep in mind that the manufacturer will have to research your product, perform its own patent search, do a competitive analysis, build prototypes, test prototypes, modify the product, build production molds, and train its people to produce and to sell your product. This takes a great deal of time, effort, and money.

Before going any further, you should, if you have not already done so, create a name for your company and print business cards and letterhead. You can rent a "mail box" from companies such as *Pak Mail* or *Mail Boxes Etc.* for approximately $25 to $50 per month. These companies allow you to use a suite number instead of post office box number on your stationery. Also they can provide other services including telex and facsimile transmission, United Parcel Service (UPS) delivery and pick-up. You should also install a company telephone line and have an answering service answer your phone when you are out. You can have the business line installed in your home; and with call forwarding, you can forward your calls to an answering service. The cost for an answering service should range from $50 to $100 per month.

SELECTING A LICENSEE

Remember that less than 1 percent of all new product ideas reach the marketplace. However, if you follow these guidelines you will greatly increase your chances of success.

1. Select a company in terms of their ability to *sell,* not their ability to produce your product. If a company specializes in selling to large department stores (like Sears), do not expect to sell them a product that rightly must be sold in small speciality stores. This is called selecting a company with a "complimentary channel of distribution."

2. Seek a company with a *similar focus* to yours. If you have a design for a new plastic molded chair, seek a plastic chair manufacturer. A company that manufactures steel chairs may not prove to be a good fit.

3. Start at the top. Always try to talk to the president of the company.

To locate potential manufacturers who could be interested in licensing your invention, the following books will be helpful:

Thomas Register of American Manufacturers
    Lists over 115,000 U.S. manufacturers with addresses, products, and occasionally, corporate officers.

Dun & Bradstreet —Million Dollar Directory
    Companies worth over $500,000 are listed together with corporate officers, directors, and summaries.

Standard & Poor's Register of Corporations, Directors and Executives
    Similar to *Dun & Bradstreet's Million Dollar Directory.*

Standard Directory of Advertisers
    Directory with officer names and products of 17,000 firms that advertise nationally.

Bacon's Publicity Checker

Industrial Arts Index

Moody's Industrial Manual

Hendrick's Commercial Register of the United States

Ask your Reference Librarian for the names of directories for specific industries.
    Let's see how Norman and Jim proceeded with this part of the job. The successful entrepreneur and the young man walked to Norman's research library where they found a set of the *Thomas Register* of 14 volumes.

Norman: First, we find the Index Volume (white pages) of the *Thomas Register* and look up "Toothbrushes" as the subject. It instructs us to refer to Volume 1, page 1656. Let's look it up together.

Jim opened Volume 1 to page 1656 and saw that under the heading (subheading) "Brushes & Tooth" there were 18 listings. Two particular entries stood out.

1. Dental Hygiene Company, Inc., P. O. Box 2247, Santa Clara, CA. Sales = $1 million
2. Colgate-Palmolive Company, 300 Park Avenue, New York, NY.

Jim: (Looking a bit puzzled,) Jim asked, But who should we contact in these companies?

Norman: Not so fast, we are not finished. We will have to refer to yet another book.

Norman took the *Dun & Bradstreet—Million Dollar Directory* from the shelf and looked in the Index (green pages) under the company names and found the following:

1. Dental Hygiene Co., Inc., *Volume III, p. 351* was listed.
2. Colgate Palmolive, *Volume I, p. 459* was listed.

The successful entrepreneur checked Volume III, page 351, and found:

Dental Hygiene Co. Inc., 3350 Scott Blvd.
Santa Clara, CA 95050
408-727-1555
Sales = $2 million
Employees = 25
President = Martin Rudnick

He then turned to Volume I, page 459, and found:

Colgate-Palmolive Co., 300 Park Avenue,
New York, NY 10022
212-751-1200
Sales = $5,261 million
Employees = 46,700
Executive Vice President = Mark Reuben

Jim: Well, that answers my question. Shall I contact them to see if they are interested?

Norman: You could to that; however, you will greatly improve your prospects if you will do your homework first.

Jim: What homework? Let me guess: You have prepared a *homework assignment form* for each manufacturer?

Norman: (*smiling*)You are perceptive. We have in fact, prepared a *Manufacturer's Evaluation Form* with a twofold purpose:

1. To evaluate whether your invention is a good match to a potential manufacturer

2. To assist as a sales aid when approaching a potential manufacturer

Companies generally have certain areas of specialty. For some, it may be in a specific manufacturing process; for others, it may be a specialized sales force. To increase the probability of licensing your invention, it is best to do as much as is possible of your homework in advance. Doing so will pay dividends in the future.

Norman gave the following evaluation form on page 128 to Jim. They reviewed it together.

Jim: That's great! I can now see why you suggested that I do my "homework" first. I can appreciate the tremendous benefit of completing the *Manufacturer's Evaluation* before contacting any company; but how can I get the answers to those questions?

Norman: Most of the questions you have already answered by completing the previous evaluation and the *Expert Evaluation*. Other questions concerning sales structure and product fit, to name two, will have to be further researched. No one procedure is correct for all situations. You will need to employ trial and error methods using creativity as well as persistence and luck.

Your stockbroker may be able to get some information on a company for you. One of my favorite sources for trade information is the trade association for that particular industry.

Jim: How do I learn about trade associations, whether they exist, or where they are?

Norman: Several sources are available that should assist you:

▶ *Encyclopedia of Associations*, Gale Research Company, Detroit, MI. 5 volumes. (A comprehensive list of all types of national trade associations and organizations of the United States.)

▶ *National Trade and Professional Associations of the United States*, Columbia Books, Inc., Washington, DC. (An alphabetical list of national trade associations, labor unions, professional and technical societies.)

▶ *World Guide to Trade Associations*, 2nd edition. (A list of over 46,000 national and international trade and professional associations.)

▶ *Business Organizations and Agencies Directory*, 2nd edition. Gale Research Company, Detroit, MI. (A descriptive directory that covers government agencies, labor unions, trade and convention centers, trade fairs, franchise companies, hotel/motel systems, publishers, data banks, and computerized services.)

▶ *Yearbook of International Organizations,* Volume 1. Gale Research Company, Detroit, MI. (A directory of over 19,000 international organizations.)

▶ *Directory of European Associations. Part 1, National Industrial, Trade & Professional Associations,* 3rd edition, 1981, 540 pages. Gale Research Company, Detroit, MI. (An industry directory of over 9,000 European associations.)

Trade shows can be excellent sources of information. To learn when the applicable trade shows are scheduled, refer to:

▶ *Trade Shows and Professional Exhibits Directory,* Gale Research Company, Detroit, MI.

Trade magazines can also provide a wealth of information on a particular industry. To locate the names of periodicals published in your industry, you can check the following:

▶ *National Magazine Directory*
▶ *The Standard Periodical Directory*
▶ *Complete Guide to U.S. and Canadian Periodicals*

And don't forget about the computerized library searches that we talked about before. The search service is available at most major public libraries and universities. Use this excellent information resource.

The young man was beginning to feel very tired and mentally drained. So much information to absorb in such a short period of time was beginning to take its toll on him. Norman sensed this and said, "All right, my friend, I think that is enough for today. Why don't you go home and think about what we have discussed so far. Call me if you have any questions."

They said their goodbyes and Jim left.

Will he stick it out? (Norman thought) Now comes the real test. Will he be able to withstand rejection. I wonder if he has enough patience, perseverance, and determination to market his product? The answer will be evident soon enough.

Norman finished some paperwork on his desk and noticed that the time was 9:45 P.M. He was reminded of those days, when he first started out, working until 1:00 or 2:00 in the morning and sometimes sleeping in the office. "Those were difficult but rewarding times," thought the successful entrepreneur. He snapped off his lights and left for the night.

Several weeks later, Jim called Norman and requested an appointment. Norman was happy to schedule a meeting.

On the appointed day and at the scheduled time, the young man was shown into Norman's office.

Jim: Completing the *Manufacturer's Evaluation* was much more difficult than I thought it would be. People were reluctant to share information with me. I tried making up stories, but people were reluctant to give me the information. Things continued to get worse. Finally my fortunes began to turn around when I began telling the truth. When requesting information, I would say that I have developed a new product and was trying to locate potential manufacturers who might be interested in the rights to it. All of a sudden people became more friendly and more willing to give me the information I needed. I still had to do additional digging on my own. By this time, I had narrowed my search to four manufacturers who I believe felt my product was a good fit with their product lines and sales channels.

MANUFACTURER'S EVALUATION

Product:

Estimated Yearly Sales: $ _____

Unit Selling Price: $ _____

Proposal To: _____ (Manufacturer's Name) _____

By: _____ (Your Company's Name) _____

Date: _____

A. Critical Aspects

1. *Need:* People perceive their need for this invention as being . . .
_____ (−2) Very low—people are unaware a problem exists
_____ (−1) Low—some people feel a problem exists
_____ (+1) Moderate—most people feel a problem exists
_____ (+2) High—most people feel a problem exists and think this invention would help solve it

2. *Sales:* Estimated annual sales are likely to be . . .
_____ (−2) Less than $500,000
_____ (−1) $500,000 to $1 million
_____ (+1) $1 million to $10 million
_____ (+2) Over $10 million

3. *Salesforce:* The salesforce required to sell this innovation is . . .
_____ (−2) Entirely different, requiring specialized sales training
_____ (−1) Many additional salespeople needed
_____ (+1) Minor additions would be required
_____ (+2) No additional sales personnel necessary.

4. *Functional Feasibility:* Will this invention do what it was intended to do?
_____ (−2) No, the concept cannot be made to work
_____ (−1) Yes, but major engineering changes might be needed
_____ (+1) Yes, but minor changes might be needed
_____ (+2) It works fine as it is

5. *Profitability:* How likely is the anticipated revenue from the invention able to cover anticipated costs such as manufacturing, (molds, new machines, etc.), advertising, selling?
_____ (−2) Might not cover any of the relevant costs
_____ (−1) Might cover some of the costs
_____ (+1) Probably will cover all costs and provide some profit
_____ (+2) Definitely will cover all costs and provide substantial profits

6. *Competition:* Existing competition for this invention appears . . .
_____ (−2) Substantial—several directly competitive products exist
_____ (−1) Moderate—several competitive products bear similarities
_____ (+1) Low—scant resemblances to a few competitive products
_____ (+2) None—no competitive products presently exist

7. *Product Differentiation:* Compared to substitutes and/or competing products or processes, the function of this innovation might be perceived as . . .

_____ (−2) Inferior
_____ (−1) Similar (approximately equal to)
_____ (+1) Superior
_____ (+2) Far superior

8. *Manufacturing Process:* The manufacturing process required to produce this product is:

_____ (−2) Entirely dissimilar. New or specially trained people required
_____ (−1) Some new personnel with some training required
_____ (+1) Few additional people needed
_____ (+2) Present personnel adequate, no additional training needed

9. *Market Penetration:* The time to reach estimated sales volume (answer from #2) would be . . .

_____ (−2) More than 10 years
_____ (−1) 5 to 10 years
_____ (+1) 2 to 5 years
_____ (+2) Less than 2 years

B. Financial and Legal Aspects

10. *Payback:* The time required to recover initial investment (molds, new machinery, etc.) is likely to be . . .

_____ (−2) Over 10 years
_____ (−1) 3 to 10 years
_____ (+1) 1 to 3 years
_____ (+2) Less than 1 year

11. *Protection:* The prospects for obtaining patents, copyrights, or other legal protection appears to be . . .

_____ (−2) None—no legal protection possible
_____ (−1) Limited legal protection possible
_____ (+1) Patent and or copyright protection possible
_____ (+2) Can definitely be patented or copyrighted

C. Product Aspects

12. *Visibility:* The advantages and benefits of this product might appear to customers to be . . .

_____ (−2) Unascertainable—cannot determine advantages
_____ (−1) Obscure—requires explanation

_____ (+1) Noticeable—advantages are noticeable to some customers

_____ (+2) Very apparent—advantages and benefits are readily obvious

13. *Durability:* Compared to competing or substitute products or processes, the durability of this product is likely to be perceived as . . .

_____ (−2) Inferior

_____ (−1) Similar or equal to

_____ (+1) Superior

_____ (+2) Far superior

14. *Societal:* The benefit to society from this invention might be . . .

_____ (−2) Definitely negative impact

_____ (−1) Neutral or mildly negative

_____ (+1) Positive

_____ (+2) Strongly positive effect on society

15. *Regulations:* In terms of the present laws and regulations, this invention . . .

_____ (−2) Might not comply

_____ (−1) Might require major changes to comply

_____ (+1) Might require minor changes

_____ (+2) No compliance problems

16. *Environment:* In terms of pollution, litter, etc., use of this product might . . .

_____ (−2) Violate environmental regulations or have dangerous environmental consequences

_____ (−1) Have some negative effect on the environment

_____ (+1) Have no effect

_____ (+2) Have positive effect on environment

17. *Safety:* Considering potential safety hazards, the use of this innovation might be . . .

_____ (−2) Dangerous when used as intended

_____ (−1) Relatively safe

_____ (+1) Safe when used as intended

_____ (+2) Very safe under all conditions including misuse

18. *Training:* The amount of training or education for correct use of the invention is likely to be . . .

_____ (−2) Extensive—consumer education essential

_____ (−1) Consumer education beneficial

_____ (+1) Little if any consumer education required

_____ (+2) No consumer education needed

19. *Product Expansion:* The potential for this product to develop into other or additional products (more styles, price ranges, quality levels) is . . .

_____ (−2) Practically nil—single product only

_____ (−1) Limited potential

_____ (+1) Moderate—multiple markets may develop

_____ (+2) High—new products and spin-offs likely

20. *Product Life:* The total market life (time until your product is obsolete) of this invention is likely to be . . .

_____ (−2) Less than 3 years

_____ (−1) 3 to 5 years

_____ (+1) 5 to 10 years

_____ (+2) More than 10 years

D. Engineering and Production

21. *Development Stage:* This invention is in the following stage of development:

_____ (−2) Idea phase—drawings only

_____ (−1) Rough prototype stage

_____ (+1) Final prototype phase—field test conducted and process modifications completed

_____ (+2) Market-ready prototype finished

22. *Investment:* The amount of money necessary to bring this invention to a market-ready stage might be . . .

_____ (−2) Extreme—costs may not be recoverable

_____ (−1) Considerable—probably recoverable

_____ (+1) Moderate—recoverable within five years

_____ (+2) Low—recoverable within two years

23. *Research and Development:* The research and development necessary to reach the production stage might be . . .

_____ (−2) Extremely involved and complex

_____ (−1) Moderately complex

_____ (+1) Relatively simple

_____ (+2) Very simple

24. *Raw Materials:* The availability of raw materials necessary to produce this invention appears to be . . .

_____ (−2) Highly problematic—extremely difficult and costly

_____ (−1) Low—limited availability

_____ (+1) Moderate—readily available

_____ (+2) Abundant—readily available and inexpensive

25. *Product Fit:* In relation to other products currently being sold by this company, this innovation . . .

_____ (−2) Does not fit in with any present product lines

_____ (−1) Fits but not advantageously

_____ (+1) Fits into present product line

_____ (+2) Compliments a present line which needs more products

26. *Manufacturing Equipment:* Manufacturing equipment needed to produce this product is . . .

_____ (−2) Entirely dissimilar; all new equipment necessary

_____ (−1) Some new equipment probably needed

_____ (+1) Can be produced with present equipment

_____ (+2) Can be produced with present idle or underutilized equipment

27. *Raw Material Compatibility:* The raw materials needed to produce this product . . .

_____ (−2) Must be purchased from new suppliers

_____ (−1) Some may be purchased from current suppliers

_____ (+1) Available from current suppliers

_____ (+2) Available from most preferred, best suppliers

28. *Quality Control:* The quality control to produce this invention is likely to be . . .

_____ (−2) Critical—precise fit essential

_____ (−1) Important—not critical

_____ (+1) Moderate—allowance for error permissible

_____ (+2) Low—no problem at all

29. *Service:* The cost and difficulty of servicing this product might be . . .

_____ (−2) Very high—frequent servicing and parts

_____ (−1) High—periodic servicing and parts

_____ (+1) Moderate—infrequent need for servicing and parts

_____ (+2) Low—little or no parts and service required

E. **Marketing Aspects**

30. *Market Potential:* The total market for products similar to the invention might be . . .

_____ (−2) Minute—very specialized or local market

_____ (−1) Small—regional market

_____ (+1) Medium—limited national market

_____ (+2) Large—broad national or international potential

31. *Market Acceptance:* Considering today's attitudes, this product's chances of being accepted are . . .

_____ (−2) Very low—people do not want to change

_____ (−1) Low—some reluctance to change

_____ (+1) Moderate—no reluctance to change

_____ (+2) High—readily accepted

32. *Price:* This invention would be priced . . .

_____ (−2) Higher than competition but with inferior or equal quality

_____ (−1) Higher than competition but better quality

_____ (+1) Similar in price but higher quality

_____ (+2) Lower price and higher quality

33. *Customer Base:* The customer base for this new product will be . . .

_____ (−2) Entirely new and different customers

_____ (−1) Mostly new customers

_____ (+1) Mostly similar customers

_____ (+2) All present customers

34. *Effect on Current Products:* The effect this innovation will have on your current products will be . . .

_____ (−2) Make current products obsolete

_____ (−1) Minor negative impact

_____ (+1) Little or no effect

_____ (+2) Increase or enhance other products' sales

35. *Potential Competition:* The expected reaction from present competitors or the competition from new entrants to this innovation is likely to be . . .

_____ (−2) Very great—short lead time

_____ (−1) Great—relatively short lead time

_____ (+1) Moderate—product lead can be relatively long

_____ (+2) Low—strong likelihood to capture and maintain market shares

36. *Demand Stability:* The fluctuation in demand is likely to be . . .

_____ (−2) Highly unstable—severe unpredictable fluctuations

_____ (−1) Unstable—moderate fluctuations expected

_____ (+1) Stable—variations are predictable

_____ (+2) Highly stable—no fluctuations

37. *Demand Trend:* The market trend for products similar to this invention appears to be . . .

_____ (−2) Declining—potentially obsolete in the near future

_____ (−1) Steady—demand expected to remain constant

_____ (+1) Growing slowly—modest growth

_____ (+2) Rapidly expanding—significant growth

38. *Promotion:* The advertising or promotion for this invention is likely to be . . .

_____ (−2) Extensive and expensive

_____ (−1) Appreciable

_____ (+1) Moderate and with limited expense

_____ (+2) Little or no promotion needed

MANUFACTURERS' EVALUATION PROFILE CHART

CRITICAL ASPECTS

	MINUS		PLUS		
-2	-1	0	+1	+2	
					NEED
					SALES
					SALES FORCE
					FUNCTIONALITY
					PROFITABILITY
					COMPETITION
					DIFFERENTIATION
					MANUFACTURING
					MARKET PENETRATION

PRODUCT: (Your product's name)

SUBMITTED TO: (Manufacturer's name)

DATE: _____

OTHER ASPECTS

	MINUS		PLUS		
-2	-1	0	+1	+2	
PAYBACK					
PROTECTION					
VISIBILITY					
DURABILITY					
SOCIETAL					
REGULATIONS					
ENVIRONMENTAL					
SAFETY					
TRAINING					
EXPANSION					
PRODUCT LIFE					
DEVELOPMENT					
INVESTMENT					
R & D					
RAW MATERIAL					
PRODUCT FIT					
EQUIPMENT					
MATERIAL SUPPLIER					
QUALITY					
SERVICE					
POTENTIAL					
ACCEPTANCE					
PRICE					
CUSTOMER BASE					
PRODUCT EFFECT					
COMPETITION					
STABILITY					
TREND					
PROMOTION					

9

Invention Brokers

Jim (*continuing his recounting of problems encountered in filling out the evaluation form*): During my research, several people told me to contact an invention broker. They said such a broker could do all the marketing work for me; they know all the ins and outs of licensing. An invention broker can find a licensing company and can negotiate the license agreement. I would have little more to do thereafter, but collect my royalties. This prospect seems great, I believe I would like to contract with one. Can you recommend such a broker to me?

Norman: You can stop your fantasy right now! There are some honest brokers who can help you license your invention; however, there are far greater numbers that are in the business to take your money but provide you almost nothing in return.

There are approximately 250 invention brokers operating in the United States, dealing with over 100,000 inventors. They reportedly are doing approximately $100 million of business each year. With so many brokers working for so many inventors and with that magnitude of business, they (brokers) must be doing a great job, right? *Wrong!* As a matter of fact, the performance statistics of invention brokers are so dismal that California State law now requires invention brokers to disclose their "records of success." The scandal uncovered was most revealing. One of the largest invention brokers in the country claimed to have performed services for over 30,000 customers. When a performance accounting was made public, it was revealed that only three out of their entire clientele had received more money than they paid out for services! This does not mean that three clients made $1,000,000 or even $100,000. All the report proved was that three lucky clients had received more than they had paid to the broker. Typical fees to the broker ranged from $1,000 to $1,500.

The New York Special Committee on Consumer Affairs investigated invention brokers in 1978, as did the Federal Trade Commission, and various Attorney Generals. The following is a summary of their findings:

Most brokers do not engage in outright fraud. They are meticulous in fulfilling the terms of their written agreement. However the services they perform for the inventor are usually of poor quality and rarely, if ever, any benefit to inventors. Just about the only people getting rich from the services of the invention developers are the developers themselves, who make their money not from selling inventions, but with their fees selling worthless contracts to starry-eyed inventors.

Brokers spend large sums of money on advertising in handyman's magazines. They offer free information on how to make money from your invention. When an inventor responds, the broker will send a packet of material with their beautiful color brochure, listing testimonials and endorsements by public officials. The inventor fills out their non-disclosure agreement and mails it to the broker. The developer promises to evaluate the invention for its commercial feasibility, which only means that they will have one of their salespeople contact the inventor.

After initial contact by the broker to the inventor and after the inventor expresses some interest, the broker will propose a preliminary agreement where a market analysis and patent search will be performed. The cost to the client is $150 to $250.

After about a month the inventor will receive a phone call suggesting the client hurry down to the broker's office. Over the phone, they may tell the inventor that their patent has great potential, or that the company has "decided to take a chance on you."

The results are reviewed with the client in abstract, complex terms ensuring the inventor not understand what the actual results of the search are. The inventor gets the impression that the broker would not proceed unless they had achieved promising results from their evaluation. However the reality is that an evaluation was never completed. They (broker) may also elude to possible sales and royalties to the client to perk the inventor's interest and anticipation. The broker may talk in terms of making millions selling to only 10% of the market.

Now the broker will explain their "deal" for the client. For $1,000 and sometimes for a percent interest in the invention the broker agrees to develop and promote the invention. This usually consists of patent application preparation, which is usually done in a shabby manner and charged to the inventor. Drawings cost approximately $100 each for poor, often incorrect schematics. Also the broker will "promote" the invention by preparing a one or two page, black and white descriptive sheet on the invention. They will usually look up companies in *Thomas Register* to obtain manufacturers in the same field and send them a cheap "Dear Sir" letter with a copy of the black and white sheet. Needless to say, the results from this shotgun approach rarely, if ever produce any results. You can do a far better job yourself, saving your money in the process."*

Norman: Now you can understand my great reluctance to having you use an invention broker. We are agreed that some brokers, who are moral as

*Reprinted from *Handbook for Inventors* by Calvin MacCracken and the *New York Law Journal*, March 30, 1978.

well as cost effective, do exist. However, your chances of finding a good one are disparagingly small. To ensure that brokers are credible, ask them the following questions. If they will not answer your questions to your satisfaction, walk out, or hang up the phone, and move on to your next name. Do not be impressed with addresses on Madison Avenue (it may be only a box number) or plush offices.

Questions to ask are:

1. Do you have a particular industry or speciality? (Start with the easy questions first.)

2. How long have you been in business?

3. What are some projects you have worked on in the past?

4. How many full-time personnel work for your company?

5. How many inventions have you handled that proved to be commercially successful? Please explain how much money your client invested and how much money they received.

6. How many active clients do you currently have?

7. I'd like three or four names, addresses, and phone numbers of people whose inventions you have successfully marketed. Have you any objection if I contact them?

8. What are your fees?

9. What services will you provide? Be specific.

If the broker has answered your questions to your satisfaction, call the Better Business Bureau in their city and the Federal Trade Commission to find out if any information on the broker is available or if any complaints have been filed.

Before revealing your invention to any broker, be sure the broker signs your *Non-Disclosure Agreement*. If he/she will not, and you have not yet submitted a patent application, you better "pass" on that broker and find another.

Jim: Now I am beginning to understand more about brokers. I was interested in using brokers because I had tried contacting several of the manufacturers myself, but could not even get past the receptionist. I thought that maybe invention brokers would have better luck than I.

Norman: Luck, has very little to do with it! However you do need finesse to get past receptionists or 'gatekeepers' as they are known. The best way is *not* to try to fool them. Be honest with them; and more likely than not, they will give you the information that you need.

10

The Licensing Procedure

Norman (*continuing*): You had the right idea calling potential companies first to attempt to stimulate their interest and to get the information you need. We have a checklist that we try to follow when licensing our own products.

They are, in their order:

1. Place a phone call to the president or sales or marketing vice president of the potential licensee to generate some interest.

2. Send the person to whom you spoke a *Non-Disclosure Agreement*. Usually, small companies (under $25 million in sales) will sign your *Non-Disclosure Agreement*. Larger companies will pose a greater challenge because they frequently have specific policies for outside submission of new products.

3. Call your contact to see if he received your Agreement and if he had any questions.

4. Ask that an authorized agent sign and return the agreement.

5. Meet with the company's representatives to present your new product.

6. Request that the representative evaluate your product and agree when to talk next, hopefully less than two weeks.

7. Negotiate the *Licensing Agreement*.

8. Sign the *License Agreement*.

Normally, the best times to reach the president are before 8 A.M. or after 6 P.M. Presidents usually arrive early and stay late. Also at these times, the "gatekeepers" should not be around, so your chances of reaching the decision maker are better. You may need to make five or six phone calls before you reach the president. Remember, try not to go into detail on the first phone conversation. Your purpose is only to generate enough interest so he or she will want to take a better look at your product.

Jim: Don't you have any guidelines to help me with this phone conversation?

Norman: In fact, I think we do have something printed. Let me get you a copy of it. (Leaving his office for a few minutes, he returned with the following form.)

FIRST PHONE CONTACT TO A POTENTIAL LICENSEE

This dialog begins with the president of the potential licensee on the phone.

Entrepreneur: Bill (use the president's first name), this is (your name) with (your company). Mr./Ms./Dr. _____ (referral, if you have one) suggested we contact you (Use "we" not "I." It sounds more professional.) regarding a new product we have developed and tested, and which we believe compliments your current product line. I understand you manufacture (their products). Is that correct (get him/her talking)?

President: Yes, it is.

Entrepreneur: Has that been a good business for your firm?

President: Not bad.

Entrepreneur: We have developed a new (your product), which has been tested and shown to be (_____) percent longer lasting, (_____) percent easier to use, safer, more convenient, and so on, than others (be specific if you have facts) on the market and can be produced (_____) percent less expensively (if known). (Try not to say too much. After this remain silent until he/she says something. It may seem like ten minutes, however do not say anything.)

President: It sounds interesting.

Entrepreneur: I think this product is a perfect match for your company. (Stop talking until he responds.)

President: We would be interested in looking at it. Send us some literature or samples.

Entrepreneur: Allright, that would be fine. However, first I'd like to send you a simple Non-Disclosure Understanding ("understanding" sounds better than "agreement"). It is about one-half page in length and just says, What's yours is yours; and what's ours is ours. After you have had a chance to sign and return the Understanding, we would be happy to share our literature, samples, tests and market study results with you. I'm sure you can understand.

President: Yes, I can.

Entrepreneur: We will send it out tomorrow and will phone you as soon as we have received your signed copy. If you have any questions, please feel free to call us.

President: Fine.

Entrepreneur: I hope we will be able to develop a long and profitable relationship. I believe this product will make money for your firm and ours. Thank you.

President: Goodbye.

Entrepreneur: Goodbye.

If you use the above procedure, getting a company to sign the Non-Disclosure Agreement will be much easier. If they refuse to sign the Agreement, you must make your decision whether or not to share your idea with them. Your risk is greatly lessened if you have:

1. Kept adequate witnessed records in your log book

2. Completed the Invention Description Form

The letter you would send to the potential licensee might read something like the one found on page 147.

After the prospective licensee has signed and returned your *Non-Disclosure Agreement*, you are ready to meet with them and to show them your idea. To facilitate their understanding of your invention, bring a prototype if one is available, for them to see and try. Also, if possible, bring testimonials from actual users (end customers) to whom you have shown your project and from those who want to buy your product, and at what price (the licensee wants to know how much money can be made and you need to help them with this).

Your meeting will most likely include the vice president of marketing, the vice president of research and development, one or two salespeople plus the president. Be properly dressed in conservative good taste.

If your presentation requires props such as projectors, screens, pointers, and so on, bring them yourself. Professionally prepared slides may cost $15 to $25 each but are well worth the cost. Everything you say and do creates an image about you and your product; you want that image to reflect nothing but positives.

Should you decide to use slides, and by all means do so whenever possible, be sure they highlight the:

1. Product by itself

2. Product in actual use

3. Competitive products in comparison to yours

4. Reasons why yours is better than the competition

5. Anticipated sales (3% of target market is a good rule of thumb). Show a realistic sales curve.

6. Anticipated earnings or profit they will realize; in 1 year, 3 years, 5 years. (To obtain this information, you may need to contact other companies who could manufacture your product. Have them sign a Non-Disclosure Agreement and ask them to quote the cost to produce your product.)

Also, carry an updated copy of your résumé that you can leave at your meeting.

After your presentation, expect the potential licensee to say they would like to evaluate your product and then get back to you. This is a critical juncture in licensing your product. You can either let them make their own decision or you can assist them in coming to a conclusion that is favorable for you. You can achieve the latter by helping them see the value of your product and marketability with their customers. You can accomplish this by telling them that you are prepared to help them in their evaluation and that you are willing to work with one of their salespeople proximate to your home city. Ask for the opportunity to call on 3 or 4 accounts with that territory's sales representative. You should be willing and eager to prove the saleability of your product. After you have demonstrated to the Licensee the acceptability of your product from their customers, they will be more eager to license your product.

The methodology promoted here assumes that you have a sales-ready prototype. It is difficult to sell a product from only a drawing or a verbal explanation of an idea.

The prototype does not have to be a full-scale, 100 percent operational prototype. If your product is extremely complex, your prototype minimally must demonstrate your products significant advantages.

Jim: Is it better to try to get a percent royalty on every unit sold, or to sell the invention outright?

Norman: In order to adequately address that issue, ask yourself the following questions:

1. How much is my idea worth today compared to what it may be worth in the future? If you feel it is worth more "today" as opposed to its future value, consider selling.

2. How much time do you expect to have before competitors copy your idea? If competition is expected within 2–3 years, consider selling.

3. For how many years do you expect a demand for your product (product lifecycle)? If the product lifecycle is short, under 5 years, consider selling.

4. How urgently do you need the money? If you need money in the near term, under two years, consider selling.

5. How eager is the acquiring company to buy your product? If they are very eager, consider selling.

LICENSING AGREEMENT

If you decide on licensing your product rather than selling it outright be certain to include the following very important factors in your Licensing Agreement.

▶ *Up-Front Payment:* Negotiate for a cash payment from $1,000 to $50,000 to help you recover some of your out-of-pocket costs like product development, patent application preparation and filing, and so on. Companies will usually not want to give you any money up-front, because they have to invest a great deal of money for molds, engineering, product testing, and so on before they see any profits. However, try to get some cash; Up-front money ensures that the licensee has some of its own money expended so the company will give your idea a little extra effort.

▶ *Exclusivity:* Most companies will want worldwide exclusive rights to market your product. Do not bargain this concession away too readily; use it for negotiating leverage later on.

▶ *Minimum Royalties:* Insist that the license contain quotas for unit sales to be met or minimum royalties to be paid. This provision will deter a company from "shelving" or holding your idea without active and consistent marketing efforts.

▶ *Monthly Reporting:* Ask that the Licensee be required to send you monthly progress reports informing you of what happened in the previous month and what is projected in the following month.

During the actual negotiation, keep the following tips in mind:

▶ Request an opportunity to open the negotiation with a statement. State your goal and encourage them to reciprocate.

▶ Do not say too much. It is usually better to say less rather than more. Do not expose your every thought at the outset.

▶ Head off objections or limitations of your invention by anticipating and overcoming them before the objection becomes a problem. Suppose, for instance, that you believe price will become an objection. Before the negative can be raised, enumerate what a great value your product is; and with all the features that you highlight, explain what a value your product is for so little extra cost.

▶ Agree on your minor points first; tackle the major issues like minimum sales and royalty rates later.

▶ To to get agreement in principle, and ask that they send you a letter of intent stating what has been agreed. Such a letter will form the basis of the final agreement.

▶ Tell good news first and bad news second.

▶ Prepare a (BATNA) *Best Alternative to a Negotiated Agreement.* Prepare an option in the event their terms are not acceptable. Remember, "No deal" is better than a "bad deal."

▶ If you need to discuss something with your partner, or counselor, take a break from the negotiation to caucus privately.

▶ Prepare a draft *License Agreement* and have it with you during the negotiations just in case they are ready to sign.

▶ Consult a patent attorney before conducting any negotiations and *before* you sign anything!

Generally, a *License Agreement* should conform to the format shown on page 149.

There are also several magazines that cater to individuals and small companies with new products to sell or license. These include:

Magazines

In Business
The JG Press
Box 323
18 South Seventh Street
Emmaus, PA 18049

Industrial Research and Development Magazine
Technical Publishing
1301 South Grove Street
Barrington, IL 60010

International Invention Register
Catalyst
P.O. Box 547
Fallbrook, CA 92028

International New Products Newsletter
6 St. James Avenue
Boston, MA 02116

Invention Management
85 Irving Street
Arlington, MA 02174

Mindsight
P.O. Box 6664
Woodland Hills, CA 91356

Product Design and Development
Chilton Company
Chilton Way
Radnor, PA 19089

The Review of Scientific Instruments
American Institute of Physics
335 45th Street
New York, NY 10017

Inventor Conventions and Exposition

Invention exhibitions are a good place to find out more about innovations in your field and to talk to others who have interests and problems similar to yours. You need not exhibit. The first time, attend merely as an observer. Information on exhibitions and conventions is available from the following organizations:

Invention Convention
International Convention Services
1645 N. Vine Street, Suite 611
Hollywood, CA 90028

INVENTECH Expo
Inventors Workshop International Education Foundation
3537 Old Conejo Road, Suite 120
Newbury Park, CA 91320

National Inventors' Week Exposition
Patent and Trademark Office
Washington, DC 20231

California Inventors' Council
Box 2096
Sunnyvale, CA 94087

New Products Technology Development Conference
P.O. Box 12793
Research Triangle Park, NC 27709

International Conventions

International Exposition of Inventions
Messezentrum Nurenberg
D-8500 Nurenberg 50
West Germany

Business World Exhibition
1801 McGill College Avenue, Suite 970
Montreal, Quebec H3A 2N4

Hanover Fair
Deutsche Messe-und
Ausstellungs-AG
Messegelande
D-3000 Hanover
West Germany

Techno Tokyo
Promotion Division
Nihon Cogyo Jimbocho, Chiyoda-ku
Tokyo, 101 Japan
(Held in odd years only, usually in the spring.)

INOVA
S.A. TECHNOEXPO
8 Rue de la Michodiere
75002, Paris, France
(Odd years only)

International Exposition Inventions
Secretariat du Salon
8, Rue du, 31 Decembre
Ch 1207 Geneve
Switzerland
(Held in April)

Flanders Technology International
International Jaarbeurs
Van Vlaanderen VZW
ICC Floraliaplaeis, B-9000
Ghent Belgium
(Odd years only)

SAMPLE NON-DISCLOSURE AGREEMENT
COVER LETTER

(Your Letterhead)

Date

Mr. President
(Their address)

Subject: (Your invention name)

Dear Mr. _____:

This letter is pursuant to our telephone conversation on __(date)__ re-garding our __(your product name)__.

This product has been tested by an independent laboratory and the results attest that our product is _____% longer lasting [or _____% safer, more durable, etc.].

Enclosed you will find two (2) copies of our Non-Disclosure Agreement. Please sign and return one copy at your earliest convenience.

I will phone you after receiving your signed form; however, if you have any questions, please feel free to call me.

I hope this is the beginning of a long and mutually profitable association.

Respectfully yours,

(Your name)

Enclosures: (2) Non-Disclosure Agreements

NON-DISCLOSURE AGREEMENT

(On Your Letterhead)

Our company agrees that, in consideration for access to information submitted to me or our employees by ___(your company)___, our company will:

    1. Keep all information relating to models, drawings, discussions, and printed material in strict confidence within our company.

    2. Disclose this information solely to individuals who have signed a Non-Disclosure Agreement with ___(your company)___ or who have written approval from ___(your company)___ to receive or have access to the information.

    3. Not make any contact or agreement of any kind with anyone outside our company on any idea submitted without prior written approval of ___(your company)___. Furthermore, we agree neither to use, directly nor indirectly, any such information provided by ___(your company)___ for our own benefit or for the benefit of any person, firm or corporation.

    Understood and agreed this

_____ day of _____ 19_____.

_____
Signature (Manufacturer's authorized representative)

_____
Print Name

_____
Title

_____
Company

_____
Signature (Your representative)   Date

_____
Print Name

SAMPLE LICENSE AGREEMENT

A. Parties to This Agreement

THIS AGREEMENT AND LICENSE is made this _____ day of
_____, 19_____, by and between:

LICENSOR: _____

having its principal place of business at

_____

_____ and

LICENSEE: _____

having its principal place of business at

_____

_____

B. Definitions

The following terms, whenever used in this Agreement, shall have the respective meanings set forth below:

(1) "Licensed Products" shall mean the products of the Licensor set forth herein when made in accordance with licensed know-how or licensed patents as hereinafter defined.

(2) "Subject Matter of this Agreement" shall mean the Licensed Products, any processes for producing the same, or any of them, and any devices for practicing or applying any such processes, or for producing the Licensed Products.

(3) "Licensed Know-How" shall mean Licensor's present and future specialized, novel, and unique techniques, inventions, practices, knowledge, skill, experience, and other proprietary information relating to the Subject Matter of this Agreement.

(4) "Affiliate" shall mean any firm, corporation, or other organization, or any person or persons (a) in which Licensee has, or which has in Licensee, at the time, directly or indirectly, a substantial stock interest or a substantial financial interest, or (b) with which Licensee has, or which has with Licensee at the time, directly or indirectly, management relations sufficient to enable it to influence the other's business policies and activities.

(5) "Agreement" shall mean this Agreement and License including all Exhibits hereto.

(6) "Licensed Territory" as specified below.

(7) "Year" shall mean each successive twelve-month period during the term of this agreement, the first of which shall commence on the date of this Agreement, or on the date of the end of the "Trial Period" if one is exercised.

C. Licensing Fee

PATENT AND KNOW-HOW ROYALTY RATE OF _____ (%) × FIRST YEAR'S SALES ESTIMATE OF _____ (UNITS) × ESTIMATED NET UNIT SELLING PRICE OF $_____ = LICENSING FEE OF $_____.

MINIMUM NUMBER OF UNITS TO BE SOLD PER YEAR = _____.

MINIMUM ANNUAL ROYALTIES TO BEGIN ____ DAY OF _____, 19_____.
UP-FRONT PAYMENT IS: _____ .

LICENSE TYPE: _____ EXCLUSIVE _____ NONEXCLUSIVE

LICENSED PRODUCT IS: _____.
LICENSED TERRITORY IS: _____.
PATENT NUMBER AND ISSUE DATE: _____
TRIAL GRANTED: _____ YES _____ NO FOR _____ NUMBER OF MONTHS.
TRIAL PREMIUM (Dollar payment for use of invention for trial period) $_____.

D. General Scope of Licensee's Activities

(1) Licensee may manufacture the Licensed Products, use, and sell such products.

(2) Licensee will neither manufacture nor use, directly or indirectly, any of the Licensed Products in any area other than the Licensed Territory, unless exempted by written agreement.

(3) Licensee will neither sell, directly nor indirectly, any of the Licensed Products in or for shipment to, or (to the best of its ability) for resale in, any area other than the Licensed Territory unless mutually agreed to by written exception.

E. Trial Option

If "Trial Period" is granted and noted in Section C, then the Patent License Grant of Section F below shall not apply except as defined in this Section; Licensor hereby grants to Licensee, for the option premium stated herein, an exclusive option to investigate Licensor's invention for the term indicated herein, such term shall commence from the date of this Agreement. Licensor will furnish to Licensee all information and know-how (if any) concerning Licensor's invention then in Licensor's possession. Licensee will thereafter investigate Licensor's invention for operability, cost, marketability, etc. Licensee shall report in writing the results of its investigation to Licensor at any time before the end of the option term. If Licensee's determination is favorable, it may thereupon exercise this option and the patent license grant of Section F below shall become effective. If however, Licensee's determination is unfavorable, then said option may not be exercised at Licensee's sole option, and should Licensee then elect not to proceed, then no Patent License grant shall take effect, and all rights hereunder shall revert to Licensor. Licensee shall then deliver to Licensor all results of its investigations for Licensor's use and benefit.

Furthermore, if Licensee's determination is unfavorable, Licensee will not make, use, nor sell the Licensed Products and will not profit in any manner, directly or indirectly from said Licensed Products. Licensee shall also keep confidential all discussions, drawings, samples and any other related material pertaining to said Licensed Products.

F. Exercised Grant or No Trial Period

If a "Trial Period" had been granted and Licensee had exercised its option, or if a "Trial Period" had not been granted, then Licensor hereby grants Licensee, subject to the terms and conditions herein, a patent license of the type (Exclusive or Nonexclusive) indicated in Section C herein. Such patent license shall include the right to use, throughout the

Licensed Territory, (1) any of the Licensed Know-how, and (2) the patents set forth in Section 1 of this Agreement and any other patent relating to the Subject Matter of this Agreement which may hereafter be issued in the Licensed Territory to the Licensor, or to a third party and then subsequently acquired by Licensor (all of which patents are herein collectively called Licensed Patents) and to make the Licensed Products and to sell such products in the Licensed Territory.

G. Disclosure of Licensed Know-How

(1) Promptly upon the execution of this Agreement, and from time to time thereafter, as the same shall become available to Licensor, the Licensor shall disclose to Licensee the Licensed Know-how.

(2) Statements, provisions, and/or Sections in this Agreement to the contrary notwithstanding, Licensor shall not be required to disclose to Licensee any Licensed Know-how,

(a) Regarding aspects of this Licensed Product still in research or development

(b) Regarding matters with respect to which patent applications are to be filed, unless or until the same shall have been filed

(c) Which Licensor shall be prevented from disclosing to Licensee by reason of any governmental regulation, or

(d) Which, by the expressed terms and provisions of any other part of this Agreement, Licensor shall not be required to disclose to Licensee.

H. Inspection of Licensee's Premises

Licensee shall permit, during normal business hours, a duly authorized representative of the Licensor, upon two (2) days advanced notice, to enter into and upon any premises of Licensee where Licensee shall be conducting operations pertaining to said Licensed Products hereunder for the purpose of ascertaining that the Licensee is complying with the provisions of this Agreement.

I. Confidential Information

All the Licensed Know-How shall be and remain the sole and exclusive property of Licensor. Said Know-how shall be used by Licensee only in connection with and for the term of this Agreement and shall be disclosed by Licensee only to those of its employees to whom such disclosure shall be absolutely necessary in order to facilitate Licensee's operations hereunder. Furthermore, said Know-how shall be kept and maintained by Licensee in strict confidence both during the term of this Agreement, as well as after the termination of this Agreement for any reason, and Licensee will take all reasonable measures to prevent its employees and others from divulging the Licensed Know-How, PROVIDED HOWEVER THAT the provisions of this paragraph shall apply only while the Licensed Know-How is not published or becomes otherwise available in the public domain from any source other than from the Licensee.

J. New Developments and Improvements

(1) If for any reason or at any time subsequent to the date of this Agreement and prior to the expiration or termination of this Agreement, any invention, new development, or improvement (including, but without limitation to licensed Know-how) relating to the Subject Matter of this Agreement and based on the Licensed Know-How or any of the Licensed Patents shall become available to Licensee or any of its Affiliates, Licensee shall promptly disclose the same, whether patentable or unpatentable, to Licensor and furnish to Licensor all relevant information pertaining thereto.

(2) Any such invention, new development, or improvement shall otherwise be and remain the sole and exclusive property of Licensor. Licensee may make, use, or sell such improvements as long as Licensee continues to pay no less than the minimum royalties required herein.

K. Licensing Fees and Royalties

(1) Licensing Fee: Unless a "Trial Period" had been granted, Licensee shall pay to Licensor upon execution of this Agreement, a nonrefundable Licensing Fee as specified in Section C hereof. This Licensing Fee shall be construed as an advance against future royalties. When Licensee actually begins selling the Licensed Product, Licensee shall certify its Actual Net Factory Sales Price, of Licensed Product, to Licensor in writing and shall pay Licensor any difference due, if the Actual Net Factory Sales Price of Licensed Product is more than the Estimated Net Unit Price, stated above, shall advise Licensor of any credit to which Licensee is entitled if the Actual Net Factory Sales Price of Licensed Product is less than the above Estimated Unit Price. In the latter case, Licensee may deduct such credit from its first royalty remittance to Licensor as stated below. If an option is granted and exercised in accordance with Section C above, then Licensee shall pay the Licensing Fee to Licensor if and when Licensee exercises said option.

(2) Minimum Annual Royalties: In the event that this is an Exclusive Agreement as noted in Section C, minimum royalties shall commence on the date specified in Section C, "Minimum Annual Royalties to Begin on . . . ." Minimum annual royalties shall be due and payable on the first day of said royalty year and upon the anniversary of each subsequent 12-month royalty year thereafter. Minimum annual royalties shall be equal to the royalty which would have been due had the "Minimum Number of Units to be Sold" (in Section C) been sold during said royalty year. If less than said minimum number of units of Licensed Product are sold in any royalty year, then the royalty payable for the fourth quarter of such year shall be increased so as to cause the royalty payments for such year to equal said minimum annual royalty. If an option is granted under Section C, then no minimum annual royalty shall be due until and unless Licensee exercises the option.

(3) Net Sales: Licensee shall pay Licensor royalties on an amount equal to the net sales of the Licensed Products as listed in Section C of this Agreement.

▸ The royalties due shall be paid by Licensee to Licensor in the following manner: On the fifteenth day following each and every successive three-month period during the term of this Agreement, Licensee shall pay to Licensor the royalties due hereunder for the immediately preceding quarter.

▸ Sales shall be deemed to have been made either when the Licensed Products shall have been shipped, or when such sales shall have been charged against a purchaser or customer on the books of said Licensee, whichever event shall first occur.

▸ Sales shall be deemed to include all sales, whether for cash or on credit, and whether the amount thereof shall be collected or uncollected, and whether made to an affiliate of Licensee or to a firm, corporation, or any other organization or person not an affiliate of Licensee.

▸ Each and every transfer or "sale" whether to an affiliate, to an associated company, or to any other entity, shall be deemed to be change of title in said Licensed Product and subject to royalty calculations.

The term "net sales" in this agreement shall mean the actual gross sale prices of the Licensed Products, f.o.b. seller's factory, less

(1) All normal trade discounts, other than discounts for prompt payment, actually allowed

(2) All sales, use, and other similar taxes paid or payable by the seller in connection with the particular transaction involved and not reimbursed or reimbursable by the purchaser or customer, and

(3) Amounts credited or refunded to the purchaser or customer for returned or defective goods.

Such actual gross sales prices of the goods involved shall not be further reduced by any discount, allowance, deduction, rebate, or franchise, income, or other taxes of any kind whatsoever.

L. Accounting for Royalties

(1) At each and every time a royalty payment is due and payable hereunder, Licensee will render to Licensor a written Statement of Account giving full disclosures regarding Licensee's sales of the Licensed Products to which royalties shall have accrued during the period then involved.

(2) Licensee shall keep, and will cause each of its affiliates to keep, full and true Books of Accounts and other records in sufficient detail to enable the royalties payable hereunder to be properly ascertained.

(3) Licensee shall permit at the request and expense of Licensor, a certified public accountant selected by Licensor, and to whom Licensee has no reasonable objection, to have access to such Books of Accounts and other records as may be necessary or desirable to insure the correctness of any statement of account or payment made under this Agreement.

M. Minimum Royalty Default

(1) In the event Licensor is operating under an "Exclusive" grant, and if sales of Licensed Products in any royalty year do not equal or exceed the minimum number of units identified in Section C hereof, Licensee may elect not to pay the minimum annual royalty due and payable. In this case, Licensee shall notify Licensor of this election by the date on which the last royalty for such year is due, i.e., within one month after any anniversary of the date identified in Section A above. Thereupon the license granted under Section C above shall automatically and without further notice be converted to a Nonexclusive Grant, and Licensor may immediately license others to a Nonexclusive Grant for the Licensed Product.

(2) Royalty payments due but not paid, as agreed herein, are subject to a penalty not to exceed 15% per year on balances late, overdue, or unpaid. Such interest shall be compounded monthly.

N. Patent Prosecution

(1) Licensor shall, at Licensor's sole expense, prosecute its above named United States Patent Application, and any continuations, divisions, continuations-in-part, substitutes, and reissues of such patent application or any patent thereon, similarly maybe prosecuted at Licensor's own expense, until all applicable patents issue or any patent application becomes finally abandoned. Licensor shall also pay any maintenance fees which become due on any patent(s) which issue on said patent application. If for any reason Licensor intends to abandon any patent application hereunder, Licensor shall notify Licensee at least two months prior to any such abandonment to permit Licensee the opportunity to assume prosecution of any such application and maintenance of any patent. If Licensee assumes prosecution, Licensor shall cooperate with Licensee in any manner Licensee requires, at Licensee's expense.

(2) If Licensee assumes prosecution of any United States patent application under sub-section (1) above, and Licensee is successful so that a patent issued, then Licensee shall pay Licensor royalties thereafter at a rate of 75% of the regular or normal royalty rate and 75% of any applicable minimum royalties. Subsequently, Licensor shall be entitled to deduct prosecution and maintenance expenses from royalty payments.

(3) Infringement: If either Party discovers that the Licensor's patent is infringed upon, the discoveror shall notify the other Party. Licensor shall thereupon have the right, but not the obligation, to take whatever action it deems necessary, including the filing of lawsuits, to protect the rights of the Parties to this Agreement and to cause such infringement to terminate. Licensee shall cooperate with Licensor if Licensor takes such action. All expenses of such action shall be borne by Licensor. If Licensor recovers any damages or compensation for any action hereunder, Licensor shall be entitled to retain 100% of such awards or damages. If Licensor elects not to take any legal action hereunder, Licensee shall then have the right, but not the obligation, to take any such action. In such event, Licensor shall cooperate with Licensee, but all of Licensee's expenses shall be borne by Licensee. Licensee shall be entitled to receive 75% of any damages or compensation recovered from any such infringement and shall pay 25% of such damages or compensation to Licensor, after deducting its costs, including attorney's fees.

O. Warranty Disclaimer

Nothing herein shall be construed as a warranty or representation given by Licensor to Licensee attesting to the scope or validity of the herein named patent application or any patent issuing thereon.

P. Default

Any obligation or duty, to be done by Licensee which Licensee fails or refuses to do or perform, shall be considered a "default."

If Licensee fails to make any payment on the date such payment is due under this Agreement, or if Licensee causes any other default under or breach of this Agreement, Licensor shall have the right to terminate this Agreement upon giving sixty (60) days written notice of intent to terminate. Said notice shall specify the failure, breach, or default. If Licensee fails to make-up any payment in arrears, or otherwise fails to cure said breach or default within sixty (60) days following written notice, then Licensor may terminate this Agreement. If this Agreement is terminated, Licensee shall not be relieved of any of its obligations to the date of termination and Licensor may act to enforce Licensee's obligations after any such termination.

Q. Termination

This Agreement may be terminated upon the occurrence of any of the following contingencies:

(1) Nothing herein to the contrary, this Agreement shall terminate, without notice from Licensor, upon (a) the bankruptcy or insolvency of Licensee, (b) the filing by Licensee of a petition therefor, (c) Licensee's assignment for the benefit of creditors, (d) the appointment of a receiver for Licensee or of any of its assets which appointment shall not be vacated within sixty (60) days thereafter, or (e) the filing of any other petition based upon an alleged bankruptcy or insolvency of Licensee.

(2) Licensor shall not be liable to Licensee, for any reason, by virtue of the termination of this Agreement, for any compensation, reimbursement, expenditure, or statutory or other indemnities, or for any investment, leases, or other commitments, or for any damages on account of the loss of prospective profits or anticipated sales, or for any other loss, damage, expense, or matter growing out of such termination.

(3) No termination of this Agreement for any reason shall relieve Licensee of or release Licensee from its obligations to be performed after such termination has become effective.

(4) Antishelving: If Licensee discontinues its sales or manufacture of Licensed Product without intent to resume, Licensee shall so notify Licensor within 30 days of such discontinuance, whereupon Licensor shall have the right to terminate this Agreement upon 30 days written

notice, even if this Agreement has been converted to a Non-Exclusive Grant. If Licensee does not begin manufacture or sales of Licensed Product within one and one-half years from either the date of this Agreement or the date of the option trial exercise if an option is granted, Licensor shall have the right to terminate this Agreement upon 30 days written notice. Licensor at Licensor's sole option, may extend an additional period of up to one (1) year to enable Licensee to resume or begin manufacture or sales.

(5) Upon the termination of this Agreement, in addition to the other matters herein provided:

(a) All rights, privileges, and licenses of Licensee hereunder shall terminate immediately and revert to Licensor, and Licensee thereafter shall not make any use whatsoever of any Licensed Know-How or of any Licensed Patent, PROVIDED HOWEVER THAT this prohibition shall apply only in relation to Licensed Know-How which is not then published or in the public domain from a source other than the Licensee.

(b) Licensee shall promptly return to Licensor all the Licensed Know-How, including, but not limited to, blueprints, drawings, and specifications.

R. Assignment and Succession

This agreement shall not be assigned, pledged, or otherwise encumbered or disposed of by Licensee, whether in whole or in part, whether voluntarily or involuntarily, by operation of law, without the prior consent of Licensor in each such instance. Licensee shall not grant any sub-licenses hereunder. Any attempt by Licensee to assign, pledge, or otherwise encumber said License, or to grant any such sub-license, without written consent from Licensor, shall be null and void, and of no force or effect. Furthermore, such attempt by Licensee to assign, encumber, or sub-license may result in the termination of this Agreement. Notwithstanding anything to the contrary contained in this Agreement, Licensee shall have the right, without the consent of Licensor, to appoint Agents on terms usual in the trade between unrelated parties to sell the Licensed Products in the Licensed Territory. And in addition where local laws or conditions make appointment of agents either necessary or desirable, the Licensee shall have the further right to appoint agents to manufacture the Licensed Product.

S. Notice

All notices, payments, or statements one Party to the other under this Agreement, shall be in writing and shall be sent by first-class certified mail, return receipt requested, postage prepaid, to the Party concerned at the address as shown on page one (1) of this Agreement, or to any substituted address given by notice hereunder. Any such notice, payment, or statement shall be considered sent or made on the day deposited in the mail and evidenced by postmark.

T. Arbitration

If any dispute arises under this Agreement, the Parties shall negotiate in good faith to settle such dispute. If the Parties cannot resolve such dispute themselves, then either Party may submit the dispute to mediation by a mediator approved by both Parties. The Parties both shall cooperate with the mediator. If the parties cannot agree to any mediator, or if either Party fails to abide by any decision of the mediator, then both Parties shall submit the dispute to arbitration by any mutually-acceptable arbitrator. If no arbitrator is mutually acceptable, then the Parties shall submit the matter to arbitration under the rules of the American Arbitration Association (AAA). Under any arbitration, both parties shall be bound by the decision of the arbitration proceeding. The arbitration hearing shall be held in the city of the arbitrator selected under the rules of AAA. Division of the costs of arbitration shall be at the discretion of the arbitrator. The arbitrator's award shall be final and enforceable in any court of competent jurisdiction.

U. Jurisdiction

This Agreement shall be interpreted under and in accordance with the laws of Licensor's State, as provided in Section A above.

V. Miscellaneous

(1) Licensor shall be held harmless and shall have no liability whatsoever to Licensee or any other Party regarding the sale, manufacture or use of the Licensed Product.

(2) If any of the terms or provisions of this Agreement are in conflict with any applicable statute or rule of law, then such terms or provisions shall be deemed inoperative to the extent that they may conflict therewith and shall be deemed to be modified to conform with such statute or rule of law. The voidance of one term does not void the entire Agreement.

(3) The failure of either Party hereto to enforce any of the terms or provisions herein shall not be deemed to be a waiver of any further or future breach of or default in any of those or any other of the terms or provisions herein. Nor shall the acceptance by Licensor of any money paid hereunder after any breach or default by Licensee of any one or more of the terms or provisions herein, whether before or after notice or knowledge thereof or by Licensor, constitute a waiver by Licensor of such breach of default.

(4) The headings of sections hereof are inserted for convenience only and are in no way to be construed as limiting any of the terms or provisions of this Agreement.

(5) If/when a patent issues, Licensee shall attach proper notices of the Licensed Patents to all of the Licensed Products manufactured by Licensee and in a manner conforming to the applicable law of the Licensed Territory or any political subdivision thereof. Patent pending markings will be appropriately attached to Licensed Product if applicable until the patent issues.

(6) This Agreement contains all the oral and written agreements, representations, arrangements, and understandings between the Parties hereto. Any rights which the respective parties hereto may have had under any previous agreements, representations, arrangement, or understandings, whether written or oral, are hereby canceled and terminated. This Agreement can be changed only by an instrument in writing executed by the Parties hereto.

(7) Nothing contained herein shall be construed as making the Parties hereto partners or joint venturers, or to render either party liable for any of the debts or obligations of the other party hereto. Licensee shall in no way be considered as being an agent or representative of Licensor in any dealings which Licensee may have with any third party, and Licensee may neither act for, nor bind, Licensor in any such dealings.

W. Signatures

AGREED:

LICENSOR

_____
(Signature)

_____
(Print name and title)

_____
(Company)

_____
(Date)

LICENSEE

_____
(Signature)

_____
(Print name and title)

_____
(Company)

_____
(Date)

11

Patenting

When is the "right" time to submit for a patent?
By following sequential steps of log-book documentation, invention description, document disclosure, and rough prototype construction, you can defer submitting for a patent until it is absolutely necessary. A patent application is expensive, possibly costing $2,500 to $5,000 or more. Therefore, it can be prudent to postpone this expense as long as possible. Furthermore, because you try to have a *Non-Disclosure Agreement* signed before showing your new product to others, the risk of their stealing your idea is reduced. However you can not ask everyone to sign your agreement. As a general rule, you should submit a patent application prior to full market introduction. One word of caution well worth repeating: You can be excluded from obtaining a patent if you have publicly disclosed your invention in a printed publication or offered it for sale more than one year prior to submitting a patent application. Even if you are awarded a patent, it may be revoked. However, as long as you confidentially disclose your innovation to others, the one year clock does not start running. One of the best, and most economical sources for information about patents is the booklet titled, "Patents, Copyrights, Trademarks, and How to Make Money with Them." You can obtain a copy from The Innovation Institute, P.O. Box 48390. Niles, IL 60648. It is well worth it.

Jim: Is my idea patentable?

Norman: Yes, I think it might be.

Jim: Is anything not patentable?

Norman: Yes. The following cannot be patented:

> 1. Thoughts, alone, cannot be patented
> 2. Abstract ideas that cannot be reduced to real things
> 3. Methods of doing business

4. Scientific principles without means of implementation

5. Perpetual motion machines

In addition, you should keep in mind that a patent does not protect; it does, however, give you the right to stop others from using your invention. Think of a patent as an offensive, not a defensive tool.

There are basically three types of patents—design patents, utility patents, and plant patents. The design patent addresses the ornamental appearance of an article of manufacture. It covers the unique shape of an invention. Typically, the design patent application consists primarily of a drawing(s) without a description or claim. Design patents are granted for a period of 14 years, provided all government maintenance fees are paid. The time of coverage begins when the patent actually is issued; not when the application is filed. The Raggedy Ann and Andy dolls are examples of design patents.

Utility patents are granted for 17 years and are usually more difficult to obtain. Utility patents cover inventions that function in a unique manner to produce a useful result; it may be a finished product, pharmaceutical drug, chemical process, method of manufacture, or a composition of matter. A new and unique computer disk drive, an electric circuit, and a trailer hitch are examples of utility patents.

Plant patents are the third type of patents. The subject matter of a plant patent is sexually or asexually reproducible plants such as a flower or a specially created lawn grass.

There are primarily three requisites for a product or process to be patentable:

▶ Is the innovation new, useful, and either a machine, method of manufacture, or composition of matter?

▶ Is the invention novel? Does the innovation have certain features that differentiate it from all prior inventions or knowledge?

▶ Is the product or process obvious? Can you show that there are features of your innovation that would not have been obvious to someone who is knowledgeable in the area to which the innovation pertains?

If you can answer "yes" to all of these questions, then the chances of your product being patentable are quite good. However keep in mind, that just because you have a patent does not mean that others will not try to copy your idea or dispute your patent.

An interference is when two individuals have each filed patent applications at essentially the same time on a similar idea. In order to prevail in these situations, you will have to demonstrate that you were the first to conceive the innovation, the first to reduce the innovation to practice (build a model), and that you were diligent after thinking of the idea to reduce it to practice (did not delay making and testing a model after you thought of the innovation).

If you thought of a new toothbrush first, but did not actively and diligently pursue building and testing a model, you would lose to another party who conceived of the idea second but diligently acted to reduce it to practice.

If you are interested in learning more about patents, read *What Every Engineer Should Know About Patents,* by Konold, Tittel, Frei, and Stallard, published by Marcel Dekker, Inc., *Patent It Yourself,* by David Pressman, Nolo Press or the booklet, "Patents, Trademarks, Copyrights, and How to Make Money with Them," by The Innovation Institute cited previously.

Jim: From what you have said, I believe that my idea should be a utility patent. Would you agree?

Norman: Yes.

Jim: Specifically, how much should getting such a patent cost?

Norman: The total cost of securing a patent is a composite of several distinct and separate services and charges:

1. An attorney who prepares the patent application may charge $2,000 to $5,000.

2. A filing fee paid to the United States Patent and Trademark Office may cost between $300 and $500.

3. Maintenance fees, payable to the Patent Office during the third, seventh, and eleventh years may cost from $200 to $1,400.

Costs for obtaining a patent are appreciable. Consequently, we want to do everything necessary before we submit for an application.

Here is a schedule of the basic fees that will have to be paid to the U.S. Patent Office. (The successful entrepreneur handed the young man the document on pages 166–168.)

Jim: Can I prepare the patent application and submit it myself? Saving the $2,000 to $5,000 attorney's fee would be a big benefit to me.

Norman: Your desire to be thrifty is commendable; nonetheless for your sake, I must recommend that you use a patent attorney. If you are able to do all the preparation and paperwork yourself and you expend the time, effort, and expense required to finish it all, wouldn't you be shattered to learn in court, during a possible patent infringement suit, that you have a patent that is so narrow in scope that it has little or no value at all?

Jim: I agree. That would be catastrophic.

Norman: I can appreciate your reluctance to spend several thousand dollars for a patent, however, if you have followed the product development phases, you should have a fairly high confidence level about your product and should be willing to spend the money for professional services at this stage.

There are several things you can do to both increase the likelihood of your getting a strong and broad patent as well as reducing the cost of preparing the patent application.

One item you can prepare in advance is a properly completed *Invention Record* that will greatly assist your patent attorney. You can also draft the application and give it to your attorney for revising and writing of the claims. The claims are the "teeth" of a patent. They outline the extent of coverage. The following is a list of items you can prepare for your attorney. (The successful entrepreneur handed Jim the outline of recommendations on page 169.)

Norman (continuing): Also, you can use your patent attorney's draftsmen or employ one yourself at the prevailing rate of $30 to $50 per hour or about $100 per sheet. Inquire at local universities' engineering or drafting departments. Engineering students or graduate students can complete your drawings for you at substantial cost savings.

Jim: Once I get my patent, for how long is it good?

Norman: Utility patents and plant patents remain in effect for 17 years as long as the maintenance fees are paid. However, design patents are valid only for 14 years beginning from the date the patent issues. Also, you must submit for a patent within one year after publicly disclosing your invention to others.

Jim: I understand. How can I find a good patent attorney?

Norman: The best way to find a good patent attorney is to do some research and use personal referrals. Many libraries have the *Martindale-Hubbell Law Directory* published by Martindale-Hubbell Inc., Summit, NJ. This Directory lists most attorneys alphabetically by city and state. There is a rating scale for very highly regarded firms, highly regarded, and fairly highly regarded. The very highly regarded implies faithful adherence to ethical standards, professional reliability, and diligence. The Directory lists the members of each firm, their educational background, the type of law the firm specializes in, such as corporate, patents, and other pertinent data, and usually lists some of their clients.

Jim: So I just have to look for an attorney with a very high rating in my own city and give him or her a call.

Norman: You could do that. However, I think a better method is calling three to five firms with a "very high" rating who are *not* practicing patent law. Ask one of the senior partners who he would recommend as a competent patent attorney. Try to get three or four recommendations. After you call several firms for referrals, soon you should begin to see that one or two names or firms are consistently on the top of the referral list. The firm whose name you hear most frequently recommended is the one you should contact first.

Jim: That sounds like excellent advice.

U.S. PATENT OFFICE FEES

A. Application Filing Fees

1. Basic fee for filing each application for an original patent, except design or plant cases:
   By a small entity (under 500 employees) $170
   By other than a small entity $340

2. In addition to the basic filing fee of an original application, for filing each additional independent claim in excess of 3 claims:
   By a small entity $17
   By other than a small entity $34

3. In addition to the basic filing fee of an original application, for filing or later presentation of each claim, whether independent or dependent, in excess of 20 claims an additional fee must be paid:
   By a small entity $6
   By other than a small entity $12

4. For filing each Design Application:
   By a small entity $70
   By other than a small entity $140

5. Basic fee for filing each Plant Application:
   By a small entity $110
   By other than a small entity $220

6. In addition to the basic filing fee in a reissue application, for filing or later presentation of each independent claim which is in excess of the number of independent claims contained in the original patent:
   By a small entity $17
   By other than a small entity $34

B. Patent Issue Fees

1. Issue fee for issuing each original or reissue patent except for design or plant patents:
   By a small entity $280
   By other than a small entity $560

2. Issue fee for a design patent:
   By a small entity $100
   By other than a small entity $200

3. Issue fee for a plant patent:
   By a small entity $140
   By other than a small entity $280

C. Post-issuance Fees

1. For maintaining an original or reissue patent, except a design or plant patent, based on an application filed on or after December 12, 1980 and before August 27, 1982, and in force more than 4 years; the fee due within 3 years and 6 months after the original grant $225

2. For maintaining an original or reissue patent, except a design or plant patent, based on an application filed on or after December 12, 1980 and before August 27, 1982, in force beyond 8 years; the fee due within 7 years and 6 months after the original grant $445

3. For maintaining an original or reissue patent, except a design or plant patent, based on an application filed on or after December 12, 1980 and before August 27, 1982, in force more than 12 years; the fee due within 11 years and 6 months after the original grant $670

4. For maintaining an original or reissue patent except a design or plant patent, based on an application filed on or after August 27, 1982, and in force more than 4 years; the fee due within 3 years and 6 months after the original grant:
   By a small entity $225
   By other than a small entity $450

5. For maintaining an original or reissue patent except a design or plant patent, based on an application filed on or after August 27, 1982, in force more than 8 years; the fee due within 7 years and 6 months after the original grant:
   By a small entity $445
   By other than a small entity $890

6. For maintaining an original or reissue patent, except a design or plant patent, based on an application filed on or after August 27, 1982, in force more than 12 years; the fee due within 11 years and 6 months after the original grant:
   By a small entity $670
   By other than a small entity $1,340

7. Surcharge for paying a maintenance fee during the 6-month grace period following the expiration of 3 years and 6 months, 7 years and 6 months, and 11 years and 6 months after the date of the original grant of a patent based on an application filed on or after December 12, 1980, and before August 27, 1982 ......$110

8. Surcharge for paying a maintenance fee during the 6-month grace period following the expiration of 3 years and 6 months, 7 years and 6 months, and 11 years and 6 months after the date of the original grant of a patent based on an application filed on or after August 27, 1982:
   By a small entity $55
   By other than a small entity $110

9. Surcharge for accepting a maintenance fee after expiration of a patent for nontimely payment of a maintenance fee where the delay in payment is shown to the satisfaction of the Commissioner to have been unavoidable $500

PRELIMINARY PATENT APPLICATION PREPARATION

1. *Title:* A heading that describes your invention.

2. *Background:* Previous patents, if any, you have submitted on this invention. This information is especially useful if this is an improvement upon one of your previous inventions.

3. *Comparison to Similar Products (Prior Art):* Discuss prior inventions with a listing of previous patent numbers and what the patents are trying to accomplish.

4. *Advantages and Disadvantages:* List the advantages of your invention and indicate why yours is specifically better than the prior art. Also, list any disadvantages you have not overcome. Your attorney may be able to make some suggestions to help you overcome these failings.

5. *Drawings:* Drawings of your invention along with sketches of other possible alternatives to your invention. Include detailed descriptions for each drawing.

6. *Descriptions:* Describe in detail how your invention works. Explain the drawings, component parts, and their functions. Describe as many alternatives as possible to accomplish the same function. Although courts base patent rights on claims, if those rights are challenged in court on an infringement issue, judges frequently review the description portion of the patent to determine the inventor's purposes and intentions.

Specific Rules for Drawings:

▶ Use a dull or matte finish white paper. Do not use shiny or gloss stock.

▶ Drawing lines must be clear and sharp. Black ink is recommended.

▶ No lines or writing of any kind in margins except "Figure Number" or "Page Number" which may appear at the bottom of the paper.

▶ Paper size should be 8 1/2 × 14 or 210 mm × 297 mm (the latter, metric size should be used if you want to file a foreign application).

Note: Keep all originals of invention records, and other documents. Send only copies!

12

Starting Your Own Company

Starting your own company to manufacture and distribute your product is also an option. Keep in mind, however, that although licensing seems difficult and involved, starting your own company is equally if not more challenging than licensing your product. Starting and operating your own company requires a great deal more risk, more planning, more time, more effort, and a lot more money.

Starting your own business is an option deserving much more careful deliberation before you make any decision. The following outline lists the steps generally needed to start a new company. Keep in mind that this is only an outline and is not intended to be all inclusive.

STEPS TO START AND RUN YOUR OWN COMPANY

1. Contact SCORE
2. Incorporate
3. Build a working model of your product
4. Secure orders or letters of intent to purchase your product
5. Prepare business plan
6. Obtain funding
7. Develop sales channels
8. Begin manufacturing the product
9. Full commercialization

The Service Corps of Retired Executives, SCORE, is a nonprofit association operating under the United States Small Business Administration. SCORE provides free business consulting to small companies. SCORE has over 10,000 retired and active executives available to assist you. The SCORE executive is a good person with whom you can start. He/she can help you with most of the steps from incorporating your business to selling and marketing your product—all at no charge!

To solicit SCORE, contact your nearest Small Business Administration (SBA) office (listed in the phone book or dial telephone information) and request a counseling form (See p. 172). A SCORE representative will call you. You can also call the U.S. SBA in Washington to get the nearest SCORE office. Their phone number is 1-800-368-5855 or in Washington, DC (202) 653-7561.

Incorporating is not particularly difficult and it is practically mandatory today. Incorporating limits your liability to the extent of your corporation's assets. This means that if things do not work out, or if something goes wrong and one of your customers sues you, they could take the assets of your company but could not seize your personal property including your house or the kids' college fund. The cost to incorporate is fairly modest considering the alternative risks. Incorporating may cost you in the range of $500 to $1,000 dollars plus another several hundred dollars per year for your accountant to prepare the necessary corporate tax returns. A good book to read if you decide to start your own company is *The Entrepreneur's Resource Guide.* It details how to incorporate your business, write a business and marketing plan along with all the forms you may need to start your own company such as: invoices, accounts payable/receivable journals, shipment logs, customer index cards, IRS forms, pricing sheets, and customer credit forms. It is available through The Innovation Institute, P.O. Box 48390, Niles, IL 60648.

The next several chapters will be devoted to discussing the steps in the outline more fully.

OMB Approval No. 3245-0091
Expiration Date: 12-31-87

U.S. SMALL BUSINESS ADMINISTRATION

REQUEST FOR COUNSELING

Please Print

Name of Company	Name of Inquirer	Telephone #

Street	City	State	County	Zip

Employer ID #	Social Security Number	Veteran	Viet Era Veteran
		Yes ☐ No ☐	Yes ☐ No ☐ Discharged:

Are you presently: Yes No | Can you furnish a recent: | Yes No
In Business? ☐ ☐ | Balance Sheet? ☐ ☐
Starting a Business? ☐ ☐ | Profit & Loss Statement? ☐ ☐
SBA Borrower? ☐ ☐

Kind of business/services (Please specify)
Retail (Selling) _____   Construction _____
Service (Kind) _____   Wholesale (Selling) _____
Manufacturing (Product) _____   Other (Specify) _____

Check the problem areas for which you seek assistance.
☐ 1. Starting a New Business
☐ 2. Sources of Credit and Financing
☐ 3. Increasing Sales
☐ 4. Advertising & Sales Promotion
☐ 5. Market Research
☐ 6. Selling to the Government
☐ 7. Bidding and Estimating
☐ 8. International Trade
☐ 9. Recordkeeping and Accounting
☐ 10. Financial Statements
☐ 11. Office or Plant Management
☐ 12. Personnel
☐ 13. Engineering and Research
☐ 14. Inventory Control
☐ 15. Purchasing
☐ 16. Credit & Collections

Please describe how SBA may be of assistance.

I request management assistance from the Small Business Administration. I understand that this assistance is free of charge. I agree to cooperate should I be selected to participate in surveys designed to evaluate SBA assistance services. I authorize SBA to furnish relevant information to the assigned management counselor although I expect that information to be held in strict confidence by him/her.

I further understand that any counselor has agreed not to: (1) recommend goods or services from sources in which he/she has an interest and (2) accept fees or commissions developing from this counseling relationship. In consideration of SBA's furnishing management or technical assistance, I waive all claims against SBA personnel or counselors arising from this assistance.

Signature and Title of Requestor	Date

SBA Form 641 (12-86) Previous editions obsolete   GPO 918-869

13

Writing a Business Plan

If you want to start your own company, you will need money. The next step in the procedural outline is to prepare a detailed strategic plan, a business plan for your business. The purpose of the business plan is to enable a prospective investor such as a bank or venture capital company to understand where your company is today, where you believe it is going (where it will be in three to five years), and how you believe it will get there.

Topics that should be covered in the plan include:

▶ *Management:* The education and past experience of principals in your organization.

▶ *Product:* The features and benefits of your product and why it is better than the competition.

▶ *Market Environment:* A general profile of your customers, the current status of your competition, and the impact of the competition on your business.

▶ *Distribution:* How your product gets from producer to consumer.

▶ *Funding:* Money needed and how it will be used.

▶ *Status of the Business:* Background and history of the company.

▶ *Future Prospects:* Likelihood of other or new products.

▶ *Financials:* What the balance sheet and income statement indicate?

HOW BUSINESS PLANS ARE READ

Before you write a business plan, it may be helpful to know how they are read and what investors look for.

To write a good plan may require several months. Such preparation may be a full time job for an entire month, working 40 hours per week. In addition to the initial document, venture capitalists or bankers will ask for more information.

They may insist that you submit your information in different forms. These changes may be extremely time consuming and tedious. There are stories of companies and individuals raising millions of dollars with relatively no effort and in as little as two or three weeks. However, for every one of these stories, there must be hundreds of others who have had to work much harder and more diligently to get funding. Venture capitalists and banks are in no hurry to simplify nor expedite this process. The conventional process acts as a screen, a first cut. Small Business Administration (SBA) has a motto: "If you got funding through the SBA, you deserved it!"

Funding can be obtained in various ways: Conventional sources such as banks, private investors (family and friends), government organizations like the SBA, Small Business Investment Corporations (SBIC), or venture capital companies. The vast majority of business plans are prepared for venture capital financing.

When you prepare a business plan, your primary goal is to raise money. Having a well conceived plan gives you an advantage. A venture capitalist may see 10 to 20 deals per day. For every 100 deals he sees, he may complete one. Because of the volume of plans seen, only five minutes may be spent on any one plan— yours included. For this reason the first section, the Executive Summary, must be written most carefully. This section is frequently the first and may be the only one read. If your reader has no interest in looking beyond the Executive Summary, then you have very little chance of receiving funding from that individual. The Executive Summary should have a one paragraph synopsis of each section of the plan such as management, product, and so on. The summary is the blood line of your application. Make it concise and interesting.

Writing a good plan, one with a reasonable chance of acquiring funding, requires the assistance of people with legal, financial (to structure the financials), and accounting (to compile the income and balance sheets) expertise. You might easily expect to spend $500 to $5,000 on outside services to prepare your plan.

However, the business plan will not only assist you in obtaining funding, it will also force you to take a logical view of your business and to develop a "road map" for the future. This exercise will help you in the long run.

Jim decided to investigate writing a business plan for his venture. Norman and Jim then laid plans on how to proceed.

Norman: I could go into more of the specifics of the business plan, however, I have a close friend who works for one of the large venture capital companies in town. If you'd like, I can set up an appointment for you to meet her. She knows all the "ins" and the "outs" of writing a business plan, and I'm sure she would be a better resource for you.

(The successful entrepreneur picked up his phone and made several calls. He then turned back to the young man.) It's all set for tomorrow morning at 8:15 A.M. Is that convenient?

Jim: Fine.

On time, Jim arrived at the venture capital company and was shown into Cheryl Jordan's office. She was on the phone.

Cheryl: We need to close the deal tomorrow. Tell them we are willing to go to $650,000 however we will need 65 percent of their company. That is our final offer. They can take it or leave it. Now you'll have to excuse me, I am late for a meeting.

Cheryl: *(Hanging up the phone, she turned to Jim, invited him to sit down, and they began to chat.)* Tell me how you know Norman?

Jim: I had an idea and I looked for someone who was willing and able to help me. I heard that Norman was experienced in new product development and marketing and was willing to help others.

Cheryl: Yes, Norman certainly knows about new product development and marketing.

Jim: Is he really as good as his reputation?

Cheryl: He is probably one of the five most successful men in the city. He did it the hard way—by marketing his own new products, not by inheritance. Perhaps you are familiar with some of the products that he directly developed or assisted in the development.

Cheryl named six products that are now household words and the young man was amazed. The successful entrepreneur never once had mentioned those to him.

Cheryl *(continuing)*:Why don't you tell me why you want to write a business plan.

Jim: I have a new product and want to start my own company to manufacture and distribute it. I am aware that it's not easy and takes perseverance, persistence, and patience. It seems that everyone says the same thing, but that doesn't discourage me.

          I have researched the market size and potential for my product; studied the competition—their strengths and weaknesses; completed independent testing showing that my product is superior; and have conducted a market study demonstrating that people will buy my product and the price they are willing to pay for it.

Cheryl: Norman has coached you well. Preparing the business plan will be much easier because you have already done a great deal of your homework.

          The plan does not have to be fancy or elaborate. It just has to address investors' questions and try to alleviate their concerns and fears. We have a general format to which we require all business plans to comply before we will even look at them.

Cheryl handed Jim a set of *Guidelines for Business Plans*. It is shown on page 176.

Cheryl gave him a copy of a detailed Business Plan for Innovation, Inc.; added to the Plan were helpful comments. She offered this sample to Jim for him to see in more detail how to develop a plan. The sample plan is reproduced on pages 178 to 189.

GUIDELINES FOR BUSINESS PLANS

CONFIDENTIAL

General Outline

    A. Cover Sheet: State name of the business, names of principals or owners, address and phone number of the business

    B. Statement of Mission or Purpose

    C. Table of Contents

    D. Summary: Briefly answer the following:
       What is the company background, date started, etc.?
       What is the product?
       Who is the competition?
       Why will people buy the product?
       How will the product be sold?
       What is the market size and its composition or demographics?
       Who are the principals with a brief history of experience?
       Why will the Company succeed?
       How much money is needed?
       What will the money be used for?

    E. The Business in Detail
       History of the company.
       Description of the business.
       Current market status.
       Competition (pricing, market share, differences between products).
       Location of business.
       Description of management.
       Why the company will succeed?
       Total funds needed.
       The expected effect of the funds.

    F. Financial Data
       Uses of funds
       Equipment list
       Balance sheet with explanations and notes
       Breakeven analysis
       Income statement and projections—prior three years (if available), three-year projections with notes, explanations, and assumptions.
       Cash flow statement, month-by-month, for the first year—with notes, explanations, and assumptions

    G. Supporting Documents
       Management résumés
       Personal financial statements of principals
       Letters of orders received or intents to purchase
       Other information

The Business Plan

Sample Contents

(SAMPLE BUSINESS PLAN)

FINANCING PROPOSAL
FOR
INNOVATION, INC.

CONFIDENTIAL

COPY # _____

January 1, 19xx

123 Innovation Lane, Anywhere, IN 46245   (219)555-1234

I. Introduction

Statement of Purpose

INNOVATION, INC. is seeking $115,600 to purchase equipment, finance inventory, hire additional personnel to fill current orders, provide adequate working capital to expand current market penetration. This sum, combined with the $15,000 of equity investment by the principals, will be sufficient to bridge the transition through the expansion phase and thus enable Innovation Inc. to turn a positive cash flow by Feb. 15, 19— and continue operating as a self-sufficient, profitable, enterprise.

This section should give the reader, a general impression of the business. The Statement of Purpose should be approximately one paragraph; the Summary should be no more than two pages followed by a one page summary of the past (if available) and projected revenues and expenses.

Basic questions that should be answered are:

- *Who is seeking money?*
- *What is the business structure (i.e. proprietorship, partnership, corporation Sub-Chapter S)?*
- *How much money is needed?*
- *Why is the money needed?*
- *How will the funds be used and benefit the business?*
- *Why does the loan/funds make good economic sense?*
- *How will the funds be repaid?*

The Executing Summary

This section may be the only one that will be read and should be a synopsis of the most important points of the Plan. It should generate excitement and interest and should briefly answer the following questions:

- Describe the nature of the business: Manufacturing? Distributing? Consulting? Etc.
- When was the business started? If not presently operating, when will it begin?
- How experienced is the management team?
- What is the future outlook for the company?
- How much money is needed?

Revenue and Expense Summary

This section should quickly give the reader an overview of past performance (if available), projected earnings and projected expenses. It should be a synopsis of the Financial Section.

INNOVATION INC.
REVENUE and EXPENSE SUMMARY
($000s)

	Actual			Projected	
	1986	1987	1988	1989	1990
Revenues	0	0	274	1,250	6,390
Expenses	27.8	46.5	323	976	5,613
Net Cash Income or (Loss)	(27.8)	(46.5)	(49)	274	777

II. The Business

This section should elaborate on the Executive Summary. The questions which should be addressed in detail are:

A. History and Description of the Business

▶ Explanation of what the business is: manufacturer, distributor, or service company.

▶ What is the history and current status of the business? Start-up company? New product development? Patent status? Etc.

▶ The business structure: Sole proprietorship, partnership, corporation?

▶ Why is or why will the business be successful?

▶ What is unique about this business?

▶ Are there any cycles in the yearly demand for the company's product? If so, how will the company address this potential problem?

B. Management

This section is one of the most important and the one which has the most significance for investors. An estimated 98 percent of all business failures are management related; less than 2 percent are due to factors other than management control. Therefore, if the company is deficient in personnel in critical areas such as marketing, manufacturing, or distribution, it is important to describe what type of people are needed and how they will be located and employed. Executive placement organizations can be helpful in locating experienced individuals.

The Management section should address:

▶ Personal histories of the principals

▶ Work related experiences (very important)

▶ Duties, responsibilities, and job descriptions

▶ Salaries and bonuses (salaries should remain low in the early years)

▶ Other personnel needed—their salaries, job descriptions, and schedules for hiring

▶ Other resources and professionals including lawyers, accountants, and consultants

C. The Market

To properly explain this section, the principal(s) must be knowledgeable about the market and the customers. The issues to answer include:

▶ What is your target market? Who specifically will buy your product?

▶ What is the present and projected market size for your product?

▶ How much of the market (market share) will the company be able to get?

▶ Why will the company be able to command the market share? Merely saying your company will get X percent is not good enough!

▶ What is the market trend? Is it increasing, decreasing, or remaining stable?

▶ How will your company get the product from producer to consumer? What is your channel of distribution?

▶ How will your product or service be priced so the company can make a profit and still be competitive?

D. Competition

The issues to address in this section are:

▶ Who are your most significant competitors?

▶ How will the company's operations be better, more efficient, or more profitable than the competition?

▶ Is the business and profitability of the competitors increasing, decreasing or stable? Why?

▶ How are competitors similar or different than your company?

▶ What are the competitors' strengths and weaknesses?

E. Location of the Business

There may be several incentives for locating a business in certain areas. Some of these incentives may include tax breaks, low interest loans, duty free ports, job training, etc. Information on these and other incentives can be obtained by contacting the Chambers of Commerce and Economic Development Departments in surrounding communities. Writing to area mayors can produce surprising results; furthermore, contacts made in the process can be helpful in the future.

This section of the plan should answer:

▶ What is the address of the business?

▶ What physical aspects does the company require (loading dock, rail access, parking, etc.)?

▶ Are renovations needed? Include remodelling quotes from contractors.

▶ Does the company need a special zoning or use permit?

▶ What other types of businesses are in the area?

▶ Why is this particular site and building desirable?

F. Expected Effect of Loan

Why will the funds be the "shot in the arm" the company needs? This section should answer:

▶ How the funds specifically are going to be used?

▶ Who will supply the items to be purchased? If equipment is needed, list the manufacturer, model number, etc.

▶ What are the prices of the items to be purchased?

▶ What will sales taxes, installation, freight charges, etc. be?

Most importantly, explain:

▶ How will the funds make the business successful or more successful?

(SAMPLE)

INNOVATION, INC.

Expected Effects of Loan

Working Capital	$81,000
Equipment Purchase	32,800
Inventory	4,500
Reserve for Contingencies	5,000
Total Funds Needed	$123,300

NOTES:

(1) Working capital will be used to hire a sales manager and pay his initial three months expenses and to cover other business expenses until the company begins to generate a positive cash flow.

(2) Additional inventory will be purchased to fill $2,000 in current orders plus an in-stock supply to support sales to new customers.

III. Financials

The Financial section supports the previous sections' conclusion, using numbers and calculations both actual (if available) and projected. To the skilled investor, a quick glance at the Financial Statements will tell the whole story even better than all the prior sections. The assistance of an accountant may be essential to complete this section properly.

Basic questions the Financials should address include:

▶ What will the funds be used for? (Refer to *Uses of Funds Statement*)

▶ Where will the money come from? (Refer to *Source of Funds Statement*)

▶ What are the assets of the company? In what form are they? (Refer to *Balance Sheet and Equipment List Statement*)

▶ What sales volume is needed to cover all the costs? (Refer to *Breakeven Statement*)

▶ What are past sales and expenses? What are they projected to be? (Refer to *Income Statement*)

▶ Will the business be able to support itself after the funds are made available? (Refer to *Pro Forma* or *Projected Cash Flow Statement*)

(SAMPLE)

INNOVATION, INC.
Sources and Uses of Funds

Sources

Venture Capital or Bank Loan	$88,000
Mortgage Loan	15,000
Owners' Investment	20,300
Total	$123,300

Uses

Equipment	$81,000
Working Capital	32,800
Inventory	4,500
Reserve for Contingencies	5,000
Total	$123,300

Equipment List

This section should describe the capital equipment that will be purchased by the company. List its cost or list price. If this Plan is for a start-up company, this list will be brief.

(SAMPLE)

INNOVATION, INC.
Equipment List

Description	List Price
IBM AT Micro Computer	$2,500
Toshiba #1445 Printer	500
Computer software (various)	5,000
Automobile for delivery (Chevrolet Truck)	15,000
Desks (various)	3,000
Filing cabinets (various)	700
Contingencies	2,000
Total	$28,700

Balance Sheet

The Balance Sheet gives the reader a "health" report of the business as of a certain date. It describes what the company *owns* and what it *owes*. Previous balance sheets, if available, should be included here. The format could be:

INNOVATION, INC.

January 1, 19_____

Balance Sheet

Current Assets
  Cash
  Accounts Receivable
  Prepaid Expenses
  Inventory
Total Current Assets

Fixed Assets
  Land
  Plant
  Patents
  Equipment
Total Fixed Assets

Total Assets

Current Liabilities
  Accounts Payable
  Notes Payable
  Taxes Payable
  Current Portion of Long-Term Debt
Total Current Liabilities

Long-Term Liabilities
  Notes Payable
  Mortgages
Total Long-Term Liabilities

Total Liabilities

Owners' Equity

Total Equity and Liabilities

Total Assets must equal the Total Equity plus Liabilities. The charges for professionally preparing the Balance Sheet and Income Statement could range from $250 to over $750 depending on the complexity. If one of the "Big 8" (the eight largest) accounting firms is employed, costs could easily be tripled; however, having their firm's name on your financial statements is worth a great deal. If an investor sees that one of the "Big 8" is your auditor, the investor will have more confidence in your figures than if a lesser known firm had completed the review. Some of the larger firms include: Deloitte Haskins and Sells; Peat, Marwick, and Main; Arthur Anderson; Arthur Young; Coopers and Lybrand; Price Waterhouse; Touche Ross; and Ernst & Whinney.

Break-even Analysis

This analysis explains how many units must be sold to cover all costs. The computation is a relatively simple exercise and is represented by the following equation:

$$BE = FC + VC$$
where BE = Breakeven, FC = Fixed Costs, and
VC = Variable Costs.

Fixed Costs are all expenses which your business will have to pay regardless of sales volume. For example, even if you had no sales, the rent, utilities, and salaries must be paid anyway. In contrast, Variable Costs are expenses that change as sales vary. These costs include sales commissions, cost of the goods sold, and labor costs.

Break-even Example:

If Fixed Costs	= $15,000 per year, and
Variable Costs	= 50% of sales, then
Break-even Sales (BES)	= $15,000 + (BES × 50%) or .5
BES − (BES × .5)	= $15,000
BES × (1 − .5)	= $15,000
BES	= 15,000/.5
BES	= $30,000

Therefore to break-even, sales must equal at least $30,000.
If your product sells for $10.00 each, then
$30,000 ÷ $10.00 per unit or 3,000 units must be sold to cover all costs for you to break-even.

Income Statement

The Income Statement shows sales and lists expenses. The result of the Income Statement is to calculate for previous years and to estimate for future years the earnings and profits of the business. The Income Statement should be viewed as a guide for the business. For the first year, this statement should be divided by month to give both the principals and investors a better insight into when specific expenses will occur. An example might be a new secretary to hire. The monthly statement would show in what month that person will be hired.

Projections need not be 100 percent on target; they seldom are. Rather they should be realistic, honest, and conservative. These statements should be prepared for three potential scenarios: Extremely conservative, most likely, and best case. If your company has access to a computer spreadsheet-software program such as Lotus 1-2-3,® these calculations will be significantly simplified.

Typical format for the Income Statement of Innovation, Inc., a hypothetical example, follows.

(SAMPLE)

INNOVATION, INC.

Income Statement: Actual and Projections

	Actual		Projection		
	1986	1987	1988	1989	1990
Sales					
Wholesale	A				
Retail	B				
Total Sales	A + B = C				
Product Cost					
Material cost	D				
Labor cost	E				
Overhead	F				
Cost of Goods Sold	D + E + F = G				
Gross Margin	C − G = H				
Operating Expenses					
Salaries	I				
Payroll taxes & benefits	J				
Utilities	K				
Research and development	L				
Advertising	M				
Accounting	N				
Legal	O				
Rent	P				
Insurance	Q				
Telephone	R				
Depreciation	S				
Sales & marketing	T				
Conventions	U				
Supplies	V				
Miscellaneous	W				
Total Operating Expenses	SUM of I through W (equal X)				
Other Expenses (Interest)	Y				
Total Expenses	X + Y = Z				
Earnings (Profit) Before Taxes	H − Z				

Depreciation varies depending on the equipment and its allowable write-off period. Your company's accountant should analyze and calculate depreciation.

The previous format should be repeated for the first year's monthly income statement. Instead of the column headings being 1986 through 1990, the headings would read "January through December." This delineation yields a more detailed look at the first year, which is usually the most critical period.

Notes and Explanations to the Income Statement

This section is more important than the income statement itself, because anyone can contend "the company will do $5 million in sales the first year." However in order for the estimates to be credible, such entries must be explained and authenticated in the "NOTES" section. This section should list all assumptions and rationale for the numbers in the Income Statement. If the business needs a company car, an explanation must follow. If sales are projected to be $5 thousand or $5 million the "whys" and "hows" must be disclosed and explained in the Notes. For every item on the income statement there should be a corresponding note or explanation.

Pro Forma Cash Flow Statement

Pro Forma is a projection. This section is the most critical for a small or start-up business, because cash flow is the life-line of the company. If the business runs out of money and can not pay its bills, the party is over; the business dies.

The Cash Flow Statement should show:

▶ How much money is needed
▶ How the money will be used

The Cash Flow Statement is an important tool for the business and may be used as a budgeting guide. A Cash Flow Statement resembles the Income Statement. The primary difference between the two is that the Cash Flow Statement does not include depreciation but does include equipment purchases. In other words, the Cash Flow Statement lists all cash expenditures; depreciation is not a cash expense.

Cash Flow Statements should be prepared for three future years. The first year's Statement should be divided into its twelve months.

After the Cash Flow Statement, a section entitled *Notes and Explanations* should follow. This section may be similar to the *Notes of the Income Statement*. All equipment purchased appears on the Cash Flow at its purchased price. The Income Statement accounts for this expenditure under the entry entitled Depreciation.

Start-up Costs

This Section should list all of the expenses needed to start operating if the company is a new entity. The following *Start-up Form* might be used:

(SAMPLE)

START-UP COSTS*

Based on sales of $_____ per year.

Monthly Estimate	Multiplier		Needed Cash
Estimated Expenses			
Salaries	× 3	=	$_____
Payroll and Taxes	× 3	=	_____
Utilities	× 3	=	_____
Research and Development	× 3	=	_____
Equipment	× 3	=	_____
Advertising	× 3	=	_____
Accounting	× 3	=	_____
Legal	× 3	=	_____
Rent	× 3	=	_____
Insurance	× 3	=	_____
Telephone	× 3	=	_____
Sales and Marketing	× 3	=	_____
Conventions	× 3	=	_____
Supplies	× 3	=	_____
Miscellaneous	× 3	=	_____
Start-Up Costs You Pay One Time:			
Fixtures and Equipment	=	=	_____
Decorating and Remodeling	=	=	_____
Fixture and Equipment Installation	=	=	_____
Starting Inventory	=	=	_____
Deposits with Public Utilities	=	=	_____
Incorporation Fees	=	=	_____
License and Permits	=	=	_____
Accounts Receivable	=	=	_____
Cash	=	=	_____
Other Expenses	=	=	_____
Total Estimated Cash Needed To Start:			$_____

*Modified from *Starting on a Shoestring* by Arnold Goldstein (New York: John Wiley & Sons).

Supporting Documents

There is no one correct format for this section of the plan. It should consist of information that adds further credibility to the proposal. Items to be included are:

▶ Résumés of principals and others involved who significantly impact the business. Résumés should be included with all business plans.
▶ Copies of purchase orders from customers
▶ Letters of intent from customers to buy your product
▶ Letters confirming positive market testing
▶ Credit information (personal financial statements)
▶ Certificate of incorporation
▶ Any other documents such as reference letters that strengthen the plan

---

(SAMPLE RÉSUMÉ FORM)

Your Name
Your Address
Your Telephone

Work Experience (Most Recent First)
Date Company City, State
      Capacity and Title
      Responsibilities
      Identifiable Accomplishments

Date Company City, State
      Capacity and Title
      Responsibilities
      Identifiable Accomplishments

Education
Date University (if attended) City, State
      Degree Earned
      Significant Honors

Special Achievements
      Affiliations and Professional Societies
      Honors and Awards

References
      Available upon request
      Date of Résumé

14

Getting Money

There are three basic questions to examine before beginning your search for funding.

1. How long to look
2. Where to look
3. What to look for

The first question, "How long to look" is never easy. Only knocking on doors will get venture capitalists or banks interested in you. Remember, they are not as familiar with your idea or your industry as you are. They tend not to be able to see the success potential as clearly as you can.

The second question, "Where you look," implies that you must not stop only with banks and the SBA. If you really believe in your idea, ask your friends and family to invest in you. Other private investors should not be overlooked. Include your doctor, lawyer, and so on.

Answering the third question, "What to look for" is more complex. If you are in an early developmental stage and you acknowledge there is a fair amount of risk, be prepared to pay interest rates as high as 25 percent. You have to be prepared to negotiate a deal. Sell, sell, sell yourself and your business.

Keep in mind other sources for capital:

▶ Suppliers. They may have interest in you as a new customer with the potential of a long and profitable relationship once you are in business. You might also try to negotiate 60-day terms, rather than 30 days with them. They may also be willing to loan you money to buy your equipment. Be creative.

▶ Charging it to Mastercard/American Express is another possibility. However, this can be very expensive money.

Probably the best place to start is with people and companies who will have the least resistance to your proposal. A priority listing in the order from easiest to most difficult sources of funding is:

1. Relatives
2. Friends
3. Suppliers
4. Community funds
5. Banks, savings & loans
6. State and federal loans and grants
7. Venture capital companies
8. Limited partnerships

Listed from easiest to most difficult: The difficulty in terms of time, documentation, and coordination required to obtain funding.

The easiest place to begin is with relatives and friends. They know you the best and are most likely to know what you have been doing. The documentation and support that relatives and friends require will be much less demanding than what others need. A full business plan may not be needed for relatives and friends. The next place to look is suppliers. They stand to profit with your success. They get a new customer if your business flourishes.

The second tier consists of community funds; state and federal funds; banks; venture capital companies; and limited partnerships. All of these potential sources will require substantial documentation and support. You will need a full, detailed, business plan for this group.

You should contact your local Chamber of Commerce or Economic Development Department in your city. They may have several programs that fit your specific needs.

Many communities have Business Development Corporations (BDC). The purpose of BDCs is not only to attract and retain business in their respective states, but also to increase employment. BDCs are not government agencies, they operate at the state level. They are specifically designed to provide assistance in many areas for small businesses. For further information on BDCs, contact those companies we talked about before when we discussed marketing research.

Small Business Administration Funding

The United States Small Business Administration (SBA) is an independent federal agency created by Congress in 1953 to assist and counsel American small businesses. Their mission is to help people get into business and to stay in business.

The SBA offers many programs to assist small businesses obtain funding. The most popular programs are listed below:

Small Business Administration Loan Programs

▶ *Regular Loan Program,* also called "the 7a Loan Program" is for general business purposes. The funds *can be used for working capital* (one of the very few programs that can be used for such funding), inventory, equipment, refinancing, or real estate and construction. You must have been turned down by two banks before becoming eligible for this program.

▸ *Local Development Company Loans* may be available to groups of local citizens whose aim is to improve the economy in their area. Loan proceeds may be used by the development company to assist specific small businesses in plant acquisition, construction, conversion, or expansion, including acquiring land, machinery, and equipment.

▸ *Small General Contractor Loans* assist small construction firms with short-term financing. Loan proceeds can be used to finance residential or commercial construction or rehabilitation of property for sale. Proceeds cannot be used for owning and operating real estate for investment purposes.

▸ *Seasonal Line of Credit Guarantees* are short-term financing for small firms having seasonal loan requirements due to cyclical business activity.

▸ *Energy Loans* are for firms engaged in manufacturing, selling, installing, servicing, or developing specific energy devices.

▸ *Handicapped Assistance Loans* are available to physically handicapped small business owners and private nonprofit organizations that employ handicapped persons and operate in their interests.

▸ *Natural Disaster Assistance Loans* are to remedy the consequence of hurricanes, floods, tornadoes, etc., that cause hardship to businesses and individuals, whose homes and businesses have been damaged or destroyed. When the President of the United States, or the administrator of the Small Business Administration declares a specific area to be a disaster area, two types of loans are offered:

1. Physical Damage Natural Disaster Recovery Loans: To homeowners, renters, businesses both large and small, and nonprofit organizations within the disaster area. Loan proceeds can be used to repair or replace damaged or destroyed homes, personal property, and businesses.

2. Economic Injury Natural Disaster Loans: To small businesses that suffer economic losses because of the disaster. Loan proceeds may be used for working capital and to meet financial obligations which the small business owners could have met had the disaster not occurred.

▸ *Pollution Control Financing* administered by the SBA assists specially qualified small businesses to finance pollution control facilities by guaranteeing their private financing. Terms may be as long as 30 years with rates as low as 5.5 percent. Up to $5 million per small business may be obtained through the private markets with a 100 percent guaranteed by the SBA.

▸ *Surety Bonds* help the SBA make the bonding process accessible to small and emerging contractors who, for whatever reasons, find bonding otherwise unavailable to them. The Agency is authorized to guarantee to a qualified surety up to 90 percent of losses incurred under bid, payment, or performance bonds issued to contractors on contracts valued up to $1 million. The contracts may be used for construction, supplies, or services provided by either a prime or subcontractor for government or nongovernment work.

SBA Eligibility Requirements

To be eligible for an SBA loan program, the business must be operated for profit and qualify as "small" under SBA's size standard criteria (except for sheltered workshops under the Handicapped Assistance Loan Program). Loans cannot be made to businesses involved in the creation or distribution of ideas or opinions. Examples of businesses excluded are newspapers, magazines, invention brokers, and academic schools. Other types of ineligible borrowers include businesses engaged in speculation or investment in (rental) real estate.

General Size Standards. For business loans, size standard eligibility is based on the average number of employees for the preceding 12 months or on sales volume averaged over the most recent three-year period.

▶ Manufacturing: Maximum number of employees may range from 500 to 1500, depending on the type of product manufactured.

▶ Wholesaling: Maximum number of employees may not exceed 500.

▶ Services: Annual receipts may not exceed $3.5 to $14.5 million, depending on the industry.

▶ Retailing: Annual receipts may not exceed $3.5 to $13.5 million, depending on the industry.

▶ Construction: General construction annual receipts may not exceed $9.5 to $17 million, depending on the industry.

▶ Special Trade Construction: Annual receipts may not exceed $7 million.

▶ Agriculture: Annual receipts may not exceed $0.5 to $3.5 million, depending on the industry.

SBA Credit Requirements. A loan applicant must:

▶ Be of good character

▶ Demonstrate sufficient management expertise and commitment for a good, successful business operation

▶ Have enough capital so that, with an SBA loan, the business can operate on a sound financial basis. For new businesses, this includes sufficient resources to withstand start-up expenses and the initial operating phase during which losses are likely to occur. SBA generally requires that owners provide a minimum of one-third to one-half of the total assets needed to launch a new business.

▶ Show that the past earnings record and/or probable future earnings will be sufficient to repay the loan in a timely manner.

Before you start spending their money, however, you should have an idea of what the SBA usually requires prior to loaning money:

1. Current balance sheet (less than 90 days old)
2. Estimated (pro forma) balance sheet
3. Current income statement for three prior years
4. Projected income statement for the first, second, and third years
5. Monthly cash flow for the first year
6. Current personal financial statement for all principals owning 20 percent or more of the stock
7. Listing of collateral to be offered as security for the loan. Include market value, original cost, date purchased, and balances of any existing liens
8. Statement showing how much money is needed and for what it will be used
9. Business plan explaining the operating details of the business

The SBA also asks that the Business Plan be in a specific form. The format for SBA Business Plans is shown on pages 195–196.

Cheryl: As you can see, the format that the SBA uses is somewhat similar to the one we require.

Jim: With all the sources of SBA funding, getting money should be a snap.

Cheryl: Don't kid yourself! Getting SBA funding is extremely difficult. There is a great deal of red tape and bureaucracy involved which further complicates matters. Perhaps it is fortunate that it is difficult to get the funds, because it is your and my tax dollars being spent. However, just in case you still want to pursue SBA funding, here are the forms required to submit for a loan. You can get copies of them and inquire about other programs that you might qualify for by calling your nearest SBA office or by contacting the SBA in Washington, DC. Their address is:

> 1441 L Street N.W.
> Washington, DC
> 1-800-368-5855 or in DC (202) 653-7561

After the forms are completed, the nearest SBA field office can direct you to a lender in your area that can process your loan application.

Cheryl gave Jim the SBA loan application forms shown on pages 199–214.

FORMAT FOR BUSINESS PLANS SUBMITTED TO THE SBA

I. Cover Letter
    A. Dollar amount requested
    B. Terms and timing
    C. Type and price of securities sought

II. Summary
    A. Business description including:
       Name
       Location and plant description
       Product
       Market and competition
       Management experience and expertise
    B. Business goals
    C. Summary of financial needs and use of funds
    D. Earnings and projections
    E. Projected return to investors

III. Market Analysis
    A. Description of total market
    B. Industry trends
    C. Target market
    D. Competition

IV. Product or Services
    A. Description of product line
    B. Proprietary Position: Patents, copyrights, legal, and technical considerations
    C. Comparison to competitors' products

V. Manufacturing Process (If applicable)
    A. Materials
    B. Sources of supply
    C. Production methods

VI. Marketing Strategy
    A. Overall strategy
    B. Pricing policy
    C. Sales terms
    D. Method of selling, distributing, and servicing products

VIII. Management Plan

    A. Form of business organization (corporation, partnership, etc.)
    B. Board of directors
    C. Officers
    D. Organizational chart and description of responsibilities
    E. Résumés of key personnel
    F. Staffing plan and number of employees
    G. Facilities plan and anticipated capital improvements
    H. Operating plan/schedule of anticipated orders for the next 1 to 2 years

VIII. Financial Data

    A. Financial history of the investors and the business
    B. Three-year financial projections (first year, monthly; second year, quarterly; third year, annually)
    C. Explanation of projections
    D. Key business ratios
    E. Explanation of use and effect of new funds
    F. Potential return to investors

U.S. Small Business Administration

AGREEMENT OF COMPLIANCE

In compliance with Executive Order 11246, as amended (Executive Order 11246, as amended prohibits discrimination because of race, color, religion, sex, or national origin, and requires affirmative action to ensure equality of opportunity in all aspects of employment by all contractors and subcontractors, performing work under a Federally assisted construction contract in excess of $10,000, regardless of the number of employees), the applicant/recipient, contractor or subcontractor agrees that in consideration of the approval and as a condition of the disbursement of all or any part of a loan by the Small Business Administration (SBA) that it will incorporate or cause to be incorporated into any contract or subcontract in excess of $10,000 for construction work, or modification thereof, as defined in the regulations of the Secretary of Labor, at 41 CFR Chapter 60, which is paid for in whole or in part with funds obtained from the Federal Government or borrowed on the credit of the Federal Government pursuant to a grant, contract, loan, insurance or guarantee, or undertaken pursuant to any Federal program involving such grant, contract, loan, insurance or guarantee, the following equal opportunity clause:

During the performance of this contract, the contractor agrees as follows:

(1)   The contractor will not discriminate against any employee or applicant for employment because of race, color, religion, sex or national origin. The contractor will take affirmative action to insure that applicants are employed, and that employees are treated during employment without regard to their race, color, religion, sex or national origin. Such action shall include, but not be limited to the following: employment, upgrading, demotion or transfer; recruitment or advertising; layoff or termination; rates of pay or other forms of compensation; and selection for training, including apprenticeship. The contractor agrees to post in conspicuous places, available to employees and applicants for employment, notices to be provided setting forth the provisions of this nondiscrimination clause.

(2)   The contractor will, in all solicitations or advertisements for employees placed by or on behalf of the contractor, state that all qualified applicants will receive consideration for employment without regard to race, color, religion, sex or national origin.

(3)   The contractor will send to each labor union or representative of workers with which he has a collective bargaining agreement or other contract or understanding, a notice to be provided advising the said labor union or workers' representative of the contractor's commitments under Executive Order 11246, as amended, and shall post copies of the notice in conspicuous places available to employees and applicants for employment.

(4)   The contractor will comply with all provisions of Executive Order 11246, as amended, and the rules and relevant orders of the Secretary of Labor created thereby.

(5)   The contractor will furnish all information and reports required by Executive Order 11246, as amended, and by the rules, regulations and orders of the Secretary of Labor, or pursuant thereto, and will permit access to books, records and accounts by SBA (See SBA Form 793) and the Secretary of Labor for purposes of investigation to ascertain compliance with such rules, regulations and orders. (The information collection requirements contained in Executive Order 11246, as amended, are approved under OMB No. 1215-0072.)

(6)   In the event of the contractor's noncompliance with the nondiscrimination clause or with any of the said rules, regulations or orders, this contract may be cancelled, terminated or suspended in whole or in part and the contractor may be declared ineligible for further Government contracts or federally assisted construction contracts in accordance with procedures authorized in Executive Order 11246, as amended, and such other sanctions may be imposed and remedies invoked as provided in the said Executive Order or by rule, regulation or order of the Secretary of Labor, or as otherwise provided by law.

The contractor will include the portion of the sentence immediately preceding paragraph (1) and the provisions of paragraphs (1) through (6) in every subcontract or purchase order unless exempted by rules, regulations or orders of the Secretary of Labor issued pursuant to Executive Order 11246, as amended, so that such provisions will be binding upon each subcontractor or vendor. The contractor will take such action with respect to any subcontract or purchase order as SBA may direct as a means of enforcing such provisions, including sanctions for noncompliance: Provided, however that in the event a contractor becomes involved in or is threatened with litigation with a subcontractor or vendor as a result of such direction by SBA, the contractor may request the United States to enter into such litigation to protect the interest of the United States.

SBA Form 601 (10-85) REF: SOP 9030   Previous editions are obsolete

The Applicant further agrees that it will be bound by the above equal opportunity clause with respect to its own employment practices when it participates in federally assisted construction work.

The Applicant agrees that is will assist and cooperate actively with SBA and the Secretary of Labor in obtaining the compliance of contractors and subcontractors with the equal opportunity clause and the rules, regulations and relevant orders of the Secretary of Labor, that it will furnish SBA and the Secretary of Labor such information as they may require for the supervision of such compliance, and that it will otherwise assist SBA in the discharge of the Agency's primary responsibility for securing compliance. The Applicant further agrees that it will refrain from entering into any contract or contract modification subject to Executive Order 11246, as amended, and will carry out such sanctions and penalties for violation of the equal opportunity clause as may be imposed upon contractors and subcontractors by SBA or the Secretary of Labor or such other sanctions and penalties for violation thereof as may, in the opinion of the Administrator, be necessary and appropriate.

In addition, the Applicant agrees that it if fails or refuses to comply with these undertakings SBA may take any or all of the following actions: cancel, terminate or suspend in whole or in part the loan; refrain from extending any further assistance to the applicant under the programs with respect to which the failure or refusal occurred until satisfactory assurance of future compliance has been received from such applicant; and refer the case to the Department of Justice for appropriate legal proceedings.

In consideration of the approval by the Small Business Administration of a loan to _____
_____ Applicant, said Applicant and _____
the general contractor, mutually promise and agree that the(y) will comply with all nondiscrimination provisions and requirements of Executive Order 11246, as amended.

Executed the _____ day of _____ 19___.

_____
Name, Address, & Phone No. of Applicant

By _____
Typed Name & Title of Authorized Official

_____
Corporate Seal   Signature of Authorized Official

_____
Name, Address, & Phone No. of Subrecipient

By _____
Typed Name & Title of Authorized Official

_____
Corporate Seal   Signature of Authorized Official

SBA Form 601 (10-85) REF: SOP 9030 Previous editions are obsolete   ☆ U.S. Government Printing Office: 1987—718-099/00813

U.S. Small Business Administration

Application for Business Loan

Applicant	Full Address

Name of Business		Tax I.D. No.

Full Street Address		Tel. No. (Inc. A/C)

City	County	State	Zip	Number of Employees (Including subsidiaries and affiliates)
Type of Business			Date Business Established	At Time of Application _____
Bank of Business Account and Address				If Loan is Approved _____
				Subsidiaries or Affiliates _____ (Separate from above)

Use of Proceeds: (Enter Gross Dollar Amounts Rounded to Nearest Hundreds)	Loan Requested	SBA USE ONLY	Collateral
Land Acquisition			If your collateral consists of (A) Land and Building, (D) Accounts Receivable and/or (E) Inventory, fill in the appropriate blanks. If you are pledging (B) Machinery and Equipment, (C) Furniture and Fixtures, and/or (F) Other, please provide an itemized list (labeled Exhibit A) that contains serial and identification numbers for all articles that had an original value greater than $500. Include a legal description of Real Estate offered as collateral.
New Construction/ Expansion/Repair			
Acquisition and/or Repair of Machinery and Equipment			
Inventory Purchase			

Working Capital (Including Accounts Payable)				Present Market Value	Present Loan Balance	SBA Use Only Collateral Valuation
Acquisition of Existing Business			A. Land and Building	$	$	$
Payoff SBA Loan			B. Machinery & Equipment			
Payoff Bank Loan (Non SBA Associated)			C. Furniture & Fixtures			
Other Debt Payment (Non SBA Associated)			D. Accounts Receivable			
All Other			E. Inventory			
Total Loan Requested			F. Other			
Term of Loan			Totals	$	$	$

PREVIOUS SBA OR OTHER GOVERNMENT FINANCING: If you or any principals or affiliates have ever requested Government Financing, complete the following:

Name of Agency	Original Amount of Loan	Date of Request	Approved or Declined	Balance	Current or Past Due
	$			$	
	$			$	

SBA Form 4 (2-85) Previous Editions Obsolete

INDEBTEDNESS: Furnish the following information on all installment debts, contracts, notes, and mortgages payable. Indicate by an asterisk (*) items to be paid by loan proceeds and reason for paying same (present balance should agree with latest balance sheet submitted).

To Whom Payable	Original Amount	Original Date	Present Balance	Rate of Interest	Maturity Date	Monthly Payment	Security	Current or Past Due
	$		$			$		
	$		$			$		
	$		$			$		
	$		$			$		

MANAGEMENT (Proprietor, partners, officers, directors and all holders of outstanding stock — <u>100% of ownership must be shown</u>). Use separate sheet if necessary.

Name and Social Security Number	Complete Address	% Owned	*Military Service From	*Military Service To	*Race	*Sex

* This data is collected for statistical purposes only. It has no bearing on the credit decision to approve or decline this application.

ASSISTANCE   List the name(s) and occupation(s) of any who assisted in preparation of this form, other than applicant.

Name and Occupation	Address	Total Fees Paid	Fees Due

Signature of Preparers if Other Than Applicant

THE FOLLOWING EXHIBITS MUST BE COMPLETED WHERE APPLICABLE. ALL QUESTIONS ANSWERED ARE MADE A PART OF THE APPLICATION.

For Guaranty Loans please provide an original and one copy (Photocopy is Acceptable) of the Application Form, and all Exhibits to the participating lender. For Direct Loans submit one original copy of application and Exhibits to SBA.

Submit SBA Form 1261 (Statements Required by Laws and Executive Orders). This form must be signed and dated by each Proprietor, Partner, Principal or Guarantor.

1. Submit SBA Form 912 (Personal History Statement) for each person e.g. owners, partners, officers, directors, major stockholders, etc.; the instructions are on SBA Form 912.

2. Furnish a signed current personal balance sheet (SBA Form 413 may be used for this purpose) for each stockholder (with 20% or greater ownership), partner, officer, and owner. Social Security number should be included on personal financial statement. Label this Exhibit B.

3. Include the statements listed below: 1, 2, 3 for the last three years; also 1, 2, 3, 4 dated within 90 days of filing the application; and statement 5, if applicable. This is Exhibit C (SBA has Management Aids that help in the preparation of financial statements.) All information must be signed and dated.

    1. Balance Sheet   2. Profit and Loss Statement
    3. Reconciliation of Net Worth
    4. Aging of Accounts Receivable and Payable
    5. Earnings projections for at least one year where financial statements for the last three years are unavailable or where requested by District Office.
       (If Profit and Loss Statement is not available, explain why and substitute Federal Income Tax Forms.)

4. Provide a brief history of your company and a paragraph describing the expected benefits it will receive from the loan. Label it Exhibit D.

ALL EXHIBITS MUST BE SIGNED AND DATED BY PERSON SIGNING THIS FORM.

SBA Form 4 (2-85) Previous Editions Obsolete

5. Provide a brief description of the educational, technical and business background for all the people listed under Management. Please mark it Exhibit E.

6. Do you have any co-signers and/or guarantors for this loan? If so, please submit their names, addresses and personal balance sheet(s) as Exhibit F.

7. Are you buying machinery or equipment with your loan money? If so, you must include a list of the equipment and cost as quoted by the seller and his name and address. This is Exhibit G.

8. Have you or any officers of your company ever been involved in bankruptcy or insolvency proceedings? If so, please provide the details as Exhibit H. If none, check here: ☐ Yes ☐ No

9. Are you or your business involved in any pending lawsuits? If yes, provide the details as Exhibit I. If none, check here: ☐ Yes ☐ No

10. Do you or your spouse or any member of your household, or anyone who owns, manages, or directs your business or their spouses or members of their households work for the Small Business Administration, Small Business Advisory Council, SCORE or ACE, any Federal Agency, or the participating lender? If so, please provide the name and address of the person and the office where employed. label this Exhibit J. If none, check here: ☐ Yes ☐ No

11. Does your business, its owners or majority stockholders own or have a controlling interest in other businesses? If yes, please provide their names and the relationship with your company along with a current balance sheet and operating statement for each. This should be Exhibit K.

12. Do you buy from, sell to, or use the services of any concern in which someone in your company has a significant financial interest? If yes, provide details on a separate sheet of paper labeled Exhibit L.

13. If your business is a franchise, include a copy of the franchise agreement and a copy of the FTC disclosure statement supplied to you by the Franchisor. Please include it as Exhibit M.

CONSTRUCTION LOANS ONLY

14. Include a separate exhibit (Exhibit N) the estimated cost of the project and a statement of the source of any additional funds.

15. File the necessary compliance document (SBA Form 601).

16. Provide copies of preliminary construction plans and specifications. Include them as Exhibit O. Final plans will be required prior to disbursement.

DIRECT LOANS ONLY

17. Include two bank declination letters with your application. These letters should include the name and telephone number of the persons contacted at the banks, the amount and terms of the loan, the reason for decline and whether or not the bank will participate with SBA. In cities with 200,000 people or less, one letter will be sufficient.

EXPORT LOANS

18. Does your business presently engage in Export Trade?
Check here ☐ Yes ☐ No

19. Do you plan to begin exporting as a result of this loan?
Check here ☐ Yes ☐ No

20. Would you like information on Exporting?
Check here ☐ Yes ☐ No

AGREEMENTS AND CERTIFICATIONS

Agreements of Nonemployment of SBA Personnel: I/We agree that if SBA approves this loan application I/We will not, for at least two years, hire as an employee or consultant anyone that was employed by the SBA during the one year period prior to the disbursement of the loan.

Certification: I/We certify: (a) I/We have not paid anyone connected with the Federal Government for help in getting this loan. I/We also agree to report to the SBA office of the Inspector General, 1441 L Street N.W., Washington, D.C. 20416 any Federal Government employee who offers, in return for any type of compensation, to help get this loan approved.

(b) All information in this application and the Exhibits are true and complete to the best of my/our knowledge and are submitted to SBA so SBA can decide whether to grant a loan or participate with a lending institution in a loan to me/us. I/We agree to pay for or reimburse SBA for the cost of any surveys, title or mortgage examinations, appraisals etc., performed by non-SBA personnel provided I/We have given my/our consent.

I/We understand that I/We need not pay anybody to deal with SBA. I/We have read and understand Form 394 which explains SBA policy on representatives and their fees.

If you make a statement that you know to be false or if you over value a security in order to help obtain a loan under the provisions of the Small Business Act, you can be fined up to $5,000 or be put in jail for up to two years, or both.

If Applicant is a proprietor or general partner, sign below:

By: _____
                                                    Date

If Applicant is a Corporation, sign below:

_____
Corporate Name and Seal   Date

By: _____
                Signature of President

Attested by: _____
                Signature of Corporate Secretary

ALL EXHIBITS MUST BE SIGNED AND DATED BY PERSON SIGNING THIS FORM.

SBA Form 4 (2-85) Previous Editions Obsolete

★U.S.GPO:1986-0-623-058/281

SMALL BUSINESS ADMINISTRATION

POLICY AND REGULATIONS CONCERNING REPRESENTATIVES AND THEIR FEES

An applicant for a loan from SBA may obtain the assistance of any attorney, accountant, engineer, appraiser or other representative to aid him in the preparation and presentation of his application to SBA; however, such representation is not mandatory. In the event a loan is approved, the services of an attorney may be necessary to assist in the preparation of closing documents, title abstracts, etc. SBA will allow the payment of reasonable fees or other compensation for services performed by such representatives on behalf of the applicant.

There are no "authorized representatives" of SBA, other than our regular salaried employees. Payment of any fee or gratuity to SBA employees is illegal and will subject the parties to such a transaction to prosecution.

SBA Regulations (Part 103, Sec. 103.13-5(c)) prohibit representatives from charging or proposing to charge any contingent fee for any services performed in connection with an SBA loan unless the amount of such fee bears a necessary and reasonable relationship to the services actually performed; or to charge any fee which is deemed by SBA to be unreasonable for the services actually performed; or to charge for any expenses whch are not deemed by SBA to have been necessary in connection with the application. The Regulations (Part 122, Sec. 122.19) also prohibit the payment of any bonus, brokerage fee or commission in connection with SBA loans.

In line with these Regulations SBA will not approve placement or finder's fees for the use or attempted use of influence in obtaining or trying to obtain an SBA loan, or fees based solely upon a percentage of the approved loan or any part thereof.

Fees which will be approved will be limited to reasonable sums for services actually rendered in connection with the application or the closing, based upon the time and effort required, the qualifications of the representative and the nature and extent of the services rendered by such representative. Representatives of loan applicants will be required to execute an agreement as to their compensation for services rendered in connection with said loan.

It is the responsibility of the applicant to set forth in the appropriate section of the application the names of all persons or firms engaged by or on behalf of the applicant. Applicants are required to advise the Regional Office in writing of the names and fees of any representatives engaged by the applicant subsequent to the filing of the application. This reporting requirement is approved under OMB Approval Number 3245-0016.

Any loan applicant having any question concerning the payment of fees, or the reasonableness of fees, should communicate with the Field Office where the application is filed.

Statements Required by Laws
and Executive Orders

Federal executive agencies, including the Small Business Administration, are required to withhold or limit financial assistance, to impose special conditions on approved loans, to provide special notices to applicants or borrowers and to require special reports and data from borrowers in order to comply with legislation passed by the Congress and Executive Orders issued by the President and by the provisions of various inter-agency agreements. SBA has issued regulations and procedures that implement these laws and executive orders and they are contained in Parts 112, 113 and 116, Title 13 Code of Federal Regulations Chapter 1, or SOPs.

This form contains a brief summary of the various laws and executive orders that affect SBA's business and disaster loan programs and gives applicants and borrowers the notices required by law or otherwise. The signatures required on the last page provide evidence that SBA has given the necessary notices.

Freedom of Information Act
(5 U.S.C. 552)

This law provides that, with some exceptions, SBA must supply information reflected in agency files and records to a person requesting it. Information about approved loans that will be automatically released includes, among other things, statistics on our loan programs (individual borrowers are not identified in the statistics) and other information such as the names of the borrowers (and their officers, directors, stockholders or partners), the collateral pledged to secure the loan, the amount of the loan, its purpose in general terms and the maturity. Proprietary data on a borrower would not routinely be made available to third parties. All requests under this Act are to be addressed to the nearest SBA office and be identified as a Freedom of Information request.

Privacy Act
(5 U.S.C. 552a)

Disaster home loan files are covered by this legislation because they are normally maintained in the names of individuals. Business loan files are maintained by business name or in the name of individuals in their entrepreneurial capacity. Thus they are not files on individuals and, therefore, are not subject to this Act. Any person can request to see or get copies of any personal information that SBA has in the request's file. Requests for information about another party may be denied unless SBA has the written permission of the individual to release the information to the requester's or unless the information is subject to disclosure under the Freedom of Information Act. (The "Acknowledgement" section of this form contains the written permission of SBA to release information when a disaster victim requests assistance under the family and individual grant program.)

NOTE: Any person concerned with the collection of information, its voluntariness, disclosure or routine use under the Privacy Act or requesting information under the Freedom of Information Act may contact the Director, Freedom of Information/Privacy Acts Division, Small Business Administration, 1441 L Street, N.W., Washington, D.C. 20416, for information about the Agency's procedures on these two subjects.

SBA FORM 1261 (12-86) REF: SOP 50 10 Previous Editions Obsolete

Right to Financial Privacy Act of 1978

(12 U.S.C. 3401)

This is notice to you, as required by the Right to Financial Privacy Act of 1978, of SBA's access rights to financial records held by financial institutions that are or have been doing business with you or your business, including any financial institution participating in a loan or loan guarantee. The law provides that SBA shall have a right of access to your financial records in connection with its consideration or administration of assistance to you in the form of a Government loan or loan guaranty agreement. SBA is required to provide a certificate of its compliance with the Act to a financial institution in connection with its first request for access to your financial records, after which no further certification is required for subsequent accesses. The law also provides that SBA's access rights continue for the term of any approved loan or loan guaranty agreement. No further notice to you of SBA's access rights is required during the term of any such agreement.

The law also authorizes SBA to transfer to another Government authority any financial records included in an application for a loan, or concerning an approved loan or loan guarantee, as necessary to process, service or foreclose a loan or loan guarantee or to collect on a defaulted loan or loan guarantee. No other transfer of your financial records to another Government authority will be permitted by SBA except as required or permitted by law.

Flood Disaster Protection Act

(42 U.S.C. 4011)

Regulations issued by the Federal Insurance Administration (FIA) and by SBA implementing this Act and its amendments. These regulations prohibit SBA from making certain loans in an FIA designated floodplain unless Federal flood insurance is purchased as a condition of the loan. Failure to maintain the required level of flood insurance makes the applicant ineligible for any future financial assistance from SBA under any program, including disaster assistance.

Executive Orders -- Floodplain Management and Wetland Protection

(42 F.R. 26951 and 42 F.R. 2961)

The SBA discourages any settlement in or development of a foodplain or a wetland. This statement is to notify all SBA loan applicants that such actions are hazardous to both life and property and should be avoided. The additional cost of flood preventive construction must be considered in addition to the possible loss of all assets and investments in future floods.

Lead-Based Paint Poisoning Prevention Act

(42 U.S.C. 4821 et seq.)

Borrowers using SBA funds for the construction or rehabilitation of a residential structure are prohibited from using lead-based paint (as defined in SBA regulations) on all interior surfaces, whether accessible or not, and exterior surfaces, such as stairs, decks, porches, railings, windows and doors, which are readily accessible to children under 7 years of age. A "residential structure" is any home, apartment, hotel, motel, orphanage, boarding school, dormitory, day care center, extended care facility, college or other school housing, hospital, group practice or community facility and all other residential or institutional structures where person reside.

Equal Credit Opportunity Act

(15 U.S.C. 1691)

The Federal Equal Credit Opportunity Act prohibits creditors from discriminating against credit applicants on the basis of race, color, religion, national origin, sex, marital status or age (provided that the applicant has the capacity to enter into a binding contract); because all or part of the applicant's income drives from any public assistance program, or because the applicant has in good faith exercised any right under the Consumer Credit Protection Act. The Federal agency that administers compliance with this law concerning this creditor is the Federal Trade Commission, Equal Credit Opportunity, Room 500, 633 Indiana Avenue, N.W., Washington, D.C. 20580.

Civil Rights Legislation

All businesses receiving SBA financial assistance must agree not to discriminate in any business practice, including employment practices and services to the public, on the basis of categories cited in 13 C.F.R., Parts 112 and 113 of SBA Regulations. This includes making their goods and services available to handicapped clients or customers. All business borrowers will be required to display the "Equal Employment Opportunity Poster" prescribed by SBA.

Executive Order 11738 -- Environmental Protection
(38 F.R. 25161)

The Executive Order charges SBA with administering its loan programs in a manner that will result in effective enforcement of the Clean Air Act, the Federal Water Pollution Act and other environmental protection legislation. SBA must, therefore, impose conditions on some loans. By acknowledging receipt of this form and presenting the application, the principals of all small businesses borrowing $100,000 or more in direct funds stipulate to the following:

1.   That any facility used, or to be used, by the subject firm is not listed on the EPA list of Violating Facilities.

2.   That subject firm will comply with all the requirements of Section 114 of the Clean Air Act and Section 308 of the Water Act relating to inspection, monitoring, entry, reports and information, as well as all other requirements specified in Section 114 and Section 308 of the respective Acts, and all regulations and guidelines issued thereunder.

3.   That subject firm will notify SBA of the receipt of any communication from the Director of the Environmental Protection Agency indicating that a facility utilized, or to be utilized, by subject firm is under consideration to be listed on EPA List of Violating Facilities.

Occupational Safety and Health Act
(15 U.S.C. 651 et seq.)

This legislation authorizes the Occupational Safety and Health Administration in the Department of Labor to require businesses to modify facilities and procedures to protect employees or pay penalty fees. In some instances the business can be forced to cease operations or be prevented from starting operations in a new facility. Therefore, in some instances SBA may require additional information from an applicant to determine whether the business will be in compliance with OSHA regulations and allowed to operate its facility after the loan is approved and disbursed.

In all instances, signing this form as borrower is a certification that the OSHA requirements that apply to the borrower's business have been determined and the borrower is, to the best of its knowledge, in compliance.

Debt Collection Act of 1982   Deficit Reduction Act of 1984
(31 U.S.C. 3701 et seq. and other titles)

These laws require SBA to aggressively collect any loan payments which become delinquent. SBA must obtain your taxpayer identification number when you apply for a loan. If you receive a loan, and do not make payments as they come due, SBA may take one or more of the following actions:

- Report the status of your loan(s) to credit bureaus
- Hire a collection agency to collect your loan
- Offset your income tax refund or other amounts due to you from the Federal Government
- Suspend or debar you or your company from doing business with the Federal Government
- Refer your loan to the Department of Justice or other attorneys for litigation
- Foreclose on collateral or take other action permitted in the loan instruments.

Consumer Credit Protection Act

(15 U.S.C. 1601 et seq.)

This legislation gives an applicant who is refused credit because of adverse information about the applicant's credit, reputation, character or mode of living an opportunity to refute or challenge the accuracy of such reports. Therefore, whenever SBA declines a loan in whole or in part because of adverse information in a credit report, the applicant will be given the name and address of the reporting agency so the applicant can seek to have that agency correct its report, if inaccurate. If SBA declines a loan in whole or in part because of adverse information received from a source other than a credit reporting agency, the applicant will be given information about the nature of the adverse information but not the source of the report.

Within 3 days after the consummation of the transaction, any recipient of an SBA loan which is secured in whole or in part by a lien on the recipient's residence or household contents may rescind such a loan in accordance with the "Regulation 2" of the Federal Reserve Board.

Applicant's Acknowledgement

My (our) signature(s) acknowledge(s) receipt of this form, that I (we) have read it and that I (we) have a copy for my (our) files. My (our) signature(s) represents my (our) agreement to comply with the requirements the Small Business Administration makes in connection with the approval of my (our) loan request and to comply, whenever applicable, with the hazard insurance, lead-based paint, civil rights or other limitations contained in this notice.

My (our) signature(s) also represent written permission, as required by the Privacy Act, for the SBA to release any information in my (our) disaster loan application to the Governor of my (our) State or the Governor's designated representative in conjunction with the State's processing of my (our) application for assistance under the Individual and Family Grant Program that is available in certain major disaster areas declared by the President.

Business Name

_____ By _____
Date   Name and Title

Proprietor, Partners, Principals and Guarantors

_____
Date   Signature

_____
Date   Signature

_____
Date   Signature

_____
Date   Signature

SBA Form 1261 (12-86)   U.S. Government Printing Office:

UNITED STATES SMALL BUSINESS ADMINISTRATION

SCHEDULE OF COLLATERAL

Exhibit A

Applicant		
Street Address		
City	State	Zip Code

LIST ALL COLLATERAL TO BE USED AS SECURITY FOR THIS LOAN

Section I—REAL ESTATE

Attach a copy of the deed(s) containing a full legal description of the land and show the location (street address) and city where the deed(s) is recorded. Following the address below, give a brief description of the improvements, such as size, type of construction, use, number of stories, and present condition (use additional sheet if more space is required).

LIST PARCELS OF REAL ESTATE					
Address	Year Acquired	Original Cost	Market Value	Amount of Lien	Name of Lienholder

Description(s):

PERSONAL FINANCIAL STATEMENT

As of _____ 19 _____

Complete this form if 1) a sole proprietorship by the proprietor; 2) a partnership by each partner; 3) a corporation by each officer and each stockholder with 20% or more ownership; 4) any other person or entity providing a guaranty on the loan.

Name _____ Residence Phone _____

Residence Address _____

City, State, & Zip _____

Business Name of Applicant/Borrower _____

ASSETS	(Omit Cents)	LIABILITIES	(Omit Cents)
Cash on hand & in Banks.............$_____		Accounts Payable.....................$_____	
Savings Accounts.......................... _____		Notes Payable (to Bk & Others	
IRA... _____		(Describe in Section 2)................. _____	
Accounts & Notes Receivable		Installment Account (Auto)	
(Describe in Section 6)................. _____		Mo. Payments $_____ _____	
Life Insurance—Cash		Installment Account (Other)	
Surrender Value Only.................. _____		Mo. Payments $_____ _____	
Stocks and Bonds		Loans on Life Insurance.................. _____	
(Describe in Section 3)................. _____		Mortgages on Real Estate.................	
Real Estate		(Describe in Section 4)................. _____	
(Describe in Section 4)................. _____		Unpaid Taxes	
Automobile—Present Value.................. _____		(Describe in Section 7)................. _____	
Other Personal Property..........		Other Liabilities	
(Describe in Section 5)................. _____		(Describe in Section 8)................. _____	
Other Assets............................			
(Describe in Section 6)................. _____		Total Liabilities............................ _____	
		Net Worth................................. _____	
Total..........................$_____		Total..........................$_____	

Section 1. Source of Income

		Contingent Liabilities
Salary.............................. $_____	As Endorser or Co-Maker...............................$_____	
Net Investment Income.............. _____	Legal Claims & Judgments............................. _____	
Real Estate Income................. _____	Provision for Fed Income Tax............................ _____	
Other Income (Describe)*.......... _____	Other Special Debt.................................. _____	

Description of Items Listed in Section I _____

_____

*(Alimony or child support payments need not be disclosed in "Other Income" unless it is desired to have such payments counted toward total income.)

Section 2. Notes Payable to Banks and Others

Name & Address of Noteholder	Original Balance	Current Balance	Payment Amount	Terms (Monthly-etc.)	How Secured or Endorsed—Type of Collateral

SBA Form 413 (10-86)   Use 11-84 edition until exhausted   Refer to SOP 50   10

(Response is required to obtain a benefit)

SECTION II—PERSONAL PROPERTY

All items listed herein must show manufacturer or make, model, year, and serial number. Items with no serial number must be clearly identified (use additional sheet if more space is required).

Description - Show Manufacturer, Model, Serial No.	Year Acquired	Original Cost	Market Value	Current Lien Balance	Name of Lienholder

All information contained herein is TRUE and CORRECT to the best of my knowledge. I understand that FALSE statements may result in forfeiture of benefits and possible fine and prosecution by the U.S. Attorney General (Ref. 18 U.S.C. 100).

_____   Date _____

_____   Date _____

SBA Form 4 Schedule A (4-87) Previous Editions Obsolete

Section 3. Stocks and Bonds: (*Use separate sheet if necessary*)

No. of Shares	Names of Securities	Cost	Market Value Quotation/Exchange	Date Amount

Section 4. Real Estate Owned. (*List each parcel separately. Use supplemental sheets if necessary. Each sheet must be identified as a supplement to this statement and signed*).

Address—Type of property	Title is in name of	Date Purchased	Original Cost	Present Value	Mortgage Balance	Amount of Payment	Status of Mortgage

Section 5. Other Personal Property. (*Describe, and if any is mortgaged, state name and address of mortgage holder and amount of mortgage, terms of payment, and if delinquent, describe delinquency.*)

Section 6. Other Assets, Notes & Accounts Receivable (Describe)

Section 7. Unpaid Taxes. (*Describe in detail, as to type, to whom payable, when due, amount, and what, if any, property the tax lien attaches*)

Section 8. Other Liabilities. (*Describe in detail*)

Section 9. Life Insurance Held (*Give face amount of policies—name of company and beneficiaries*)

SBA/Lender is authorized to make all inquiries deemed necessary to verify the accuracy of the statements made herein and to determine my/our creditworthiness.

(I) or (We) certify the above and the statements contained in the schedules herein are a true and accurate statement of (my) or (our) financial condition as of the date stated herein. This statement is given for the purpose of: (*Check one of the following*)

☐ Inducing S.B.A. to grant a loan as requested in the application, to the individual or firm whose name appears herein.

☐ Furnishing a statement of (my) or (our) financial condition, pursuant to the terms of the guaranty executed by (me) or (us) at the same time S.B.A. granted a loan to the individual or firm, whose name appears herein.

Signature	Signature	Date

SOCIAL SECURITY NO.   SOCIAL SECURITY NO.

SBA Form 413 (10-86)

*U.S. GOVERNMENT PRINTING OFFICE:1986- 716-533

Return Executed Copies 1, 2 and 3 to SBA

OMB APPROVAL NO. 3245-0178
Expiration Date: 3-31-87

United States of America

SMALL BUSINESS ADMINISTRATION

STATEMENT OF PERSONAL HISTORY

Please Read Carefully - Print or Type

Each member of the small business concern requesting assistance or the development company must submit this form in TRIPLICATE for filing with the SBA application. This form must be filled out and submitted by:

1. If a sole proprietorship by the proprietor.
2. If a partnership by each partner.
3. If a corporation or a development company, by each officer, director, and additionally by each holder of 20% or more of the voting stock.
4. Any other person including a hired manager, who has authority to speak for and commit the borrower in the management of the business.

| Name and Address of Applicant (Firm Name)(Street, City, State and ZIP Code) | SBA District Office and City |
| | Amount Applied for: |

1. Personal Statement of: (State name in full, if no middle name, state (NMN), or if initial only, indicate initial). List all former names used, and dates each name was used. Use separate sheet if necessary.

First   Middle   Last

2. Date of Birth: (Month, day and year)

3. Place of Birth: (City & State or Foreign Country).

U.S. Citizen? ☐ YES ☐ NO
If no, give alien registration number:
#

4. Give the percentage of ownership or stock owned or to be owned in the small business concern or the Development Company.

Social Security No.

5. Present residence address:
From: To: Address:

City   State

Home Telephone No. (Include A/C):

Business Telephone No. (Include A/C):

Immediate past residence address:
From: To: Address:

BE SURE TO ANSWER THE NEXT 3 QUESTIONS CORRECTLY BECAUSE THEY ARE IMPORTANT.

THE FACT THAT YOU HAVE AN ARREST OR CONVICTION RECORD WILL NOT NECESSARILY DISQUALIFY YOU. BUT AN INCORRECT ANSWER WILL PROBABLY CAUSE YOUR APPLICATION TO BE TURNED DOWN.

6. Are you presently under indictment, on parole or probation?

☐ Yes   ☐ No   If yes, furnish details in a separate exhibit. List name(s) under which held, if applicable.

7. Have you ever been charged with or arrested for any criminal offense other than a minor motor vehicle violation?

☐ Yes   ☐ No   If yes, furnish details in a separate exhibit. List name(s) under which charged, if applicable.

8. Have you ever been convicted of any criminal offense other than a minor motor vehicle violation?

☐ Yes   ☐ No   If yes, furnish details in a separate exhibit. List name(s) under which convicted, if applicable.

9. Name and address of participating bank

The information on this form will be used in connection with an investigation of your character. Any information you wish to submit, that you feel will expedite this investigation should be set forth.

Whoever makes any statement knowing it to be false, for the purpose of obtaining for himself or for any applicant, any loan, or loan extension by renewal, deferment or otherwise, or for the purpose of obtaining, or influencing SBA toward, anything of value under the Small Business Act, as amended, shall be punished under Section 16(a) of that Act, by a fine of not more than $5000, or by imprisonment for not more than 2 years, or both.

| Signature | Title | Date |

It is against SBA's policy to provide assistance to persons not of good character and therefore consideration is given to the qualities and personality traits of a person, favorable and unfavorable, relating thereto, including behavior, integrity, candor and disposition toward criminal actions. It is also against SBA's policy to provide assistance not in the best interests of the United States, for example, if there is reason to believe that the effect of such assistance will be to encourage or support, directly or indirectly, activities inimical to the Security of the United States. Anyone concerned with the collection of this information, as to its voluntariness, disclosure or routine uses may contact the FOIA Office, 1441 "L" Street, N.W., and a copy of §9 "Agency Collection of Information" from SOP 40 04 will be provided.

SBA FORM 912 (6-85) SOP 9020 PREVIOUS EDITIONS ARE OBSOLETE

1. SBA FILE COPY

| 2 SBA Office Code | | U.S. SMALL BUSINESS ADMINISTRATION
LENDER'S APPLICATION FOR GUARANTY
OR PARTICIPATION
(Numbers in circles or squares are SBA codes only) | | SBA Loan Number
1
1 |

Name of Applicant:

30

WE PROPOSE TO MAKE A (Check One)

	Lenders Share	SBA Share	Term of Loan	Monthly Payment
Guaranteed Loan	%	%	Years	$
	Lenders Share	SBA Share	Lenders Interest Rate	Payment Beginning
Immediate Participation Loan (Lender to make and service)	%	%	% Per Annum	_____ Months from Date of Note

Amount of Loan $

If Interest Rate is to be Variable		Rate Adjustment	Base Rate Source
		Other	
Base Rate:	Spread:	☐ Quarterly ☐ (Specify)	

TERMS AND CONDITIONS OF LENDER: *(Attach additional sheets if more space is needed.)*

I approve this application to SBA subject to the terms and conditions outlined above. Without the participation of SBA to the extent applied for we would not be willing to make this loan, and in our opinion the financial assistance applied for is not otherwise available on reasonable terms. I certify that none of the Lender's employees, officers, directors or substantial stockholders (more than 10%) have a financial interest in the applicant.

Signature:	Title:	Date:

Name of Lender	Telephone (Inc A/C)	Financial Institution I.D. Code
40		41
Street Address	City	State	Zip
42	43	44	45

FOR SBA USE ONLY

Loan Officers Recommendation   ☐ Approve   ☐ Decline State Reason(s).

Signature:	Title:	Date: 3

Other Recommendation, if Required   ☐ Approve   ☐ Decline State Reason(s)

Signature:	Title:	Date:

THIS BLOCK TO BE COMPLETED BY SBA OFFICIAL TAKING FINAL ACTION

☐ Approve   ☐ Decline State Reason(s)

Signature:	Title:	Date:

BUSINESS LOANS ONLY

4 Program Struct. Code	6 MTY (MOS)	9 SMR	46 No. of Employees	47 Franchise Code	48 New Bus 1-No 2-Yes	49 Women 1-No 2-Yes	50 Viet Vet. 1-No 2-Yes	51 Organ. Code 1-Indiv. 2-Part. 3-Corp.
10 City Code	11 State Code	12 Loan Type (1) Dir. (4) IPSBA (3) IPBK (7) Guar.	52 SIC Code	53 Location 1-Urban 2-Rural	54 EOL Family Income ($ Only) $	55 Poll. Code	56	
13 Sub Program Code	14 County Code	15	SBA LOAN PAY OFFS: LIST ALL SBA LOANS BEING REFUNDED					

			(15a) Loan Number	(15b) Loan Type	(15c) Loan Status	(15d) Amount
Loan Amount Approved	% Participation	Interest Rate	cc 11-20	cc 21 (1) Direct (2) Part. (3) Guar.	cc 22 (1) Curr. (4) C/D (2) P/D (5) Liq. (3) Del.	$
16 SBA	19	21				
	%	%				
17 Bank	20	22	cc 29-38	cc 39 (1) Direct (2) Part. (3) Guar.	cc 40 (1) Curr. (4) C/D (2) P/D (5) Liq. (3) Del.	$
	%	%				
18 Total			cc 11-20	cc 21 (1) Direct (2) Part. (3) Guar.	cc 22 (1) Curr. (4) C/D (2) P/D (5) Liq. (3) Del.	$

23 Minority Code	24 O/S SBA Loan 1-No 2-Yes	25 Const. Cont. Amt. $	IF MORE THAN 3 LOANS ARE PAID OFF ENTER TOTAL OF REMAINING LOANS	16 $

26 New Construction 1-No 2-Yes	27 Real Collateral 1-No 2-Yes	28	PRIOR SBA LOANS: LIST LOAN NUMBERS OF ALL PRIOR SBA LOANS TO BORROWER		
29	31 Soc. Sec. No.		(17a) cc 11-20	(17b) cc 21-30	(17c) cc 31-40
33 Employer ID No.		35 Borrower Alpha Code			

SBA Form 4-1 (10-85) REF SOP 50 10   USE 2-84 EDITION UNTIL EXHAUSTED

INSTRUCTIONS: The information requested below must be supplied with the application package.

FINANCIAL SPREAD

BALANCE SHEET	As of	Fiscal Year Ends	AUDITED ☐	UNAUDITED ☐
		DEBIT	CREDIT	PRO FORMA
Assets				
Cash	$	$	$	$
Accounts Rec.				
Inventory				
Other				
Total Current Assets				
Fixed Assets				
Other Assets				
Total Assets	$	$	$	$
Liabilities & Net Worth				
Accounts Payable	$	$	$	$
Notes Payable				
Taxes				
Other				
SBA				
Total Current Liabilities	$	$	$	$
Notes Payable	$	$	$	$
SBA				
Other				
Total Liabilities	$	$	$	$
Net Worth	$	$	$	$
Total Liab. & Net Worth	$	$	$	$
Profit & Loss	YEAR	YEAR	YEAR	YEAR
Sales	$	$	$	$
Depreciation				
Income Taxes				
W/D Officer Comp.				
Net Profit After Tax/Deprec.	$	$	$	$

PRO FORMA SCHEDULE OF FIXED OBLIGATIONS

	YEAR 1	YEAR 2	YEAR 3	YEAR 4
	$	$	$	$

Lender should comment on the following (Continue on separate sheet if needed):

1. Balance sheet and ratio analysis - comment on trends, debt to worth and current ratio.
2. Lenders analysis of repayment ability.
3. Management skill of the applicant.
4. Collateral offered and lien position, and analysis of collateral adequacy.
5. Lenders credit experience with the applicant.
6. Schedule of insurance requirements, standby agreements and other requirements.

Lenders Analysis:

U.S. GOVERNMENT PRINTING OFFICE : 1985 O - 489-160

ESTIMATED PROJECTION AND FORECAST OF TWO YEARS' EARNINGS

(ATTACH NARRATIVE EXPLAINING BASIS FOR FIGURES SHOWING RECEIPTS, EXPENSES, AND PROFITS)

YEAR _____ _____ _____%

PERCENTAGE OF SALES

GROSS RECEIPTS			
COST OF GOODS SOLD			
OPENING INVENTORY			
MATERIALS			
DIRECT LABOR			
SUBCONTRACT COSTS			
PURCHASES			
OVERHEAD			
TOTAL			
LESS ENDING INVENTORY			
COST OF GOODS SOLD			
GROSS PROFIT			
EXPENSES			
OFFICERS' SALARIES . . . . (IF CORPORATION)			
EMPLOYEE WAGES			
ACCOUNTING & LEGAL FEES			
ADVERTISING			
RENT			
DEPRECIATION			
SUPPLIES			
ELECTRICITY			
TELEPHONE			
INTEREST			
REPAIRS			
TAXES			
INSURANCE			
BAD DEBTS			
MISCELLANEOUS** . . . . (POSTAGE, ETC.)			
TOTAL EXPENSES			
NET PROFIT			
LESS: FEDERAL INCOME TAXES			
LESS: STATE INCOME TAXES			
NET PROFIT AFTER TAXES			
LESS WITHDRAWALS . . . . (PROPRIETORSHIP/PARTNERSHIP)			
NET PROFIT REMAINING FOR LOAN PAYMENT	$		

**IF SUM IS LARGE, PLEASE ITEMIZE.

OVERHEAD TO BE BROKEN DOWN INTO MAJOR EXPENSE CATEGORIES SUCH AS: SUPPLIES, DIRECT LABOR, ETC., ON SEPARATE SCHEDULES.

_____   _____
NAME   TITLE

MWR FORM 1 (4-72)

15

Venture Capital

If you attempt to get venture capital funding there are a few issues you should be aware of. Venture capital companies will usually ask for an equity percentage of your business ranging from 10 to 80 percent depending upon your company's stage of development. If you already are in production, have production samples completed, or have customer orders in hand you may be able to negotiate the percentage they demand to something under 50 percent. However, venture capital companies usually want control of your company. If that is agreeable with you and you are still interested in venture capital financing, you may be wondering how to interest a venture capital company.

After you have completed your Business Plan, should you mail it to all the venture capital companies; that is, employ the proverbial shotgun approach? The answer is a simple and emphatic, No! With the hundreds of plans that cross venture capitalists' desks on a continuing basis, yours will just be one of the crowd. A far better way is to ask for a referral from your attorney, accountant (here is one place where using one of the larger accounting firms helps), bankers, stockbrokers, and the like. If one of them will call the venture capitalist and arrange an introduction and meeting with the three of you, that is by far the best approach. In the event this prospect is not a viable option, then the next best option is to find the venture capital companies that specialize in your particular field and call them.

An early hour (7:45 A.M.) or a late afternoon (6:15 P.M.), are usually the best times to reach the venture capitalist without the secretary screening your call. Let's suppose you called a venture capital company and the receptionist answered:

Receptionist: Good morning, XYZ Venture Capital Company.

Entrepreneur: Good morning. This is _____. I understand your firm specializes in _____ investments. Is that true?

Receptionist: Yes.

Entrepreneur: Could you please tell me which partner specializes in the _____ Industry?

Receptionist: His name is Mr. _____.

Entrepreneur: Thank you. I know he must be extremely busy; however, I have a potential opportunity for him in the _____ field. My product has been fully tested by independent labs; and the market research has been completed. The results of the tests and research has shown our product to be _____. I believe he'll be interested in making an assessment of this innovation. When would you suggest would be the best time for me to talk to him?

Receptionist: That is really hard to say. He is in and out of town so much.

Entrepreneur: What is his secretary's name?

Receptionist: Ms. _____.

Entrepreneur: Thank you. Is she in?

Receptionist: One minute.

Secretary: Mr. _____'s office.

Entrepreneur: Ms. _____, (very important to call her by name) this is _____. (If you were referred to this Venture Capital Company, use the referral's name.) I understand your firm specializes in _____ investments. Is that true (important to get her involved)?

Secretary: Yes, it is.

Entrepreneur: We (better to say "we" rather than "I") have been working on our business proposal for _____ months for a new _____. We believe it is a much better product than any other currently available. It has been fully tested; and the market research has been completed. The results are so positive and encouraging I would like the opportunity of personally giving Mr. _____ a copy of our business plan. Can you help me make an appointment to meet briefly with him?

Secretary: He is a very busy man. You might try calling next Thursday.

Entrepreneur: What time would be better? Morning or afternoon? (Always offer a choice.)

Secretary: Morning would be best.

Entrepreneur: Thank you. Goodbye.

Thursday 8:00 A.M.

Receptionist: Good morning, XYZ Venture Capital Company.

Entrepreneur: Ms. (secretary) please.

Secretary: Mr. _____'s office.

Entrepreneur: Ms. _____, this is _____, we spoke last week. Is Mr. _____ in?

Secretary: I'm sorry he is on the phone. May I take a message?

Entrepreneur: Yes, could you please mention to him I called—_____—with _____ Inc.

Secretary: Your phone number?

Entrepreneur: I am in and out of the office a great deal. It is pretty difficult to reach me. I'll try again later. When would you recommend I try again? (Let her tell you when to call, because when you do call the next time, she will be more likely to put your call through.)

Secretary: Try next Monday morning.

Entrepreneur: Thank you.

This process will likely be repeated four or five times. When you are finally able to get through you might say:

Entrepreneur: Mr. _____, this is _____, with _____ Inc. (If you have a referral, use it now.) Mr. Referral with the Law Firm of Referral & Referral mentioned your company to us and suggested I speak to you. He said your firm specializes in the _____ industry. Is that true (get him saying "yes")?

Mr. _____: Yes, we do.

Entrepreneur: Our firm has designed a new _____. It has been tested at _____ (name of testing facility). Our product can be produced at _____ % savings over current models and has been shown to be _____ % more effective. The market potential for it is _____ (dollars). And market research has shown people prefer it _____ % more than other competitive products. However, in order for us to set-up an adequate facility (or purchase adequate inventory), we need additional funding. Can your firm help us? (If he says "No," be sure to ask why and who he would recommend that might be able to help. Now you'll have a referral source.)

Mr. _____: Perhaps.

Entrepreneur: Is it possible to meet next week; I have a business plan and would like to give you a copy? Would the beginning or the end of the week be better? (Always offer a choice.)

Mr. _____: The next few weeks are very busy for me. Can you just mail it?

Entrepreneur: I would prefer to drop it off. You can probably appreciate how important this is to us. A great deal of time and effort went into the Plan and just mailing would not do justice to it. How would breakfast be? Would Thursday or Friday be better?

Mr. _____: Friday.

Entrepreneur: What time would be most convenient?

Mr. _____: How about 7:30 the Union League Club?

Entrepreneur: That's fine. I will see you Friday at 7:30 A.M. at the Union League Club.

Mr. _____: See you then.

HOW A BUSINESS PLAN IS ANALYZED

After you give the venture capitalist your plan, he will usually review it spending less than one minute on each section he/she will:

1. Want to determine the characteristics of the company and industry.
2. Determine the terms of the deal.
3. Read the latest balance sheet.
4. Analyze the caliber of the management team.
5. Determine what is different or significant about this deal.
6. Give the rest of the plan a quick once-over.

Step 1: Determine the characteristics of the company and the industry. Most venture capitalists have a preference for a certain industry. Some like computers, others prefer health care, others like retail projects, and so on. Venture capitalists usually try to remain within an area of speciality. If your business is outside their area of familiarity, they will no longer continue reading your plan. If your deal is rejected, knowing why is important. If your plan has been rejected by a venture capital company because the firm is not in your industry, ask who they know who deals in your industry. Once you have one or two names of other venture capital companies, you have a referral. And a referral from one venture capital company to another is one of the best kinds of introduction. The reason for this is because people in the venture capital industry usually know and tend to respect each other.

Step 2: Determine the terms of the deal. How much of the company is to be sold and for what price? Does the valuation seem reasonable? Is the entrepreneur asking for a great deal of money but willing to give up very little equity?

How do you know how much of your company to offer? Venture capitalists have a relatively simple formula for quickly valuing your deal. The calculation is based on how much the venture capital company needs to invest and what the return on their money will be. This is known as *Return on Investment* or ROI. They calculate ROI in a very unique way based on the Price to Earnings Ratio (P/E). The P/E Ratio represents not only current earnings but also what people expect future earnings will be.

Most industries have an average P/E Ratio (stock price divided by the earnings per share) for each of their respective industries. The telecommunication industry, for example has a P/E Ratio of approximately 18. AT&T's P/E Ratio ranges from about 20 to 25. The computer industry has a P/E Ratio of about 22, with IBM at 18 to 23. Genentec (Genetic Engineering) enjoyed a P/E of over 200 at one time. This was even before they had any sales! You can find P/E Ratios in *Barrons Weekly Newspaper* available at most newspaper stands.

The P/E Ratio is represented by:

$$P/E \ Ratio = \frac{SP}{EPS \times SO}$$

where SP = stock price in dollars, EPS = earnings per share in dollars, and SO = number of shares outstanding.

Venture capitalists often use this ratio to calculate what their investment (what your stock) will be worth after you "go public," are bought out by another company, or you buy the venture capitalist out. This calculation gives them a rule-of-thumb measure to estimate the percentage of your company they will demand in exchange for funding your company.

Let's say you are in an industry with a P/E Ratio of 15. Let's also say that your realistic sales projections and estimate of your profits (after taxes) to be $100,000 after the third year. If you issued one million shares of stock, your per share stock price would be worth $1.50:

$$SP = P/E \times EPS$$
$$SP = 15 \times (\$100,000/1,000,000 \text{ shares}) = \$1.50/\text{share}$$

Since your stock price would be projected at $1.50 per share, your company would be valued or worth:

$$1,000,000 \text{ shares} \times \$1.50 \text{ per share} = \$1,500,000$$

Venture capitalists usually target a return on their investment (ROI) of around 30 percent per year. To calculate how much you'll have to give up, use the following approach:

Let's say you need funding of $250,000. That $250,000 should grow 30 percent per year (for the venture capitalist), and after the third year, when it is time to go public, their investment should be worth approximately [250,000 × 1.3 (1st year) × 1.3 (2nd year) × 1.3 (3rd year)] or $550,000.

Since $550,000 is 36.6 percent of $1,500,000 ($550,000/1,500,000), you should expect to give away about 37 percent of your company if you need $250,000.

You can see how decreasing the amount of funding needed or improving earnings will lower the venture capitalist's stake in your business.

Now you can see why venture capitalists prefer certain industries—those with high P/E's, because their returns can be very attractive.

Step 3: Review the Balance Sheet, performing a couple of quick calculations will give a better understanding of your financials. The calculations are:

$$\text{Current Ratio (CR)} = \frac{\text{Current Assets (CA)}}{\text{Current Liabilities (CL)}}$$

This ratio shows how financially solid your company is over the short term. The CR should be greater than 1, and generally speaking, the higher the number the better. Current Assets are items including cash, accounts receivable, inventory and marketable securities. Current Liabilities include accounts payable, short-term debt, and taxes payable.

$$\text{Debt to Equity (DE) Ratio} = \frac{\text{Total amount of short and long-term loans (debt) (TL)}}{\text{Total equity in the business (TE)}}$$

This ratio reveals how much credit a bank (or other lending institution) has already extended to the company. DE Ratio should be no more than approximately

50 percent, which means that for every dollar invested as equity a lender has lent fifty cents:

Step 4: Analyze the caliber of the management team. This step is the single most important aspect of the business plan. A company is only as good as the people who run it. Investors look for someone in the company with whom they are familiar. They also want to evaluate the reputation and competency of the management team.

Particular questions investors look for include:

▸ What is the track record of the founders?

▸ How much balance is there in the management team? (Do they have competent personnel in sales, marketing finance, engineering, and general management?)

▸ Who is the financial officer? (What are his or her credentials?)

Step 5: Determine what is special about this deal. Are there any unusual features in the product? Is it patented? How much of a lead does the company have over the competition? Does the company have the potential to open up a whole new industry as companies like Polaroid, Xerox, or Apple Computer did? Is the company in a modest growth area, one with a limited future?

Step 6: Give the rest of the plan a quick review. After the previous analyses, venture capitalists probably will spend the final moments glancing through the plan. They will look at product literature, letters of recommendation, purchase orders, and letters of intent to purchase.

When all the steps have undergone this cursory review, the investor may then request additional information or he may reject the deal and return the plan to you. Your chances of approval are roughly a scant one in a hundred.

How should the plan be packaged? Does a thick plan and a fancy cover give a better chance of getting funding?

No! Venture capitalists are not impressed by expensive, elaborate covers. Rather, more attention is paid to those plans with a unique or an interesting name and logo. The next most important criterion is the company's location. The last factor is thickness of the plan. Shorter, more concise plans tend to receive greater attention.

These suggestions should help increase your chances of funding. However, there is one more consideration you should be aware of: Selecting the right venture capital company.

SELECTING THE RIGHT VENTURE CAPITAL COMPANY

Being successful in attracting funding is, of course, important. However, merely getting funding, by itself, is only half the task. Equally important is finding a venture capital company compatible with your company, one that can help you in the months and years that follow. Additional funding and managerial guidance are just a few examples of services you may need. Venture capitalists have a saying: "It's not how much but whose money you get."

Ask questions of the venture capital firm. Do not be fearful of asking questions; in fact, it is to your advantage. Questions indicate to the venture capitalist that you are not naive, that you know selecting the correct investor will increase your chances of success, and selecting the correct venture firm will be better for you and for the venture capital company. Enough of the lecture, now for the questions:

1. Does the venture firm fund deals in your industry? How many has it done? What was the total funding of the deals? How much of the total did your firm invest? What are the status of the deals now?

2. How easy is the venture firm to work with? Get a list of companies they funded in the past together with presidents' names and phone numbers. (Asking these questions, should not be posed until the venture firm has met with you several times and prospects look favorable. You do not want to scare them off by asking for too much too soon.)

3. What experience does the partner have that is reviewing your particular deal? How long has he/she worked for the firm? Is he/she a junior associate or senior partner? Does he/she have decision-making responsibilities?

4. How much time and effort will the venture capital company spend with your company if your firm needs help? The company should be willing to meet with you at least once a month if necessary.

5. Is the firm profitable? Where has it invested money, and how are the investments doing? If the venture firm is having problems, how can it help you if you need help. Expect to need assistance in the future.

6. Are the venture capitalist's goals for your company the same as yours? Are you willing to "go public" or to be bought out in three to five years if that is what the venture firm wants?

7. Has the venture firm and its representative working on your project been through any economic down-turns? If it has, the investors will remain calm and will not panic if major problems arise.

Asking insightful questions will enable you to make a wiser investor selection. Here are some additional sources you may find helpful.

FUNDING RESOURCES

The Insider's Guide to Small Business Resources by David Gumpert and Jeffry Timmons (New York: Doubleday Books).

Up Front Financing by A. David Silver (New York: John Wiley & Sons).

The Small Business Guide to Borrowing Money by Richard Rubin and Philip Goldberg (New York: McGraw-Hill).

The Guide to Venture Capital Sources (Wellesley Hills, MA: Capital Publishing).

Business Planning Guide (Dover, NH: The Upstart Publishing Company, Inc.)

Guide to Venture Capital Sourcing by Stanley Pratt. (Wellesley Hills, MA: Capital Publishing).

How to Raise Venture Capital Sourcing by Stanley Pratt. (Wellesley Hills, MA: Capital Publishing).

The Entrepreneurs Resource Guide (Niles, IL: The Innovation Institute).

16

Contract Manufacturing

Several days later after Jim had a chance to re-read all the material he had received, he called the successful entrepreneur and requested a meeting. The young man was looking forward to talking to Norman. He had worked diligently and felt that he was making real progress. He had learned a great deal but had more questions to ask.

On his appointment day, Jim met with Norman and told him how helpful Cheryl had been and what she had told him about financing. The young man said, "I have been giving starting my own manufacturing company a great deal of thought over the past couple days. I have talked to several friends who have their own manufacturing company. All of them say they are operating at 50 to 70 percent of capacity. Then I thought of the possibility of using their manufacturing facility instead of starting my own."

Norman replied, "Very intuitive. In fact, many companies are now using outside manufacturing, or as it is called, "contract manufacturing", to have their products produced. Why start your own company if so many others have excess capacity and may be willing to make your products for you at cost plus a fair margin to help pay their fixed costs?"

The successful entrepreneur continued, "Estimating how much should be outside contracted depends on how much you want to do or can do in-house. If you have some questions or doubts about your capacity to produce your product, you are wiser to let an outside source handle more, rather than less, of the process."

There are several reasons why contract manufacturing makes sense. These include:

1. No investment in plant and equipment
2. Lesser personnel needs
3. Reduced capital requirements
4. Reduced start-up time
5. Avoidance of plant maintenance and equipment obsolescence

But remember, selecting the correct manufacturer is far more important than merely selecting the lowest bidder. Questions you may ask to help you formulate criteria to determine the best manufacturer include:

▶ Is their production technology complimentary to the technology needed to produce your product? Don't seek a tire manufacturer if you need to produce a car.

▶ Can they do most of the manufacturing in-house? If they have their own painting lines or chrome plating capability that your product requires, you will be able to save money. If the contract manufacturer has to look to subcontractors, your product manufacturing costs will probably increase.

▶ What is the quality of their other products (i.e. clean welds, smooth paint coatings, no rough or jagged edges, finished corners, no material fraying, or improper assembling)?

▶ Do you have to pay for molds, forms, dies, etc.? If so, are costs payable in advance or may they be amortized (spread out) over a pre-determined number of units?

▶ Who owns the molds? If you take your business elsewhere, can you take the molds also?

▶ How solid is their main line of business? You don't want them going out of business unexpectedly.

▶ How many quality control and design engineers do they have?

▶ Do they fabricate from raw material (i.e. do they make their tubing from flat sheet stock or do they buy ready made tubing)? If they fabricate their own materials the cost will usually be lower and frequently with better quality.

▶ Do they have references of other customers for whom they contract manufacture? Ask for four names, phone numbers and contact persons?

▶ How long will it take for molds, dies, etc., to be finished if required?

▶ When will the first production samples be ready? What assurances can they give?

You should have a written agreement with any manufacturer before you make any commitment with them. Contract manufacturing agreements vary with different products and circumstances. You should prepare a draft understanding for your particular situation using the following agreement then have it reviewed by your attorney. The cost, if you prepare the draft and ask for a professional review, would be about $200 to $500 compared to $1000 to $2500 if an attorney writes the entire contract from scratch.

SAMPLE CONTRACT
MANUFACTURING LETTER AGREEMENT

(Your Letterhead)

(Date)

TO:

Subject: Contract Manufacturing Agreement

Dear Mr. _____:

    We are pleased to submit this proposal for __[The Manufacturer's Name]__, hereinafter called the "Manufacturer," to perform contract manufacturing services to ___[Your Company's Name]___ hereinafter called the "Company," for our __[Your Product]__ hereinafter called the "Product."

    The Parties herein agreed that:

    The Company shall purchase from Manufacturer and Manufacturer shall exclusively supply to the Company items and products listed in Exhibit 1 attached. The Parties further agree that only Company's orders shall be valid and binding when written on Company's purchase orders and transmitted from the Company to the Manufacturer.

    The Company may, at its option, cancel this Agreement before the stated termination date upon the occurrence of:

    1. Presentation of a true and verified proposal from a competitive manufacturer of a unit price of 5% or greater, LESS THAN THE PRICE stipulated in this Agreement. However the Manufacturer has an option to modify the cost by reducing the unit cost to within 3% of the verified competitive proposal and thereby render this Agreement NOT subject to cancellation under this provision.

    2. Delays of 30 days or more in production from the date of the Company's postmarked purchase order to the Manufacturer's shipment date unless waived in writing from the Company.

    3. Manufacturer's declaration of bankruptcy or insolvency.

    4. Acquisition of Manufacturer by another company, or entity.

    5. Majority of stock issued by Manufacturer being purchased, or acquired by another firm or person.

Payment terms are two percent (2%) ten days, net thirty (30) days. The Manufacturer is not required to continue shipping if the Company does not meet its payment terms.

The Parties hereto further agree that all products, drawings and samples, whether complete or in process, are the property of the Company. The Manufacturer agrees to assign all patents and product improvements to the Company. In the event of termination of this Agreement, if the Company changes its source of supply as above listed, the Manufacturer agrees not to manufacture Products listed in Exhibit 1 for any other firm or person, for a period of no less than five (5) years beginning from the termination date.

The Manufacturer agrees that the Company owns all molds, dies and fixtures used in the manufacture of the Company's Products, except for those that the Company has not paid or has been invoiced. In the event the Company elects to change its source of supply, as stated above, the Manufacturer either will immediately deliver (delivery carrier to be specified by the Company) to the Company all such tools, dies, molds and fixtures or will sell all said tools, dies, molds and fixtures at their current book value as calculated by generally accepted accounting standards, at the Company's option. (The proceeds of said sale will also immediately be delivered to said Company). The Company shall be entitled to seek immediate injunctive relief to obtain possession of these items.

The Manufacturer also agrees that no employee will use knowledge of any of the Company's Products gained during their employ with the Manufacturer to manufacture or market the Company's Products or similar products either directly or indirectly or to advise, counsel or in any way assist any third party to compete with the Company. Furthermore the Manufacturer agrees not to use any information provided by the Company, directly or indirectly, for the Manufacturer's own benefit or for the benefit of any other person, firm or corporation.

The Manufacturer agrees to use its best efforts to ensure high quality products and workmanship. The Manufacturer warrants all products sold to the Company under this Agreement will be free from defects due to poor workmanship or material for a period of thirteen (13) months. If Products are defective the Manufacturer will be responsible to replace the defective Products without charge, credit the Company's account, or issue the Company a refund, at the Company's option. This warranty shall supersede all previous warranties of any kind whether written or implied.

The Company agrees to keep the Manufacturer apprised of product sales; and the Company further agrees to use its best efforts to sell the Products.

The Company agrees to hold the Manufacturer harmless from any patent infringement.

Either Party may terminate this Agreement by giving ninety (90) days written notice sent via Certified U.S. Mail, Return Receipt Requested. If this Agreement is terminated, the Company has the sole option to purchase the Manufacturer's inventory of said Products over a six (6) months period. If the Company elects not to purchase the Manufacturer's inventory of Products, the Manufacturer may dispose of such finished goods inventory in any method it chooses.

The terms of this Agreement shall survive in the event of termination.

This Agreement is not assignable by either Party except by written agreement by both Parties. If this agreement is assigned, the assignee shall be bound by the terms and conditions of this Agreement.

Correspondence shall be addressed to the individuals on Page 1 of this Agreement.

Exhibit 1   Products

Product(s) to be manufactured or supplied by the Manufacturer:

1.

2.

3.

Agreed:

By: _____
       (Manufacturer)
       _____
       (Signature of officer)
       _____
       (Print name and title)
       _____
       (Date)
       _____
       (Company)
       _____
       (Signature of officer)
       _____
       (Print name and title)
       _____
       (Date)

17

Pricing

The young man asked, "If I am able to get my product produced, how do I know what price to charge and how to sell it?"

"A valid question," replied the successful entrepreneur.

Some "experts" say that as a general rule, you should charge 30 percent above your cost; others say 50 or 60 percent. All are wrong! Your product's costs are irrelevant in the pricing or marketing analysis. Costs, are however, extremely relevant in your profitability analysis.

You need to find a price which consumers are willing to pay for your product. If your cost (material, labor, etc.) is $1.00 but consumers think your product is worth only $.50 you have a problem. However if your cost is $1.00 but your customers perceive the value of your product to be $3.50, your item should be priced $3.50 and the difference is reward for your diligent and innovative work.

You therefore need to assess what people are willing to pay for your product.

Jim: We already know what people are willing to pay from our market research.

Norman: That's exactly right. However now we additionally need to make sure there is enough profit to run our business.

To make profit, you need to consider more than just the product cost. We also need to account for the following additional costs:

▶ Inventory storage cost per unit

▶ Order processing per unit (How much does it cost to fill an order, and the average order quantity)

▶ Loan interest per unit

$$\text{Loan Interest Per Unit} = \frac{\text{Yearly loan interest}}{\text{Estimated yearly unit sales}}$$

▶ Shipping cost per unit

▸ Indirect cost per unit

Indirect cost per unit = IC/YUS

where IC = Indirect costs not related to manufacture, such as rent, salaries, utilities, telephone, etc. and YUS = Yearly unit sales.

▸ Sales commissions per unit.

▸ Discounts to distributors and mark-ups for retailers.

A good rule of thumb is to make a product for 3–4 times under what the selling price is. This will hold if you are selling through distributors who sell to retailers.

Jim: How do I market my product? And if I can find salespeople to sell my product, what are fair sales commissions?

Norman: I believe you are really catching on. You have to select the channel of distribution based on how you need to get your product to your consumer.

18

Distribution

The successful entrepreneur began explaining to Jim about distribution, explaining that there are four basic methods for getting your product to the consumer:

▶ Your own salespeople

▶ Direct mail

▶ Wholesaler/Distributor/Retailer

▶ Manufacturers' representatives

HIRE YOUR OWN SALESPEOPLE

The cost to cover hotels, food, transportation, and miscellaneous expenses, to put your own salesperson on the road today is approximately $50,000 per year. This figure does *not* include salary! If you pay a base salary of $30,000 per year or more plus commission, the cost totals about $80,000 to $100,000 *plus* commission. This is an extremely expensive channel of distribution. However, your own salespeople can be quite effective because they will "push" your product exclusively. Nonetheless, the costs may render this option prohibitive. If you have an entire line of products, having your own salespeople makes more economic sense because you can spread your selling costs over more products, thus reducing your selling cost per unit.

DIRECT MAIL

Direct mail is another selling method; however it is not the easiest nor the cheapest. Costs to consider are:

- ▸ Printing ($.25 to $.75 for each letter with one page enclosure)
- ▸ Typing the cover letter, using a computer ($.15 each)
- ▸ Envelop and labeling ($.10 each)
- ▸ Stuffing and sorting for bulk mail ($.03 each)
- ▸ Bulkrate Postage ($.20 each)
- ▸ Mailing list ($.05 each)
- ▸ Total = $.96 per mailing

If you mail 1000 pieces, your cost would be approximately $960.00 based on the above breakdown. Direct mail may generate a 5 percent response rate. Of the 5 percent that respond, perhaps 10 percent will actually buy. This would yield total sales of 5 units:

$$1000 \text{ units} \times 5\% \text{ response} \times 10\% \text{ sales} = 5 \text{ units sold}$$

Therefore you have to add enough profit in selling 5 units to cover almost $1000 in expenses.

If you are interested in direct mail, some books you may want to read include:

The Dartnell Direct Mail and Mail Order Handbook, Richard S. Hodgson, 3d edition (Chicago: Dartnell Corp., 1980) 1,538 pp. (Covers techniques and problems of direct mail marketing. It includes practical illustrations and examples.)

The Direct Marketing Handbook, Edward L. Nash (New York: McGraw-Hill, 1984) 946 pp. (A thorough resource for mail order information.)

Building a Mail Order Business: A Complete Manual for Success, William A. Cohen (New York: Wiley, 1982) 442 pp. (A comprehensive and practical book that covers most topics and techniques in mail order.)

Direct Marketing: Strategy, Planning, Execution, Edward L. Nash (New York: McGraw-Hill, 1982) 423 pp. (A step-by-step guide for direct mail marketing, covering mailing lists, various media placement, research, testing, and other topics.)

How to Start and Operate a Mail-Order Business, Julian L. Simon, 3d edition (New York: McGraw-Hill, 1981) 536 pp. (For both newcomers and for experienced mail-order operators. Illustrates what to do when starting and operating a mail-order business.)

Direct Mail List Rates and Data (Wilmette, IL: Standard Rate & Data Service) [Semiannual]. (Gives sources, rental rates, commissions, and more, for over 50,000 direct mail lists.)

Mail Order Business Directory (Coral Springs, FL: B. Klein Publications) [Biennial]. (Lists 7,500 U.S. mail-order and catalog houses, arranged geographically.)

Inside the Leading Mail Order Houses, Maxwell Sroge with Bradley Highum, 1982. (Profiles 200 leading mail-order houses. Brief data includes nature of businesses, officers, history, sales, income and earnings for each.)

WHOLESALERS/DISTRIBUTORS/RETAILERS

Wholesalers, distributors, and retailers are other possible channels. The wholesaler or distributor will handle functions like warehousing, sales, customer billing, and sometimes advertising. The wholesaler or distributor will usually mark the price up 20 to 60 percent.

You therefore must leave enough "room" in your price for the distributor and the retailer; because you probably do not have the time, resources or desire to sell directly to each retailer. You personally do not want to have to sell to every drugstore, discounter, and department store. However with as few as ten distributors, you may be able to cover the entire U.S.A. As an example, let's say your product's factory cost (material and labor) is $1.00, and the market value is $4.00, using a 50 percent mark-up as a general rule, your profit margin calculation would be:

For the Retailer:

$$\$4.00 \text{ per unit} \times 50\% \text{ mark-up} = \$2.00 \text{ cost}$$

The retailer would have to buy the product for $2.00 to be able to sell it for $4.00 and make 50%.

For the Distributor:

$$\$2.00 \text{ per unit} \times (100\% - 30\% \text{ mark-up}) = \$1.40$$

The distributor would need to buy the product for $1.40 to be able to sell it to the retailer for $2.00 and make 30%.

What all this means is that your profit margin would be about 29% [1 − ($1.00 ÷ $1.40) = 29%]. This is about the minimum you should be shooting for (try to average a profit margin of 30% to 50%). You may therefore want to try to re-design your product with a few more "bells and whistles" which adds substantial perceived value at small additional cost. This advice is sound; implementation will not be so easy.

MANUFACTURERS' REPRESENTATIVES

Manufacturers' representatives are professional, usually independent salespeople, who handle a number of products in a given geographical area for several manufacturers. Such representatives will normally not stock inventory nor bill the customer. You will have to keep adequate inventory, arrange deliveries, and perform the billing. Because representatives perform fewer functions than the distributor, their payments or commissions are lower.

Representatives are of most value when extra selling effort is required. Distributors may carry hundreds, sometimes thousands of products. It is unrealistic to assume their salespeople will spend a great deal of time selling your product. In contrast, representatives may only carry a handful of usually complimentary lines. Consequently your product will be taken out of their "bag" and shown more often. With a new product, your product's sales are directly proportional to how often it is shown to customers.

Payment to a representative is based on commission rather than a mark up. Typical commissions range from five percent for well established lines that require little selling effort to forty percent or more for a new product requiring a great deal of sales effort. Representatives are not naive. They know how much money they will make on every product they sell and will spend proportionately more time on the products that will make them the most money. Therefore it is better to overpay at the beginning and get the product out in the field and accepted by consumers rather than underpay a sales representative and not generate any meaningful sales for several months or years.

If your contract manufacturer will keep an adequate inventory on hand for you, or if production time is relatively short (less than two to three weeks), using a sales representative has many advantages for a new, unique, and innovative product.

How do you find the right sales representatives or distributors? You can seek sales representatives by:

▶ Placing a classified advertisement in trade journals for your industry.

▶ Determining if your industry has an independent representative or distributor trade association; most industries do.

▶ Asking customers who they currently buy from or which salespeople they like.

▶ Calling noncompeting companies in the same industry and asking them for references. Sometimes they may even give you a list of their entire representative or distributor sales organization.

After you have your distributors or sales representatives selected, you will need to negotiate agreements with them.

Norman showed Jim a copy of his Sales Representative Agreement pages 234–239. "You will need to alter it to fit your particular application. It will, nevertheless be a good place to start for you."

Norman: (*continuing*) The Sales Representative Agreement, is our standard contract. As you can see, it is very restrictive on the representative; some are reluctant to sign it. When refusal is apparent and we believe that the representative is highly desirable to our firm, we will use an alternative letter agreement which simply states:

1. The Representative will do his best efforts.

2. The Company can cancel the agreement with thirty (30) days notice.

3. If the Agreement is terminated, the Company will pay the Representative 100 percent of the stated commission on current customers that the Representative has already sold Products, for a period of 2 months after termination, and 50 percent of the stated commission for the period 2 to 6 months after termination.

4. Unresolved disputes will be settled by the American Arbitration Association.

If the representative is hesitant to sign our standard agreement, the brief agreement usually will calm his fears. This makes it easier for both of us to get together to see if the representative will do a good for our firm, and for representative to determine if our product is a good fit for his company.

Jim: Thank you. What else do you think I need to know?

Norman: That is it. I've taught you everything I know. Your future and your success are now in your own hands.

Jim: You have taught me well. I have a much clearer idea of what has to be done; the ball is now in my court. I greatly appreciate all your help, advice and patience. I hope one day I can repay you for your generous cooperation.

They said their good-byes, and the young man left. Two weeks later the successful entrepreneur received a heartfelt note of thanks from Jim expressing his gratitude.

Several months passed, and Norman thought about the young man often. Although the successful entrepreneur had seen many people come to him for advice, Jim really seemed like that 1 in 100 with enough fortitude and ambition to achieve success. Norman hoped the young man would prove to have the courage and persistence necessary to overcome the countless obstacles that lay ahead of him.

Finally, almost four years later, the successful entrepreneur read in the newspaper that a company, Smile, Inc. was sold to a major, multinational company for a substantial sum of money. A picture of the president of Smile accompanied the story; it was Jim. The successful entrepreneur felt rewarded that Jim had been able to turn his ideas into a success.

A short time later, Norman received a phone call and was very surprised to hear Jim's voice.

Jim: I wanted to call to thank you personally. Your advice and guidance has made me a wealthy man. Success did not come easily however. My first idea failed, my second invention made a little money and it wasn't until I had my fourth invention that my business started to do well.

Norman: I am glad to hear that. Now that you have sold your business, what are you going to do?

Jim: Before I came to you, I knew almost nothing about taking an idea from the concept stage through the marketing stage. You were such a tremendous help to me, I think I'd like to help others do the same.

Norman: Why don't you come to work here? We have individuals coming to us for help all the time. You could add a new dimension to our firm with your experience.

The details were quickly settled and the next week, Jim began his first day at his new job.

SALES REPRESENTATIVE AGREEMENT

(Your Company Letterhead)

ARTICLE 1. APPOINTMENT OF SALES REPRESENTATIVE

(Your Company Name) , a company, with its offices and principal business at: _____ (hereinafter called the "Company"), hereby appoints _____ (hereinafter called the "Representative") having its principal place of business at: _____ as authorized exclusive Representative for the _____ Market segment [retail, wholesale, export, or all markets] (hereinafter called "Served Market").

The Company hereby engages the Representative to provide services in accordance with the terms and conditions of this Agreement for the sale of the products and services (hereinafter called "Products) which are: _____

ARTICLE 2. TERRITORY

The geographic area (hereinafter called "Territory") in which the Representative shall undertake the duties specified in this Agreement is: _____ .

ARTICLE 3. TERM AND SCOPE

This Agreement shall remain in effect for an initial period of six (6) months beginning _____, 19_____, and ending _____, 19_____, and be subject to consecutive renewal periods of one (1) year ending _____ _____, 19_____ hereafter, if the Representative solicited and the Company shipped at least those amounts listed in Schedule I in net invoice value.

The Company has the right to terminate this Agreement in accordance with Article 10 if Representative does not meet the minimums in Schedule I in any period. The Company has the right to terminate this Agreement at the end of a renewal period with a sixty (60) day written notice, in the event of which the Company agrees to continue to pay the Representative fifty percent (50%) of its standard commission listed in Article 13 on orders received from customers who had previously been introduced to the Company by the Representative during the preceding one (1) year period; these commissions are to continue for a period of six (6) months following termination.

ARTICLE 4. COMPANY RESPONSIBILITIES

The Company agrees that during the term of this Agreement, it will, subject to and in accordance with the terms and conditions herein expressed:

a) Keep the Representative advised of new prospects and objectives with respect to Products for Served Market Customers in the Territory.

b) Pay compensation as provided in Article 13 hereof on orders for Products received and accepted by the Company from Served Market Customers in the Territory. As used in this Agreement, the terms "order" or "orders" include contracts executed by the Company for Products with Served Market Customers in the Territory.

ARTICLE 5. REPRESENTATIVE'S RESPONSIBILITIES

The Representative agrees that during the term of this Agreement, will, subject to the terms and conditions herein expressed:

a) Solicit orders for the Products, on behalf of and in the name of the Company, quoting only prices and terms mutually established in writing by the Company and the Representative.

b) Forward to the Company all orders so obtained for acceptance by the Company. Orders will be deemed to have been accepted when notice of acceptance is received by the Customer from the Company.

c) Maintain an adequate sales organization and use its best efforts to assist the Company in the sale of Products to Served Market Customers in the Territory.

d) Keep the Company fully informed of all contracts and bids which do or could affect the sale of Products to Served Market Customers in the Territory.

JOINT RESPONSIBILITIES

In addition to duties directly related to the promotion and sales of the Products, the Representative and the Company agree that:

a) The Company will bill all customers directly.

b) The Company expressly reserves the right to change its terms of sale at its own discretion.

c) The Representative will not have the authority on behalf of the Company to accept the return of or make any allowance with respect to any of the Products without the prior approval of an authorized representative of the Company.

d) The Representative will bear all responsibilities for expenses and disbursements incurred by the Representative in connection with this Agreement. The Representative does not have, nor will he/she hold himself out as having, any authority to create any contract or obligation, either expressed or implied, on behalf of, or in the name of, or binding upon, the Company, unless the Company consents thereto in writing. The Representative will have the right to appoint, and will solely be responsible for his own salesmen, employees, agents and representatives, who will be at the Representative's sole risk, expense and supervision, and none of whom will have any claim against the Company for compensation nor reimbursement.

e) The Representative will have no power to bind the Company to delivery dates or warranties not expressly authorized in writing by the Company to the Representative.

f) The Representative, during the term of this Agreement, will not engage in the manufacture or sale, directly or indirectly, or any competing products without the expressed written consent of the Company.

g) The Representative shall not communicate during the continuance of this Agreement or at any time subsequent, any information relating to the trade or commercial secrets of which he/she then had or might, from time to time, acquire pertaining to any aspect of the business of the Company to any person not a member of the Company's corporation, except as exempted, in writing, by the Company. In case of violation of this covenant, the Representative agrees to be responsible to the Company for the Company's damages caused by that divulging of information. This provision will be enforceable by mandatory injunction.

ARTICLE 6. COMPENSATION

a) The Company will pay the Representative, as compensation for services performed under this Agreement, a commission in accordance with Article 13. Said calculations due herein shall be made on net invoice exclusive of freight, trade discounts, etc., of all shipments of the Products from a Served Market Customer in the Territory on orders obtained by the Representative. The compensation herein due to be paid to the Representative when and if collected by the Company.

b) Compensation due will be paid to the Representative on the first day of each month.

c) Payment of any taxes attributable to commissions paid to the Representative under this Agreement shall be remitted by the Representative.

ARTICLE 7. LIMITATION OF LIABILITY

Neither Party to this Agreement shall have liability to the other Party with respect to claims arising out of, in connection with, or resulting from, this Agreement, whether in contract, tort (including negligence of any degree) or otherwise, except as provided under the terms of this Agreement.

ARTICLE 8. COMPANY TRADEMARKS AND TRADE NAMES

The Representative at all times that it will comply with the rules and regulations furnished to the Representative by the Company with respect to the use of the Company's trademarks and trade names. Representative shall and identify properly the "representative" relationship with the Company for Products and that the Representative will not publish or cause to be published any statement or approval any advertising or practice which might be detrimental to the good name, trademarks, good will or reputation of the Company or its products. The Representative further agrees upon request to withdraw any statement and discontinue any advertising or practice deemed by the Company to have such effect.

ARTICLE 9. FAILURE TO ENFORCE

The failure at any time of either Party to enforce the provisions herein in accordance with its terms shall not be construed to be a waiver of such provision or of the right of such Party thereafter to enforce each and every provision.

ARTICLE 10. TERMINATION

a) This Agreement will automatically expire and terminate if the Representative does not meet or exceed the minimum sales levels of Products as listed in Schedule I.

b) This Agreement may be terminated hereof:

1) By mutual written consent of the Parties hereto.

2) By either party at will or without cause upon not less than sixty (60) days notice in writing by registered mail to the other party.

3) By the Company upon one (1) day's like notice in the event the Representative attempts to assign this Agreement or any right hereunder without the Company's prior written consent, or there is a change in control or management of the Representative unacceptable to the Company.

4) If Representative acts in any manner deemed by the Company to be detrimental to the best interests of the Company. The foregoing events shall without limitation be deemed to be cause for termination by the Company.

c) Neither Party shall be liable by reason of the termination or nor expiration of the Agreement to the other Party for compensation, reimbursement or damages on account of expenditures, or commitments in connection with the business or goodwill of the Company or Representative or otherwise.

ARTICLE 11. DISPUTE RESOLUTION

Any controversy or claim arising out of or relating to this Agreement which cannot be amicably settled between the Parties will be settled by arbitration in accordance of the American Arbitration Association.

ARTICLE 12. MISCELLANEOUS

a) This Agreement constitutes the only and entire agreement between the Parties respecting the Representative and the Served Market of Products specified in Article 1.

b) This Agreement cancels, terminates and supersedes any and all previous negotiations, commitments and agreements between the Parties with respect to Products.

ARTICLE 13. COMPENSATION

The Company will pay to the Representative commission based on FOB net sales price according to the following schedule:

_____% on initial and repeat orders.

SCHEDULE I

MINIMUM SALES LEVELS*

6 months, ending _____ 19___: ____ units totaling _____ dollars

1st year, ending _____ 19___: ____ units totaling _____ dollars

2nd year, ending _____ 19___: ____ units totaling _____ dollars

3rd year, and after ending _____: ____ units totaling _____

*May be altered by written mutual consent.

IN WITNESS WHEREOF, this Agreement has been executed by both parties.

Agreed:

(Your Company Name)

_____

_____
Signature

_____
Print name and title

_____
Date

(The Representative)

_____
Print name

_____
Signature

_____
Date

Bibliography

Attorneys and Agents Registered to Practice Before the U.S. Patent and Trademark Office 1985. (Washington, DC: U.S. Department of Commerce, U.S. Government Printing Office, August 1985) 360 pages.

Baker, Kenneth G. *The Comparative Analysis of Models for Use in New Product Screening Decisions.* Ph.D. diss. University of Oregon, 1980.

Betts, Jim, and Noreen Heimbold. *New Products.* (Point Pleasant, NJ: Point Publishing Co., 1984).

Betts, Jim. *The Million Dollar Idea.* Point Pleasant, NJ: Point Publishing Co., 1985.

Blanchard, Kenneth, and Spencer Johnson. *The One Minute Manager.* (New York: Berkley Books, 1982).

Buggie, Frederick, D. *New Product Development Strategies.* (New York: Amacom, 1981).

Business Planning Guide. (Dover, NH: The Upstart Publishing Company).

Business Publication Rates and Data. (Wilmette, IL: Standard Rate and Data Service, 1987).

Business Services and Information: The Guide to the Federal Government. (Philadelphia, PA: Management Information Exchange, 1978).

Casis User's Manual. (Washington, DC: U.S. Government Printing Office, 1985).

Churchill, Gilbert, Jr. *Marketing Research,* 3rd Ed. (New York: Dryden Press, 1983).

Colgate, Craig, Jr. *National Trade and Professional Associations of the U.S. 1987.* (Washington, DC: Columbia Books, Inc., 1987).

Conlin, Gholz, Hennessey, Kayton, Kirn, Schwaab, Sutton. *Patent Preparation and Prosecution Practice.* (Washington, DC: Patent Resources Institute, Inc., 1985).

Daniells, Lorna M. *Business Information Sources.* (Berkeley, CA: University of California Press, 1985).

Direct Mail List: Rates and Data. (Wilmette, IL: Standard Rate and Data Service, 1987).

Dougherty, David E. *From Technical Professional to Entrepreneur.* (New York: John Wiley, 1986).

Dufour, Patrick, and Carol Niemir. *Idea Screening in the U.S.* Ph.D. dissertation, Northwestern University, 1978.

Eisenberg, Richard. "Financing Your Venture." *Money* (December 1982): 73–94.

Elster, Robert. *Trade Shows and Professional Exhibits Directory.* (Detroit, MI: Gale Research Company, 1985).

Famualao, Joseph. *Handbook of Personnel, Forms, Records, & Reports.* (New York: McGraw-Hill, 1982).

Federal Government Directory of Information Resources in the U.S. (Washington, DC: Government Printing Office, 1974).

Freimer, Marshall, and Leonard Simon. "The Evaluation of Potential New Product Alternative." *Management Science* (February 1967): 279–292.

Gendron, Mary. "Here Are Ten Factors that Determine HBA Product Success." *Supermarket* (May 1977): 31: + .

Goldscheider, Robert. *Eckstrom's Licensing in Foreign & Domestic Operations.* (New York: Clark Boardman, 1984).

Goldscheider, Robert, and Gregory Maier. *1986 Licensing Law Handbook.* (New York: Clark Boardman, 1986).

Gregory, James, and Kevin Mulligan. *The Patent Book.* (New York: A & W Publishers, 1979).

Groosswirth, Marvin. *The Mechanix Illustrated Guide to How to Patent and Market Your Invention.* (New York: McKay, 1978).

Gruenwald, George. "Seven Steps Toward New Product Success." *Advertising Age* (April 27, 1981): 52: + .

Gruenwald, George. *New Product Development.* (Lincolnwood, IL: NTC Business Books, 1985).

Hamburg, Bruce. *1984–1985 Patent Law Handbook.* (New York: Clark Boardman, 1984).

Hart, A. "A Chart for Evaluating Product Research and Development Projects." *Operational Research Quarterly* (December 1966).

Hartman, Susan, and Norman Parrish. *Inventors' Source Book.* (Berkeley, CA: Inventors Resource Center Publishers, 1978).

Hopkins, David S. *New Product Winners and Lowers.* (New York: The Conference Board, 1980).

Jacob and Jacob. *Patent and Trademark Forms.* (Brooklyn, NY: Central Book Company, 1967).

Jansson, J. David. "Idea Evaluation." Massachusetts Institute of Technology, Speech (1982).

Juilland, Jeanne. "Grilling a Venture Capitalist." *Venture Magazine* (August 1987).

Kasunic, Vivian, and Anne Wallis. *Lawyer's Register by Specialities & Fields of Law,* 2d Ed. Cleveland, OH: The Lawyer to Lawyer Consultation Panel, 1979. (753 pp.).

Kenyon, Joan (Ed.). *The American Lawyers' Guide to Leading Law Firms.* (New York: American Law Publishing, 1983). 1125 pp.

Konold, William, Bruce G. Tittel, Donald F. Frei, and David S. Stallard. *What Every Engineer Should Know About Patents.* (New York: Dekker, 1979).

Kotler, Philip. *Marketing Management: Analysis, Planning and Control,* 6th Ed. (Englewood Cliffs, NJ: Prentice-Hall, 1988).

Kuczmarski, Thomas D. *Managing New Products.* (Englewood Cliffs, NJ: Prentice-Hall, 1988).

Lent, Constantin. *How to Invent, What to Invent.* (New York: Pen-Ink Publishing, 1966).

Leonard-Barton, D., and W.A. Kraus. "Implementing New Technology." *Harvard Business Review* (Nov.–Dec. 1985): 102–110.

Lindenberger, Paul H. *Invention Licensing and Royalty Rate Structure.* U.S.A., 1970.

MacCrachen, Calvin. *A Handbook for Inventors.* (New York: Scribner's, 1983).

Mancuso, Joseph R. "How a Business Plan Is Read." *Business Horizons* (August 1974).

Manual of Patent Examining Procedure. Rev. October 1986. Washington, DC: U.S. Department of Commerce, Patent & Trademark Office, 1983.

Martindale-Hubbell Law Directory. (Summitt, NJ: Martindale-Hubbell, 1987).

McGuire, Patrick E. *Evaluating New Product Proposal.* (New York: The Conference Board, 1973).

McGuire, Patrick E. *Generating New Product Ideas.* (New York: The Conference Board, 1972).

Midendorf, William. *What Every Engineer Should Know about Inventing.* (New York: Dekker, 1981).

Midgley, David F. *Innovating and New Product Marketing.* (New York: Halsted Press, 1977).

More, Roger A. "Risk Factors in Accepted and Rejected New Industrial Products." *Industrial Marketing Management* (February 1982): 9–15.

O'Meara, John T., Jr. "Selecting Profitable Products." *Harvard Business Review* (January 1961).

Paige, Richard E. *Complete Guide to Making Money with Your Ideas & Inventions.* (New York: Barnes & Noble Books, 1973).

Park, Robert. *The Inventor's Handbook.* (White Hall, VA: Betterway Publications, 1986).

Patents and Trademarks Style Manual. (Washington, DC: U.S. Patent and Trademark Office, U.S. Government Printing Office, 1984).

Pessemier, Edgar A. *New Product Decisions.* (New York: McGraw-Hill, 1966).

Pope, Jeffrey. *Practical Marketing Research.* (New York: Amacom, 1981).

Pratt, Stanley. *Guide to Venture Capital Sourcing.* (Dover, NH: Capital Publishing).

Pratt, Stanley. *How to Raise Venture Capital Sourcing.* (Dover, NH: Capital Publishing).

Pressman, David. *Patent It Yourself.* (Berkeley, CA: Nolo Press, 1985).

Quelch, J. "How to Build a Product Licensing Program." *Harvard Business Review* (May–June 1985): 186–197.

Rivkin, Bernard. *Patenting and Marketing Your Invention.* (New York: Van Nostrand Reinhold, 1986).

Rom, Walter O., and Frederick W. Winter. "New Product Evaluation Using a Bayesian Dynamic Program." *Journal of the Operational Research Society* (March 1981): 223–232.

Rosenbloom, Richard S., and Francis W. Wolek. *Technology & Information Transfer.* (Boston, MA: Harvard University Press, 1970).

Rubin, Richard, and Philip Goldberg. *The Small Business Guide to Borrowing Money.* (New York: McGraw-Hill).

Sheth, Jagdish N., and S. Ram. *Bringing Innovation to Market.* (New York: John Wiley, 1987).

Silver, David A. *Up Front Financing.* (New York: John Wiley).

Standard & Poors Industry Surveys. (New York: Standard & Poors Corp., 1985).

Statistical Abstract of the U.S. —1986, 106th Ed. (Washington, DC: U.S. Department of Commerce, U.S. Government Printing Office, 1986).

Technology Crossing Borders. Robert Stobaugh and Louis Wells, Jr. (Eds.). (Boston, MA: Harvard Business School Press, 1984).

Technology Transfer. A. Coskun (Ed.). (Westport, CT: Quorum Books, 1985).

The Guide to Venture Capital Sources. (Wellesley Hills, MA: Capital Publishing).

The Lawyer's List. (The Law List Publishing Company, 1984).

"The 1986 Exhibits Schedule." *Successful Meetings Magazine* (1986).

Udell, Gerald G., and Kenneth G. Baker. *Pies II Manual for Innovation Evaluation.* (Whitewater, WI: University of Wisconsin, 1980).

Urban, Glen, and John R. Hauser. *Design and Marketing of New Products.* (Englewood Cliffs, NJ: Prentice-Hall Inc., 1980).

1988 U.S. Industrial Outlook. (Washington, DC: U.S. Department of Commerce, U.S. Government Printing Office, 1988).

Verified Directory of Manufacturers' Representatives. (New York: Manufacturing Agreement Publishing Company, 1982).

Weller, Don. "Protecting Your Product." *International Trade Forum* (January 1982): 13–15.

Index